presumably you now
about. It
pretty intense business as
far as artillery is concerned,
& a new experience for us,
for we practically overlook
the ground in dispute.
I am expecting leave
shortly, so will reserve
further account. [Please
don't tell Aunt B! or
anyone I am coming]

Please thank D. for
letter (I forget if I wrote to
her before or after getting
it) & also tobacco parcel
which was quite correct.

George

From Downing Street
to the Trenches

From Downing Street to the Trenches

FIRST-HAND ACCOUNTS FROM THE GREAT WAR, 1914–1916

Mike Webb

Bodleian Library
UNIVERSITY OF OXFORD

Dedicated to the memory of
John Angus MacLeod of Balallan, Isle of Lewis (1953–2013)

First published in 2014 by the Bodleian Library
Broad Street
Oxford OX1 3BG

www.bodleianbookshop.co.uk

ISBN 978 1 85124 393 8

Foreword © Hew Strachan
Introduction and selection © Bodleian Library, University of Oxford, 2014

All images, unless specified on pp. 257–8,
© Bodleian Library, University of Oxford, 2014

Cover image: Parliamentary Recruiting Committee poster
no. 104. Oxford, Bodleian Library, John Johnson Collection.
© Bodleian Library, University of Oxford, 2014

Extracts from MS. Macmillan dep. c. 452 are reproduced with the kind
permission of the Trustees of the Harold Macmillan Book Trust.

Extracts from Bertrand Russell's correspondence is
© The Bertrand Russell Peace Foundation Ltd.

Extracts from Francis Macdonald Cornford's correspondence is reproduced
by permission of the Francis Macdonald Cornford Will Trust.

Extracts from the papers of H.H. Asquith and Margot Asquith
© Bonham Carter Trustees.

Extract from *Yeats: Collected Letters*, letter from W.B. Yeats to Gilbert Murray,
15 September 1914, by permission of Oxford University Press.

Every effort has been made to obtain permission to use
material which is in copyright. The publisher would welcome
any omissions being brought to their attention.

Cover design by Dot Little at the Bodleian Library
Designed and typeset in 11½ on 14 Monotype Bulmer by illuminati, Grosmont
Printed and Bound in Great Britain by TJ International Ltd, Padstow,
Cornwall on 80 gsm Premium Munken Cream

British Library Catalogue in Publishing Data
A CIP record of this publication is available from the British Library

Contents

Acknowledgements

I WOULD LIKE TO THANK a number of people for their help in bringing this book together. Professor Sir Hew Strachan very generously read the draft and kindly pointed out areas that needed reinterpretation or explanation. Mike Page also read the text and made helpful suggestions. Professor Richard Sheppard provided me at very short notice with a lively translation of the extracts from Ernst Stadler's war diary. I have had help in transcribing extracts of various letters and diaries from Dunja Irwin, Kalika Sands, Larisa Roberts, Chrissie Webb and Sandrine Decoux. Sandrine also translated the letter from a Belgian officer. The staff of the Special Collections Reading Room have been endlessly patient with my constant demands for more First World War manuscripts. Helen Langley, curator of Modern Political Papers, has been helpful with suggestions and advice over many years about the papers under her care. The book would not have been possible without the continuing support of families and trusts connected with the manuscript collections held in the Bodleian Libraries. I am grateful to the Trustees of the Harold Macmillan Book Trust, the Bonham Carter Trustees, the Seven Pillars of Wisdom Trust, Bishop John Bickersteth, James Munson, Colin Oberlin-Harris, Virginia Makins, Alexander Murray, Anne, Countess Attlee, Professor John Postgate, the Bertrand Russell Peace Foundation Ltd, the Francis Macdonald Cornford Will Trust, Oxford University Press, Sophie Ilbert Decaudaveine, James Best Shaw, and Sir Guy Acland. I would also like to thank Anthony Pitt-Rivers and Philip Athill for allowing the reproduction of photographs for the book, and for the information they provided. Janet Phillips and Samuel Fanous of Bodleian Library Publishing have been helpful with advice throughout the project and have guided the book through to completion.

MIKE WEBB

Foreword

SIR HEW STRACHAN

THE STORY of the First World War has been told many times—so much so that the voices of those who lived through it have too often been swamped by the constructions and simplifications of hindsight. This book centres on the experiences of ten men and women, all British but drawn from very different walks of life. From prime minister to parish priest, whether in Cabinet meetings or in the trenches, they reflected in their correspondence and private papers on the impact of the war from day to day, so capturing history as it unfolded.

Running through their accounts is another thread: their papers came to the Bodleian Library because of their connection with Oxford University. For Oxford, as for so many other institutions, the First World War was both a culmination and a caesura. It was a culmination because in the decade and more since the South African War the University had identified with public life, with the capacity to prepare undergraduates to lead the nation and with the need to generate fresh solutions to match the demands created by Britain's sprawling responsibilities. Today such ambitions sound both elitist and arrogant—elitist because one university more than any other claimed this role, and arrogant because it did so in the name not just of Britain but also of the empire.

In many respects such accusations are well founded. There can be something insufferably and suffocatingly inappropriate about the presumption of many Oxonians before 1914. In 1902 Cecil Rhodes's will provided for the education at Oxford of future leaders of the empire as well as of the United States. Sir William Anson, the warden of All Souls College from 1881 until his death on the eve of the Great War, revivified the college in part through stressing its responsibility to produce men of affairs. All Souls supported chairs in international and civil law, government and the history of war, so linking the academic world to the making of policy. Of the undergraduate colleges, Balliol in particular, but also Christ Church, Magdalen and New College, nurtured the sense that those they taught were destined not solely for the Church or for education but also for Parliament, the law and public administration. Political societies and groups, like Lord Milner's Kindergarten and its more liberal offshoot, Philip Kerr's Round Table, designed to promote debate and discussion, as well as awareness and fresh thinking, flourished. They provided a bridge from Oxford to Whitehall and Westminster, and they were supported by those who had passed through the University and now held senior office. In July 1914 both the prime minister, Herbert Henry Asquith, and the foreign secretary, Sir Edward Grey, were Balliol men.

By 3 August 1914 Asquith and Grey were persuaded that Britain had to support France, morally because of the entente between the two countries signed in 1904 and practically because under the terms of the Anglo-French naval agreement of 1912 France was relying on the Royal Navy to protect its northern coast. For Grey in particular Britain's global and imperial position had become indivisible from its European policy. The understandings not just with republican France but also—more controversially—in 1907 with autocratic Russia were conditioned by the need to resolve tensions in North Africa and Asia, but their consequence was a renewed British commitment to the balance of power in Europe. In other words, Oxford's preoccupation with Britain's position was prompted as much by an awareness of British vulnerabilities as by any sense of superiority. The City of London was still the world's financial, shipping and insurance capital, but Oxonians were thinking through new political solutions—from tariff reform to imperial federation—precisely because Britain, the world's first industrialized nation, now ranked third to the United States and Germany in terms of gross national output. And whereas Asquith and Grey concluded, with heavy hearts and real reluctance, that the answer in 1914 was war, others with equal conscientiousness decided it was not. John Morley, a graduate of Lincoln College and Gladstone's biographer, was one of two ministers who resigned from the Cabinet. Several more senior Liberals, including the secretary of state for the colonies Lewis Harcourt, who is well represented in the pages that follow, teetered on the edge of doing so but ultimately decided against.

viii

Most affected by the decisions of this older generation were those who found themselves donning the uniform of the British Army as newly commissioned subalterns, many of them to be killed and all to be marked in other ways, both physically and psychologically. Here another prime minister and Balliol man, Harold Macmillan, thrice wounded with the Grenadier Guards, stands out. Like many other young men for whom the war was the defining experience of early adulthood, or even of late adolescence, the effects never left him. Macmillan was wont to say that military service had exposed him to the working classes and developed within him a respect and affection for them which proved central to his political life. For others of equally refined dispositions, the forced conviviality, the boorishness of the army, and the lack of time for introspection were more powerful.

Oxford's links with the army before 1914 were exiguous but not insignificant. The University produced not just subalterns but also generals, including the best known of them all, Douglas Haig, who had been at Brasenose College. Haig's academic career was undistinguished and so was his time at the Staff College, but here he was taught by one of the army's most inspirational intellects, Colonel G.F.R. Henderson, Camberley's professor of military art and history between 1892 and 1899. Henderson was a scholar of St John's College who died young, in 1903, but not before he had shaped the thinking not just of Haig but also of other makers of Britain's wartime strategy, including Edmund Allenby, conqueror of the Turks in Palestine in 1917–18, and the most important of them all, William Robertson, the chief of the imperial general staff from 1915 to 1918.

The portal to army life for most Oxford undergraduates after 1908 was the Officers Training Corps, remodelled from the Oxford University Rifle Volunteers. In 1909 its strength stood at 649 cadets and 28 officers; Cambridge mustered 520 cadets with 26 officers. When war broke out, recent graduates and current undergraduates who wished to enlist did so by returning to Oxford and joining the OTC with a view to taking commissions in Kitchener's 'New Armies'. In the popular view of the First World War these men would all die; in fact most did not. Of those who joined the British armed forces in the First World War, 12 per cent were killed. However, for Oxford the rate rose to 18 per cent, and for New College and Worcester specifically over 20 per cent. Of the men who served from New College, 258 were killed. At the opposite end of the scale, St Edmund Hall, with 21 killed out of the 213 who served, suffered losses much closer to the national average. Casualties were particularly high in the cohort who came up between 1910 and 1913, rising to 28 per cent. The premature deaths of these young men were what created the belief that interwar Britain had lost a generation. This was indeed an elitist take on the war, because while it was not true in purely demographic terms it was true in the sense that the 'best and the brightest' had been disproportionately affected. Oxford's members had never before taken part so fully or so actively in a war, and it left those who were responsible for running the University bereft.

The dons' disorientation was prompted not just by bereavement. When the war broke out college fellows responded as men like Warden Anson had hoped. They engaged with their minds. Many were in awe of Germany's contribution to scholarship and research, and saw in its universities models for the future. But those links, both intellectual and personal, did not prevent the Oxford Faculty of Modern History from producing within the first few weeks of the war both a collaborative volume, *Why We Are at War: Britain's Case*, and a series of more widely ranging pamphlets. Gilbert Murray, who was a classicist rather than a historian, was one of their authors: his resolve was all the more powerful for his credentials as an internationalist and Germanophile. The Faculty's response was not a government-sponsored initiative, but an example of 'self-mobilization': the first meeting to enlist British authors for propaganda purposes was not held until 2 September and Murray attended it.

Lucky were those who were sucked out of Oxford to war work in London and elsewhere. Charles Oman, professor of modern history and Fellow of All Souls, who was in the middle of writing his history of the Peninsular War, advised the Press Bureau, created in August to censor the press and in due course to produce stories. Oman edited the official publication of British documents on the war's outbreak. Of a younger generation, John Buchan, who had followed Murray from Glasgow to Oxford, and specifically Brasenose, found that his fictional story of pre-war German spies in Britain, *The Thirty-Nine Steps*, reached the best-seller list in 1915. The book's hero, Richard Hannay, went on to further adventures in the war in *Greenmantle* (1916) and *Mr Standfast* (1919), but Buchan's real war work was a history of the war, written as it unfolded and published in twenty-four volumes for Thomas Nelson. He continued its punishing schedule while simultaneously becoming engaged from 1915 onwards in the delivery of British official propaganda.

For those who stayed in Oxford, finding purpose was harder. The University had emptied by 1915. Those undergraduates who were still in residence, including J.R.R. Tolkien, spent at least half their day on OTC exercises and drills. While himself a student, Oman had been a member of the *Kriegsspiel* (war games) club, set up in 1876 by a scholar of Merton College and member of the Oxford University Rifle Volunteers, Spenser Wilkinson. In 1909 Wilkinson, by then a noted military commentator, returned to Oxford as the University's first professor of military history. Having begun his war with trenchant articles in the *Morning Post*, he found himself progressively marginalized, unconsulted by government and short of anybody to lecture to in Oxford. Younger dons went off to fight, and many of them died. Of Wilkinson's colleagues at All Souls, Raymond Asquith, the prime minister's son, was killed on the Somme and so too were his own son (with the Royal Flying Corps) and Sir Foster Cunliffe, who had done so much before the war to persuade the university to take the study of war seriously. The helplessness and ineffectiveness of the academic community by 1916 were as galling to it as was the knowledge that its sons and students were dying.

This book closes in 1916. It was a year in which the war tested the resolve of all those caught up in it as never before. And yet what is clear is that, both for those at the front and for those left, like Wilkinson, feeling powerless in Oxford, the experience of the Somme did not diminish their determination to carry on. By December Asquith would be out of office, but when the new prime minister, David Lloyd George, had the opportunity to negotiate an end to the war, he could see no basis for doing so.

The war had two more years to run, and in its immediate aftermath many other conflicts would follow across the British Empire. By then the war's legacy for Oxford would be obvious in multiple ways, and Oxonians in turn shaped its legacy for the nation—in the development of British war aims in 1917–18 and in the effort to give them effect at Versailles in 1919; in poetry and literature written after the war; and in the appeasement favoured by many of the 'men of affairs' of the 1930s. But never again would Oxford have to rise to the challenge of war so directly. In the Second World War, the British government gave more care to the employment of the University's graduates, from the armed forces to operational research, from intelligence to economic planning—and so the culmination in 1914–18 was itself its own caesura.

Introduction

THIS BOOK is based on the words of participants in the Great War. These words were written as immediate reactions to events—they are not memoirs or literary reflections, but thoughts and descriptions written on the spur of the moment, usually in an attempt to explain to another person an extraordinary, momentous, frightening or even routine event beyond the usual understanding of that person. Letters to family or friends were the vehicles for these explanations, and diaries could fulfil a similar purpose, some being compiled in the expectation that family members would see them in due course, though such documents must also have helped their compilers to come to terms with the scarcely believable circumstances in which they found themselves.

The book does not attempt to explain the First World War. Instead it conveys an impressionistic and subjective view of the war, using the letters and diaries of participants, military and civilian, on the Western front and in other areas of conflict across the British Empire, and at home. The correspondents and diarists are all associated with the University of Oxford and so we see the war from the perspective of a well-educated group: and their writings reflect not only their experiences, but also their ideas and thoughts about the war. Such people found themselves thrust into positions of leadership and responsibility, and the subjects include political leaders, military officers and opinion-formers, for and against the war. This of course provides only a partial perspective, but it is an important one that can be put alongside the many published letters, diaries and memoirs of men and women who were involved in the war to help round out our understanding of that conflict. The sources used reflect the nature of the papers acquired by the Bodleian Libraries over the last hundred years. Although inevitably they provide only a partial glimpse of the war, the important fact about archival collections such as these is that although they were accumulated because of their historical interest, they were not usually created for that purpose. Unlike literary productions such as memoirs or poems, contemporary letters and diaries were not intended for a wide reading public and reflect immediate concerns and reactions to events. They are truly contemporary voices and a direct link to the past. Thirty or forty years later their authors may have been surprised, perhaps even ashamed, of what they had written, but that might be because their opinions had changed under the burdens of wisdom and historical knowledge; they would not be able to deny that their younger selves were expressing their genuine feelings and thoughts.

The book covers only the first two years of the war, from the British intervention in 1914 to the fall of the prime minister, H.H. Asquith, in December 1916. When I began the process of researching the collections held in the Bodleian Libraries I soon realized that the huge quantity of papers and the richness of the sources would make it difficult to do justice to the story of the whole war. Many of the subjects of the book were out of the war by 1916 for one reason or another, and the personal stories of 1917 to 1918 would have to be taken up by others. It would require another book to do this, and give due consideration to the experiences of the latter half of the war, the Armistice, the peace treaty and the aftermath of the conflict. However, there are other reasons why stopping at the end of 1916 helps us to understand the war from a contemporary perspective. Of course, no one in 1914, or even in 1916, had any clear idea when the war would end. The 'over by Christmas' idea was certainly present, but there were others who knew that this was unlikely and predicted a war of two or three years duration. By early 1916 the government and the generals believed that the 'Big Push' in France, in combination with the naval blockade, would bring Germany to sue for peace. The failure to deliver this final blow by the end of 1916 was one of the main reasons for the fall of Asquith's government; any illusions of a short war were gone. By looking at the ideas and experiences of 1914 to 1916 we leave the possibilities for the future open-ended, which was exactly how it was for the participants. We now know that by the end of 1916 the naval blockade was so serious for Germany that she was forced to return to unrestricted submarine warfare, and that this would bring the Americans into the war in April 1917; we know that Russia was on the brink of revolution and would be knocked out

Herbert Henry Asquith

of the war altogether in 1917; we know that further great and costly battles were to be fought on the Western Front in 1917; we know too that Germany would stake all on a huge offensive in the spring of 1918 and that the effort would break her. None of these things was certain at the end of 1916. The choice facing all the combatants was to make peace on the best possible terms or to continue the fight. The battle of the Somme, in many ways the defining battle of the First World War for Britain, had come to a close in November 1916. George Butterworth, one of the subjects of this book, was dead, and another, Harold Macmillan, was seriously wounded, and would not return to the front. Conscription had been brought in against much opposition in March 1916, and the age of Kitchener's volunteer army had come to an end. In the Middle East at the end of 1916, T.E. Lawrence had come out from behind his desk at the Arab Bureau in Cairo and taken the first steps of his path to fame in the Arab Revolt. In Britain, the fall of Asquith and his replacement by Lloyd George signified that a choice had been made: the war would continue, and there would be no peace without victory.

The extracts from contemporary sources used in this book produce a kaleidoscopic effect, and serve to remind us what it was like to live through the war without any of the prejudices of hindsight. It is worth reflecting on our understanding of the Great War from a 2014 perspective. Some of the most memorable images and impressions of the war have come to us through poetry and memoirs; in more recent years, the reminiscences of the last survivors of the war received considerable coverage in television interviews and books. These insights are compelling because we can, with hindsight, see the tragedy and waste of the 'war to end all wars', looking back on a century that saw an even greater conflict and the spread of totalitarianism. It is very difficult to go back to 1914 and see the war through the eyes of those engaged in it, and imagine how it must have seemed to them without any knowledge of what was to come. On 19 December 1916 the new prime minister, Lloyd George, made a rousing speech in the House of Commons in which he quoted the words of Abraham Lincoln: 'We accepted this war for an object, and a worthy object, and the war will end when that object is attained. Under God I hope it will never end until that time.' He went on to outline the British cause:

T.E. Lawrence, 1919

a challenge had been sent to civilisation to decide an issue higher than party, deeper than party, wider than all parties—an issue upon the settlement of which will depend the fate of men in this world for generations, when existing parties will have fallen like dead leaves on the highway. ... This is a struggle for international right, international honour, international good faith.... The plain sense of fair play amongst nations, the growth of an international conscience, the protection of the weak against the strong by the stronger, the consciousness that justice has a more powerful backing in this world than greed, the knowledge that any outrage upon fair dealing between nations, great or small, will meet with prompt and meritable chastisement—these constitute the causeway along which humanity was progressing slowly to higher things. The triumph of Prussia would sweep it all away and leave mankind to struggle helpless in the morass. That is why, since this War began, I have known but one political aim. For that I have fought with a single eye. That is the rescue of mankind from the most overwhelming catastrophe that has ever yet menaced its well-being.[1]

With the knowledge we have now of the course and consequences of the Great War, these words may seem hollow. However, when considering what the war meant to the Edwardian generation, we should not assume that these words were any less sincere than those of the much more widely known speeches of Winston Churchill in the Second World War, or that the sense of a threat to civilization seemed any less real. This view of the war was certainly one endorsed by many of the people whose papers are the sources for this book.

The University of Oxford in 1914 was an elite institution, self-consciously aiming to produce leaders of society. It was male-dominated, and overwhelming upper- or upper-middle-class in its student intake. Inevitably when war came the University assumed a leading role. In 1920, just two years after the Armistice of 11 November 1918, the Clarendon Press at Oxford published a remarkable work. This was the *Oxford University Roll of Service*, edited by E.S. Craig, the Assistant Registrar of the University, and Winifred Gibson. The *Roll* includes the names of 14,561 Oxford alumni who served in the military and naval forces of the Crown during the Great War. The introduction admits that the *Roll* might have been three times as long to acknowledge the part played by the University in training officers, caring for the wounded and scientific research in the art of both taking and saving lives. Nor does the *Roll* include the names of the thousands of men who were briefly enrolled into collegiate life, not as academic students, but in order to learn soldiering, in the Cadet Battalions formed at Oxford and quartered in various colleges. By March 1916 about three thousand men had passed through the School of Instruction for young officers set up in January 1915. A further thousand cadets passed through the School of Military Aeronautics, set up to train young officers but soon transformed into a cadet school.

There are, of course, further omissions from the *Roll* whose absence is not admitted by the editors. There are no women named, not even nurses who served near the battlefields or behind the lines, let alone those who tended the wounded in military hospitals up and down the country. A glance at the annual reports of the women's college Somerville shows a huge contribution towards a whole range of war-related work, Vera Brittain being but one name among many. Those older alumni who served the state in other capacities, such as politicians, diplomats and writers, would not be included in a work centred on active service in the field. There is, however, a group of serving men who were not included: the Oxford alumni who fought in the armies of Germany. More than fifty German Rhodes Scholars fought for Germany, among them the son of the German chancellor Bethmann Hollweg, and Manfred von Richthofen, a cousin of the 'Red Baron'.

Of the names recorded in the *University Roll of Service*, the overwhelming majority served as junior officers, and this was the quintessential experience of young Oxford graduates. Douglas Haig, himself an alumnus of Brasenose, wrote in his diary that when he met General Sclater at the War Office in November 1914, he told him that he wanted 'patriots who knew the importance of the cause for which we are fighting' and stressed the importance of good leadership. In his opinion, as there was a shortage of officers, Sclater should 'send out young Oxford and Cambridge men as officers; they understand the crisis in which the British Empire is involved.'[2] Many of the letters and diaries in this book were written by young lieutenants, including a future prime minister, Harold Macmillan; a folk-dancer and composer, George Butterworth; a future academic, John Burgon Bickersteth; and a German poet, Ernst Stadler.

The public school education and ethos of young British officers led to a widespread belief among this group that war was something noble, chivalric and the ultimate test of manliness. Although predominantly serving on the Western front where the main British war effort was concentrated, they were to be found in all the theatres of war: T.E. Lawrence is forever associated with the Middle East and the Arab Revolt; views from Mesopotamia, India, Nigeria, Salonika and the Dardanelles are represented in this book. Looking back at the letters written in 1914 from our modern perspective it can make uncomfortable reading to see how willingly so many young men took up arms and how keen they were to do what they regarded as a duty. Historians have contrasted the naivety and idealism with the reality of the war they entered, and Wilfred Owen's poem 'Dulce et Decorum Est' is a heartfelt and bitter attack on those ideals, contrasting the reality of an agonizing death with the noble ideal of self-sacrifice.

It would seem inevitable that such ideals would be destroyed in the storm of modern warfare, and many officers did become disillusioned. Yet Harold Macmillan, having lived through two years of war, and writing to his mother from the Somme amid the smell of corpses, was still able to say that death in battle was 'noble and glorious', though he recognized its 'revolting' and 'horrid' aspects. Burgon Bickersteth's disillusion was at first caused more by the inaction of his cavalry brigade than by the continuing carnage. We may be out of tune with their values, but we cannot dismiss them out of hand.

Many Britons went to war in 1914 convinced of the righteousness of the cause, and many, both soldiers and civilians, continued to feel this throughout the war; others began fairly quickly to feel that the price to be paid was far too high. There is no simple paradigm to explain the trajectory of peoples' thoughts; different people were affected by the war in different ways, had different values, beliefs and priorities. It is perhaps instructive to consider what people believed the options were in 1914, as yet unaffected by the knowledge of vast casualty lists and the seemingly relentless wastage of trench warfare. We can argue with their understanding of events, but most people felt that the German attack on France and the violation of neutral Belgium left them with a stark choice—German domination of Europe or war.

Harold Macmillan, September 1915

at Vermelles n. Loos, at
2.30 p.m. Monday. Sept! 28th 1915
before the attack n Hill 70"

It has to be questioned too just how naive and unprepared these officers were. The idea that everyone rushed to the colours as soon as war broke out in the expectation of excitement and an easy victory must be modified in the light of contrary evidence. The composer George Butterworth noted in his diary a surge in recruitment in September 1914 when news of serious reverses had come through. Many of these men joined when they knew that the fighting had become desperate and in the belief that Britain was in danger. However, Butterworth also relates the chaos caused by the inability of the recruiting organization to cope with such huge numbers, so that surges may simply reflect administrative bottlenecks. Nor should the many social and economic pressures compelling individuals to join up or resist recruitment be left out of this equation.

There is an idea prevalent that the war created a huge gulf between soldiers and civilians, and between serving sons or daughters and their parents. The letters in this book provide plenty of evidence to the contrary, at least in the early part of the war. Not only did men like Macmillan, Bickersteth and Butterworth write regularly about their experiences to their parents, sometimes with a surprising degree of frankness; they also enjoyed reading letters from home and mention quite often how much they needed to hear domestic news.

Junior officers were also a pivotal connection between the senior officers and the men. Socially they were often closely connected with senior officers, and had to attend regularly at brigade or battalion headquarters, being the conduit through which higher orders were transferred to the smaller tactical units on the battlefield. They were directly connected to ordinary soldiers as they lived in close proximity to them, led them in battle, and generally had to look after their interests, finding them billets when on the march, censoring their letters, writing to their relatives when they were killed or wounded, and working with them in a range of other duties. The bonds between officers and men could be strong, Macmillan and Butterworth for example both displaying huge respect and affection for their men, which seems to have been reciprocated.

The trenches of the Western Front were a defining experience for soldiers and have come to symbolize the whole war, often invoked to describe its lethal and futile nature. The accounts in this book put the trenches into their contemporary perspective; they were not all the same, not all equally dangerous, and indeed were often reported in letters as a relatively safe place to be during shelling, which was of course the reason they were created in the first place.

The real horrors of war are rarely mentioned in the letters, though several indicate an uncomfortable proximity to death or carnage. There are several reasons why this should be so. The most obvious one is that for much of the time there was no severe danger. A British soldier before 1916 could expect to spend just ten days a month on the front line in normal trench warfare conditions, and rotation of battalions and divisions could mean that units were assigned to quieter sections after serving in more active areas. Then again, we have to take into account the possibility that the recipient of the letter was being spared the worst

(John) Burgon Bickersteth (*left*) with two other officers of the 1st Royal Dragoons, Rouen, May 1915

George Butterworth (*back row, second left*) with the troupe of the English Folk Dance Society at Stratford, summer 1914

of the details to prevent distress. We know that the weapons used in the First World War, particularly shells, caused horrific maiming and could literally blow a man to pieces. It is perhaps not surprising that, contemplating such horrors, letter writers were reluctant to dwell on the meaning of this for themselves, and it would have seemed wrong to allow loved ones to share in their worst fears. The nearest anyone comes to describing the real horror is Burgon Bickersteth in his account of the death of several colleagues when a shell hit their trench. The effects are not described graphically, one Waterhouse being 'terribly wounded', but small details convey the sense of shock and bewilderment, such as the look on the wounded man's face which Bickersteth knew to mean that he would not live, and the mug of tea and bacon left in the hands of the troop sergeant at the moment of his death.

But even if they spare their audiences the gory details, the letter writers make no attempt to hide from their relatives the nature of the dangers they are facing, and we can only assume that they knew that the people at home were well informed about the trenches and that there was no point in pretending that there was no risk. When Macmillan assures his mother that he is perfectly safe and that she should not worry about him, we can see that his descriptions have caused her unease. By September 1916, Bickersteth, disillusioned and sickened by his experiences on the Somme, begins to talk in general terms about the war as a 'horrible, fearful thing'.

Another factor that makes it difficult sometimes to assess the degree of truthfulness in young officers' letters is a cultural one. Ironic humour was prevalent among Oxford-educated men, and there are a number of examples of a self-conscious downplaying of the seriousness of the situation. Macmillan is fond of portraying the war as unreal in comparison to his student and home lives; Butterworth is self-deprecating about his own efforts, and T.E. Lawrence and Godfrey Elton refer to their work, or the war, as a 'joke'. This was no doubt a way of coping with the war, and indeed writing letters and receiving them fulfilled an important need. Not only was letter-writing a useful distraction in time of stress or boredom; it also reminded the writer that there was another reality, that the war would one day end and the armies would return home.

While younger men trained to be soldiers, University professors engaged in public discourse about the war's causes, aims and meaning. Gilbert Murray, Professor of Greek, produced pamphlets in support of the British cause, and engaged in correspondence on a range of issues including conscientious objection, African native rights and the post-war political settlement. Oxford-educated men could be found everywhere that the war was organized, fought or debated. The prime minister H.H. Asquith, his foreign secretary Sir Edward Grey and two other members of his wartime Cabinets were alumni of Balliol College; another four were Oxford men. Their papers reflect the continual struggles over strategy and direction of the war, among politicians and between the politicians and the military, and the impact of events on public opinion. Both Murray and Asquith were deeply engaged in the war in another way too: for these public figures the war was also a desperate private struggle, as, in common with many of their age and status, they had sons serving with the British forces. Asquith had three sons involved in the war, one of whom, Raymond, was killed in the battle of the Somme in September 1916, and another of whom, Arthur, was in the Dardanelles campaign of 1915; Gilbert Murray's son Denis was shot down off the Belgian coast while serving with the Royal Naval Air Squadron in February 1915 and interned in the Netherlands for the rest of the war.

Other men and women decided to record their thoughts more privately in diaries, though the rector of Great Leighs in Essex felt that his record of what was happening in his village in wartime was of such public interest that at the end of each year he parcelled up the pages of his diary and sent them to the Bodleian Library. Andrew Clark's 'Echoes of the Great War' is thus an invaluable contemporary source for understanding public perception of the war in an ordinary village.

Although inevitably women's voices are not prominent in these papers, nevertheless they are never far from the stories in this book. The letters in the book were part of a dialogue, and many of the

Professor Gilbert Murray, 1934

recipients of these letters were women: Macmillan, Bickersteth and T.E. Lawrence maintained a constant correspondence with their mothers. Asquith confided his political troubles to two successive female confidantes, Venetia Stanley and then her sister Sylvia Henley. His wife Margot provides a further commentary on his political and personal life through her diary. The wives and daughters of prominent public figures were determined to support the war effort by making appropriate sacrifices in recognition of the hardships that the nation as a whole was suffering. Homes were opened up as hospitals, Lewis Harcourt's large Georgian mansion at Nuneham Courtenay, for example, being used for convalescent Belgian and then Canadian officers under the care of Mrs Mary Harcourt. Asquith's daughters volunteered for nursing work, and his confidante Sylvia Henley served in canteens. Margot Asquith used her position to arrange a visit to the front in December 1914 where she met troops and distributed gifts. Sarah Angelina Acland, daughter of the late Herbert Acland, Regius Professor of Medicine in Oxford until 1900, sent parcels of food and clothing to servicemen. As a result she received regular letters from ordinary soldiers whose opinions and experiences added to the range of information available to those on the home front.

The accounts in this book range from the Cabinet table at 10 Downing Street to the trenches on the Western Front, and from a village in Essex to outposts of the empire in Africa. They include the perspectives of Cabinet ministers, soldiers and civilians. The accounts are filtered through the lives of particular Oxford alumni, but take into account their wider connections, friends, wives, parents and colleagues, whose perspectives add a further dimension to their stories. They are not meant to be comprehensive or definitive—it should become apparent in reading them that the war meant many different things to different people. The letters and diaries that form the book convey impressions—fear, excitement, bewilderment and fascination are to be found in equal measure. Inevitably, given the nature of the collections in the Bodleian Library, the stories are very much centred on the British experience of the war, though this requires the Imperial dimension to be taken into account.

NOTE ON EDITORIAL CONVENTIONS

The spelling and punctuation of the original documents have been left where possible, including obvious mistakes, which were inevitable given the trying circumstances in which many of the letters were written, often in great haste. Occasionally I have silently introduced punctuation where the meaning of the original would otherwise be obscure, particularly when punctuation in the original is entirely lacking, as is the case with many of Margot Asquith's hurried diary entries. Square brackets have been used for editorial interpolations; square brackets in the original text have been changed to {brace brackets}. I have replaced '&' with 'and' throughout, and have capitalized letters at the beginning of sentences without comment.

Short biographies
of key figures

THE PRIME MINISTER AND HIS CIRCLE

HERBERT HENRY ASQUITH, first earl of Oxford and Asquith (1852–1928).

Asquith won a classical scholarship to Balliol College, Oxford, in 1869, and was a Fellow of Balliol from 1874 to 1882. He was home secretary and chancellor of the exchequer before becoming prime minister in 1908. As leader of the Liberal government Asquith was the prime minister who took the United Kingdom to war in August 1914. Under increasing pressure from the Unionist opposition and from members of his own government, Asquith was forced to form a coalition in May 1915. A series of crises in 1916 led to his downfall and replacement by David Lloyd George.

Asquith's perspective is seen through his correspondence with two confidantes. BEATRICE VENETIA STANLEY, later Montagu (1887–1948), was the daughter of the 4th Baron Sheffield and Stanley of Alderley. She met Asquith through her friendship with his daughter, Violet. They began writing to one another in 1910, but Asquith seems to have fallen in love with her around 1912 and their correspondence increased. By 1915, when the relationship ended following Venetia's marriage to one of Asquith's Cabinet ministers, Edwin Montagu, Asquith was writing up to three times a day, and seeking advice on all sorts of political and even military issues. SYLVIA LAURA HENLEY, née Stanley (1882–1980), was Venetia Stanley's older sister. She was the wife of the Hon. Anthony Morton Henley, who was a captain on Sir John French's staff in this period. Very soon after the end of Asquith's relationship with Venetia, Sylvia began to take her place as Asquith's confidante, and soon began to receive regular correspondence full of confidential observations and opinions on political and military matters. Asquith's letters to the two Stanley sisters form a remarkable insight into his thinking during the First World War.

Margaret Emma Alice (Margot) Asquith, née Tennant, Countess of Oxford and Asquith (1864–1945), political hostess and diarist.

Margot was the second wife of H.H. Asquith (they were married in 1894). Before she met Asquith she was part of a social group nicknamed the 'Souls', which included among others Arthur Balfour, the Conservative prime minister 1902 to 1906, later First Lord of the Admiralty in Asquith's coalition government; and Ettie Grenfell, Lady Desborough, mother of the soldier and poet Julian Grenfell. Outspoken, passionate and willing to use her position to try to influence politics, she provides in her diary a very personal insight into personalities and events of Asquith's government.

Lewis Vernon Harcourt, 1st Viscount Harcourt (1863–1922), politician.

Lewis Harcourt, known as 'Loulou', was the son of Sir William Harcourt, who had served under Gladstone as home secretary and chancellor of the exchequer. His political career began as his father's private secretary. Only after the death of Sir William in 1904 did he fully enter politics. His period as a Cabinet minister, 1907 to 1916, largely coincided with Asquith's premiership. He was president of the board of works 1907–10 and 1915–16, and colonial secretary 1910–15. Harcourt was fond of gossip and political intrigue. He sat next to Asquith at the Cabinet table and spoke to him quietly, which did not endear him to all his colleagues. One Cabinet minister described him as 'subtle, secretive, adroit'.[3] Asquith and Harcourt were also neighbours on the Thames, then the Oxfordshire–Berkshire border, at Sutton Courtenay and Nuneham Courtenay.

Harcourt's diary provides a remarkable insight into the politics and personalities of Asquith's government. He kept notes of Cabinet meetings, though asked more than once not to do so. Harcourt's political career ended with the fall of Asquith. In 1917 he received an honorary DCL degree from Oxford University, and was raised to the peerage as Viscount Harcourt of Stanton Harcourt. Apparently enmeshed in sexual scandal involving an Eton schoolboy, he died suddenly in 1922, quite probably at his own hand. His diary did not see the light of day until its transfer to the Bodleian in 2008. An obituary in the *Daily Sketch* relates a story that Harcourt admitted keeping a secret diary, and that it was so full that it would probably be burned by the public hangman.

TWO CAVALRY OFFICERS

JOHN BURGON BICKERSTETH (1888–1979), academic administrator.

Bickersteth studied history at Christ Church, Oxford, graduating in 1911. After two years as a lay missionary with the Anglican Church in western Canada, he spent 1913–14 at the Sorbonne. On the outbreak of war he joined the 1st Royal Dragoons and served with them in France as a lieutenant from 1915 to 1919. During periods of cavalry inactivity Bickersteth began writing the *History of the 6th Cavalry Brigade*, published in 1919. He was twice awarded the Military Cross. His older brother the Revd K.J.F. (Julian) Bickersteth served as a chaplain to the forces, becoming senior chaplain in the 56th Division in 1916. A younger brother, R.M. (Morris) Bickersteth, served as captain in the West Yorkshire Regiment, and was killed on the first day of the Somme, 1 July 1916. In many ways epitomizing the attitude of the public-school- and Oxbridge-educated young man, Burgon embraced the war in 1914 with patriotism and an eagerness to see action; by 1916 he was attacked by severe doubts about the nature and purpose of the war. Despite appearing to reject all the war stood for in 1916, he served to the end and won the Military Cross in 1917. By 1917 he still could talk about the 'greatness of the cause', but his main motivation was the '"camaraderie" and friendship of the life out here', and he was able to say that he felt 'no rancour against the German rank and file.'[4]

All three brothers wrote detailed letters to their parents during the war, and their mother, Ella, copied these into the so-called 'Bickersteth Diaries'.[5]

After the war Bickersteth went to Canada, becoming warden of Hart House in the University of Toronto. He returned to England in 1940 to join the Canterbury Home Guard at the height of the invasion scare.

SIR ERNEST MAKINS (1869–1959) British officer.

Makins was educated at Winchester College and Christ Church, Oxford. He fought in the Boer War, attaining the rank of major. In September 1914 he was appointed temporary brigadier-general of the

Brigadier-general Ernest Makins

6th Cavalry Brigade, and was with the brigade in the fighting around Ypres in the autumn and early winter of 1914 before returning home sick in November. He returned to the front with the 1st Cavalry Brigade and was with the Cavalry Division on the Somme in 1916. He served with the Brigade for the rest of the war. After the war he was the Conservative MP for Knutsford, 1922 to 1945. He was made colonel of the Royal Dragoons in 1931.

FOUR INFANTRY OFFICERS

GEORGE SAINTON KAYE BUTTERWORTH (1885–1916), British composer and folk dancer.

Butterworth was educated at Eton and Trinity College, Oxford. He had been brought up in York, where his father was general manager of the North Eastern Railway Company. At Oxford he studied 'Greats' (Classics), and was president of the university musical club 1906 to 1907. At this time he began to collect folk songs and dance tunes with Ralph Vaughan Williams, and joined the Folk-Song Society. In 1911 he helped to found the English Folk Dance Society.

Butterworth's most notable compositions were *The Banks of Green Willow* (1913) and his setting for Alfred Edward Housman's *A Shropshire Lad* (1912). He seems to have given up composing after 1914, and may even have destroyed some of his music.

In August 1914 Butterworth enlisted as a private with the Duke of Cornwall's Light Infantry, and then received a commission as a lieutenant with the 13th Battalion of the Durham Light Infantry.

Butterworth served in France, winning the Military Cross during the Somme campaign, for his actions in defending a trench at Pozières, 17–19 July 1916. He was killed shortly afterwards leading a raid near Pozières on 5 August 1916. His body was never found and so his name is inscribed on the Thiépval Memorial to the Missing.

THOMAS EDWARD LAWRENCE (1888–1935), British intelligence officer and author.

Lawrence studied history at Jesus College, Oxford, 1907 to 1910. Here he was noticed by Dr D.G. Hogarth, keeper of the Ashmolean Museum, and through him found employment on the British Museum's excavations at Carchemish in Syria. Living and working there from 1911 to 1914, Lawrence became familiar with the culture and politics of the region, becoming sympathetic to Arab traditions and hostile to modernizing influences, both European and Turkish. In 1912 Lawrence wrote: 'I don't think anyone who tasted the East as I have would give it up half-way, for a seat at high table and a chair in the Bodleian.'[6] With this background, Lawrence was recruited by the War Office and sent to Cairo as a subaltern attached to the military intelligence department of the Egyptian Expeditionary Force. Up to the spring of 1916 Lawrence was largely confined to the office in Cairo, but in April 1916 he went with Aubrey Herbert to Kut to negotiate the extrication of the Anglo-Indian army trapped by the Turks there. In June 1916 Sharif Hussein of Hejaz rebelled against Turkish rule. Lawrence as an intelligence officer had been involved with the preliminary planning of the Arab uprising, and in October 1916 was ordered to Jiddah to assess the military situation. This was the beginning of his direct connection with the Arab Revolt, recorded in his highly personal account, *Seven Pillars of Wisdom*, printed for private circulation in 1926 and published in 1935.

MAURICE HAROLD MACMILLAN, 1st Earl of Stockton (1894–1986), prime minister.

Harold Macmillan was born in Chelsea. His father was the publisher Maurice Crawford Macmillan, and his mother was Helen Artie Tarleton (Nellie) Belles (1856–1937), an artist from Spencer, Indiana, USA. He was at Summer Fields School, Oxford, from 1903 to 1906 and then Eton, 1906 to 1910. He went up to Balliol College, Oxford, in 1912, where he achieved a first in 'Mods', though the war prevented him from taking 'Greats'. He became involved with political societies, and supported the Liberal Party at this stage in his life.

When war broke out in August 1914 Macmillan was recovering from appendicitis, but soon joined the King's Royal Rifle Corps as a second lieutenant. Finding this regiment uncongenial, he managed, with the help of his mother, to effect a transfer to the prestigious Grenadier Guards in 1915. With the 2nd Battalion he saw action in Belgium and France, being wounded at Loos in September 1915, and again near Ypres in July 1916. In September 1916, during the battle of Flers–Courcelette, part of the Somme offensive, he was severely wounded, and for the rest of the war spent long periods in hospital. He did not return to the front.

After the war, Macmillan joined the family publishing company, but retained his interest in politics. Believing that the Liberal Party had no future, he joined the Conservatives and in 1924 was elected as MP for Stockton-on-Tees. He was on the left of the party and believed in the need for social reform. A strong critic of the appeasement policies of the 1930s, he was invited by Winston Churchill to join his wartime government in 1940. After the Second World War he became successively minister of housing, minister of defence, foreign secretary and chancellor of the exchequer before serving as prime minister from 1957 to 1963.

CIVILIANS

ANDREW CLARK (1856–1922), Church of England clergyman, scholar and diarist.

Clark was born at Dollarfield near Dollar, Clackmannanshire, and educated at the University of St Andrews before matriculating from Balliol College, Oxford and winning a scholarship at Lincoln College in 1876. In 1880 he was elected a fellow of Lincoln, and was ordained in 1884. He was chaplain of Lincoln, and vicar of All Saints, and of St Michael's, Northgate, both in Oxford. In 1894 he became rector of Great Leighs in Essex, a Lincoln College living.

Clark was a notable editor of historical texts, and a frequent user of the archives in the Bodleian Library and the Oxford colleges. Among many works produced for the Oxford Historical Society was his three-volume edition of Anthony Wood's *Antiquities of the City of Oxford* (1889–99); between 1891 and 1900 he produced the five-volume compendium *The Life and Times of Anthony Wood*. In 1898 he produced *John Aubrey's Brief Lives* (1898).

During the First World War, Clark turned his literary energy towards compiling a record of the effects of the war on his parish at Great Leighs, which he deposited in the Bodleian Library in instalments between 1915 and 1919. It comprises ninety-two exercise books, and includes letters from his family and parishioners, and many other papers collected from a variety of sources.

The Reverend Andrew Clark

GEORGE GILBERT AIMÉ MURRAY (1866–1957), classical scholar and internationalist.

Murray was born in Sydney, Australia, in 1866, coming to Britain with his widowed mother in 1877. He was educated at Merchant Taylors' School and St John's College, Oxford. He was Professor of Greek at the University of Glasgow from 1889 to 1899 before returning to Oxford as a Fellow of New College. From 1908 to 1936 he was Regius Professor of Greek. A Liberal, he occasionally spoke in public on political issues; following the outbreak of war, he became more closely involved in public affairs, writing several pamphlets for the Bureau of Information and contributing to discussions about international peace, often within the League of Nations Society. In 1916 he became vice president of the Society. The following year, he began work for the Board of Education. In this role he was able to intervene on behalf of men imprisoned as conscientious objectors. Murray later worked for the League of Nations Union and was a prominent figure in the League of Nations (founded in 1920) in the interwar years. He was elected president of the United Nations Association three times after the Second World War.

OTHER FIGURES

SARAH ANGELINA ACLAND (1849–1930), daughter of Sir Henry Wentworth Acland; pioneer of colour photography. Sent parcels of food and clothing to men on active service, and in return received letters of thanks which give some insight into the outlook of ordinary soldiers.

CLEMENT ATTLEE (1883–1967), 1st Earl Attlee, prime minister 1945–51; alumnus of University College, Oxford; served with South Lancashire Regiment.

LIONEL BERNERS CHOLMONDELEY (1858–1945), chaplain of the British embassy in Tokyo during the First World War; alumnus of Oriel College, Oxford.

RICHARD DOUGLAS DENMAN (1876–1957), Liberal MP for Carlisle, 1910–18; Labour MP for Leeds, 1929–45; alumnus of Balliol College, Oxford; served with Royal Field Artillery.

CHARLES DENNIS FISHER (1877–1916), academic; alumnus of Christ Church, Oxford; served in Royal Army Medical Corps, and lieutenant in the Royal Naval Volunteer Reserve.

HARRY J.G. MILLER-STIRLING (d. 1917), colonial administrator; alumnus of Keble College, Oxford; served with the West African Frontier Force.

ERNST MARIA RICHARD STADLER (1883–1914), German Expressionist poet; alumnus of Magdalen College, Oxford and Rhodes scholar; served with the German 80th Field Artillery Regiment.

Letters and diaries, 1914–1916

'We talked about the probable Austro-Servian War'

LEWIS HARCOURT AND THE PEACE PARTY

What we know of the deliberations of the British Cabinet in the momentous week of 28 July to 4 August 1914 when the war between Austria and Serbia transformed into a world conflict can only be derived from surviving letters and diaries of those who were present. Cabinet meetings were informal in that there were no minutes (until December 1916), and no votes were taken. Decisions were made collectively after debate, and so there was no record of individual statements or arguments. In the Bodleian Library there is a remarkable journal kept by a member of Asquith's Cabinet. Lewis 'Loulou' Harcourt (1863–1922) was colonial secretary in 1914–15. As the debates raged around the table, he jotted down notes, sometimes recording conversations almost verbatim, on the backs and in the margins of Foreign Office telegrams. In July 1914 he records that during a discussion on Ireland 'Winston [Churchill] at this point remonstrated with me for taking notes of Cabinet proceedings, so I desisted—the following were made from memory later.' As the war crisis deepened, however, we find copious diary notes on Foreign Office telegrams as well as transcripts clearly copied from the notes after the meetings.

In July 1914 Harcourt was one of a group of Cabinet ministers who argued the case for neutrality. According to his own account his opposition to intervention was very strong, and he ascribes to himself a leading role in galvanizing a 'Peace Party'.

On 26 July 1914, as the European crisis deepened, Harcourt records that he motored from his home at Nuneham Courtenay in Oxfordshire, across the River Thames to see Prime Minister Asquith at his home, The Wharf, in nearby Sutton Courtenay:

We talked about the probable Austro-Servian War (Austria has refused the Servian reply) and I told him that under no circs. could I be a party to our participation in a European War.

I warned him [Asquith] that he ought to order Churchill to move no ship anywhere without instructions from the Cabinet. I have a profound distrust of Winston's judgment and loyalty and I believe that if the German fleet moved out into the Channel (agst. France—not us) he would be capable of launching our fleet at them without reference to the Cabinet.

The P.M. pooh poohed the idea—but I think he is wrong not to take this precaution.

At the next day's Cabinet meeting we find Harcourt determined to resist any slide towards war, but we also learn that this position is not unconditional. The Germans have attempted to secure British neutrality with a promise of no annexations in France—she would be content with some French colonies:

> I said it was inconceivable that we should take part in a European War on a Servian issue, but still more inconceivable that we should base our abstention on such a bargain. ...
>
> After the Cabinet I had talks with several colleagues in order to form a Peace party which if necessary shall break up the Cabinet in the interest of our abstention.
>
> I think I can already count on 11.
>
> Self, J. Morley, Runciman, McKinnon Wood, Pease, McKenna, Beauchamp, Burns, Simon, Hobhouse, Birrell (probably also Samuel and Masterman). If we destroyed this Govt. to prevent war, no other cd. make it.[7]

On 29 July he records the debate in the Cabinet about obligations to Belgium, noting that the Russians say a declaration of support for France would prevent war, but that the Germans are saying that a declaration of neutrality would prevent war:

> I am determined not to remain in the Cabinet if they decide to join in a war—but they cannot so decide as I am certain now I can take at least 9 colleagues out with me on resignation viz. Morley, Burns, Beauchamp, McK[innon] Wood, Pease, Samuel, Hobhouse, Runciman, Simon.

Cabinet Journal of Lewis Harcourt, 26–29 July 1914

'We've sent ... "the precautionary telegram" to every office in the Empire'

MARGOT ASQUITH AND THE PRIME MINISTER ON THE EVE OF WAR

An insight into the private side of international politics is provided by Margot Asquith's diary. As the prime minister's wife she was privy to some of the innermost thoughts, arguments and ideas in the highest political circles, and recorded her impressions in her diary. Margot tried to write up her diary early each morning, and admitted that she had neither the time nor the inclination to go back and reconsider what she had written. She was a passionate and opinionated woman, and many of the diary entries appear to have been written in emotional bursts of energy. The result is an extraordinarily subjective and interesting account of British politics and personalities of the era.

> July 29th 1914   Bad news from abroad
> I was lying in bed resting 7.30 p.m.: the strain from hour-to-hour—waiting for telegrams—late at night—standing stunned and unable to read or write—2 cabinets a day—crowds thro wh. to pass cheering Henry wildly—all this contributed to making me tired. H. came into my room. I saw by his face that something momentous had happened—I sat up and looked at him. For once he stood still and did not walk up and down the room.
> H. Well! We've sent what is called 'the precautionary telegram' to every office in the Empire—War, Navy, Post Office etc to be ready for war. This is what the Committee of Defence have been discussing and settling for the last 2 years. It has never been done before and I am <u>very</u> curious to see what effect it will have. All these wires were sent between 2 and 3.30 marvellously quickly.
> I never saw Henry so keen outwardly—his face looked quite small and handsome. He sat on the foot of my bed.
> M. (passionately moved I sat up and felt 10 feet high) How <u>thrilling</u>! Oh! tell me aren't you xcited darling[?]
> H. (who generally smiles with his eye brows slightly turned) quite gravely kissed me and said it will be very interesting.

> *Margot Asquith's diary, 29 July 1914*

'Pray God I can still smash our Cabinet before they can commit the crime'

LEWIS HARCOURT AND THE COLONIES

Harcourt's journal entry for 30 July 1914, written on Colonial Office writing paper, runs to several pages. It vividly illustrates both the divisions within the Cabinet and the practical steps that the minister responsible for the colonies had to take, whatever his personal views. Harcourt's journal records not only Cabinet meetings, but also ad hoc meetings of interest groups and conversations with individuals.

> Sent special fresh warnings by tel. to all Domins. and Cols. to prevent search—am much afraid of an 'incident' over search on some German vessel.
>
> Lambert of Admlty told me Churchill last night hired 'Acquitania' (Cunard)? What for? Transport of troops to Belgium or for guard ship in Mersey? Also commandeered all coal in South Wales—Cardiff paralysed: he is sd. to have incurred expenditure of over £1,000,000—he told us at Cab. yesterday 'Precautionary' stage expenses wd. not exceed £10,000. I think he has gone mad. Every room in admiralty lighted and men at work when I passed at 2 a.m. this morning. I fear he is carrying his preparations too far and getting prematurely in the war stage. . . .
>
> On Front Bench at Question Time Grey told me he had recd. from Bethman Holweg[8] (I suppose thro' Goschen[9] at Berlin) shameful proposal that we should declare our neutrality on promise from Germ. Govt. that they wd. respect neutrality of Holland: ditto of Belgium <u>after they had violated it to attack France</u>: wd. not, after crushing France, annex European territories (tho' take her Colonies): subsequently offer us a European neutrality and friendship in general affairs. Grey of course without hesitation rejected offer with (I think) some contumely.
>
> Cambon (Fr. Ambass.) is coming this aft. to Grey to put <u>the</u> question 'are we going to help France if war breaks out.' Grey told me he will say to Cambon 'I cannot answer without a Cabinet (tomorrow morning) but tell him that in pres. circs. public opinion here not support or enable H.M.G. to give an affirmative answer.'
>
> Cambon if wise will accept non-committal answer sooner than negative.

Simon, J. Morley, Hobhouse, Beauchamp, Pease, Runciman, Montagu, Birrell all been in my room this afternoon—all with me, but Hobhouse with some reservations as to Belgium (he was of course a soldier). ...

I sent Sir F. Miles (Govr. of Gib.) back to his post today—pledged on word of honour to avoid any 'incident'.

Simon sd. to me pointing to Pease 'my views are those of <u>his</u> forebears'.

Lambert tells me Winston's mad commandeering of coal has been cancelled this afternoon.

My prescribed duty in 'precautionary stage' to ask Australia to place her fleet at our disposal and put under command of Admiralty.

I declined to send this tel. this morn. on ground premature, unnecessary and that I wanted initiative to be taken by Australia—if initiative failed I wd. tel (priv. and pers.) to R.M. Ferguson [Governor-General] to try to produce it. At 5 p.m. recd. acknlgmt. fr. Austral. of my 'warning' tel. with unofficial offer of their fleet for our purposes.

Sent tel. to Admlty and P.M.—Admlty asked me to tel to Austr. for fleet to go to 'War stations'. I did so with regret (cd. not take responsibil. of refusing)—I think premature, but possibly justified on ground of great distances for their fleet e.g. The Australia [warship] has got to go to coast of West. Australia.

Hobhouse hears from Pres. of Dresdener Bank that Germany has given Russia 24 hours to explain her mobilisation, failing which Germany will mobilise.

Emmott and Vernon (of C.O.) came to me this morn. to say French delegates to New Hebrides Commiss. must return to France on Sat. (convinced war will be declared by Monday) and Commiss. must meet at 10 am. tomorrow morn to conclude report etc. ...

J. Morley told me this aft. he was prepared to resign at my signal, but I don't think it will be tomorrow.

Ld. Bryce has been to me—and separately Molteno M.P. on behalf of Radicals to ask situation. Both sd. they were confident in me and as long as I stayed in Cabinet they wd. assume that peace was assured. I am to let them know if <u>that</u> situation alters.

At the end of the day, Harcourt is vehemently for peace:

War situation I fear much worse tonight. Pray God I can still smash our Cabinet before they can commit the crime.

Cabinet Journal of Lewis Harcourt, 30 July 1914

'We agreed to refuse to go to war merely on a violation of Belgian neutrality'

THE CABINET ON THE EVE OF WAR

Harcourt's account of the Cabinet meeting held between 11 a.m. and 1.55 p.m. gives a detailed picture of the slide into war and the tensions this created in the government. News of German military movements continually affected the individual and collective response of Cabinet members to the unfolding drama.

The pre-war Anglo-French naval agreements had resulted in a plan whereby in the event of war with Germany, the British fleet would take responsibility for the defence of the Channel and the northern coast of France. Harcourt's version of events indicates varying degrees of opinion as to the importance of the violation of Belgian neutrality. In the reality of an impending German attack, it was clear that if the British did not want Germany to be able to launch a naval offensive against an undefended French coast, then she would be obliged to intervene, and this would commit the British to war whether Belgium was invaded or not.

> Sunday   2.8.14
>   Simon and Illingworth came to me at 14 B. Sq. [14 Berkeley Square, Harcourt's London residence] at midnight last night to ask me to come to Ll. Geo. at 11 Down. St. at 10 this morn. I suggested other Peace colleagues.
>   Went there at 10. We had Pease, Mc K[innon] Wood, Beauchamp, Simon, Runciman, Ll. Geo. and self.
>   Settled we wd. not go to war for mere violation of Belgian territory and hold up if possible any decision today.
>
> 11.0 a.m. Before Cab. Ll. Geo. and I went to P.M. and sd we represented 8–10 colleagues who wd. not go to war for Belgium. P.M. listened, sd. nothing. Birrell added his name to others before Ll. G. and I went up.

At Cabinet   11–1.55

Moratorium Bill approved.—Ditto arrangts. with Priv. Banks and Bk of Engl. as to deposit of £15 mills of gold and 35 mills. securities and issue of notes agst. both.

Issue £1 and 10/- Bk notes will take at least 3 weeks: in mean time we can make Postal notes legal tender: we have £2,500,000 in stock and can get £500,000 per diem.

War risk sea insurance (Huth Jackson's scheme) approved.

War is declar. by Germany on Russia.

Luxemburg is invaded by Germans—Duchy has protested to us. Germ. troops are moving <u>south</u> as if they did not mean to enter Belgium.

The Germ. Ambass. saw P.M. this morning—he was in tears and sd. it is not France but my country wh. is going to be crushed—he thinks his Govt. mad.

Grey saw the Fr. Ambass. yesterday—he also in tears. Grey told him we shd. not send troops to France to defend the Franco-Belg. frontier (this now less necess. as Italy has declared her neutrality and thus releases 6 divs. of Fr. troops fr. the Ital. frontier).

Grey also told Cambon that we took yesterday no decis. as to Belgian neutrality or as to our action if Germ. fleet came into Channel.

But Grey sd. it was <u>vital</u> to him that he shd. today assure Cambon that if the Germ. Fleet attacked French coast we wd. prevent it and use all our naval power. And he must say this in Parlt. tomorrow.

Nothing is to be sd. today to Cambon (whom Grey sees at 2.30) as to our attitude to a breach of Belg. neutrality.

Grey is much stronger than before for joining in war and wd. <u>like</u> to promise France our help today.

Crewe[10] from all he sd. this morning seems to be with 'us'.

Bonar Law[11] wrote to P.M. during Cabinet that he and Lansdowne as represent. Un[ionist] Pty. are prepared to support Govt. in war and think it "wd. be fatal to the honour and security of the U.K. to hesitate".

On Belg. neutrality Winston sd. 'If Germ violates Belg. neutrality I want to go to war—if you don't I must resign'. J Morley sd. 'if you <u>do</u> go to war <u>I</u> resign'. J Morley very angry at Fleet reserves being mobilised during last night—contrary to Winston's promise to Cab. It still may not be necess. to issue Proclamation till tomorrow.

J. Burns sd. he could not agree to Grey's formula to Cambon this afternoon as to German fleet attack on Fr. coast and must resign at once—almost in tears. We all begged him to take time to think and to come back to Cabinet at 6.30 this evening. He promised to do this.

At 2 p.m. I went to lunch with Beauchamp in Belgrave Sq. J. Morley, Simon, Samuel, Ll. Geo. also came. We telephoned for Pease, Mc K[innon] Wood and Runciman who joined us after luncheon and discussed plans for afternoon. Beauchamp feels we were 'jockeyed' this morning over Germ. Fleet; Simon agrees and thinks we ought to have resigned with Burns. I differ as I think the prevention of a German fleet attack and capture of French territory on shore of Channel a British interest.

We agreed to refuse to go to war merely on a violation of Belg. neutrality by a traverse for invasion purposes of territory but to regard any permanent danger or threat to Belg. independence (such as occupation) as a vital Brit. interest.'

Cabinet Journal of Lewis Harcourt, 2 August 1914

'We have no obligation of any kind either to France or Russia'

THE PRIME MINISTER EXPLAINS
THE CASE FOR PEACE OR WAR

In his letter of 1 August to his confidante Venetia Stanley, Asquith described the frantic attempts to rein in the Russians, whose mobilization orders threaten to wreck the last hope of a settlement. Having drafted a letter to be sent on behalf of King George to his cousin Czar Nicholas, Asquith and several colleagues took it by taxi to Buckingham Palace where the King was 'hauled out of his bed' at 1.30 a.m. The King agreed to send the letter, adding only a personal touch 'by the insertion of the words "My dear Nicky"—and the addition at the end of the signature "Georgie"!' Asquith told Venetia about the Cabinet that morning, noting that 'Winston occupied at least half the time', and

Winston Churchill and Venetia Stanley on the beach at Penrhos in 1910

describing the cracks appearing at the heart of the government: 'We came, every now and again, near to the parting of the ways.' Asquith talked of Morley and possibly Simon as being on the 'Manchester Guardian tack—that we should declare now and at once that in no circumstances will we take a hand'. The *Manchester Guardian* was the strongest advocate of non-intervention among a group of Liberal papers that took this line. He was in no doubt that the majority of the party was against intervention, but Grey had said that he would have to go if Britain did not support France, and Churchill was 'very bellicose and demanding immediate mobilisation. ... The main controversy pivots upon Belgium and its neutrality.' Asquith summarized the position for Venetia:

I am still <u>not quite</u> hopeless about peace, tho' far from hopeful. But if it comes to war I feel sure (this is entirely between you and me) that we shall have <u>some</u> split in the Cabinet. Of course, if Grey went I should go, and the whole thing would break up. On the other hand, we may have to contemplate with such equanimity as we can command the loss of Morley, and possibly (tho' I don't think it) of the Impeccable [this was Asquith's nickname for Simon].

On Sunday 2 August Asquith wrote to Venetia just after the Cabinet meeting described by Harcourt (see pp. 33–5) that ended at about 2 p.m. Among items of news about the Cabinet, and an emotional meeting with the German ambassador Lichnowsky who had wept and blamed his own government for not restraining Austria, Asquith laid out his own views on the crisis in six points:

Happily I am quite clear in my own mind as to what is right and wrong. ...
  (1) We have no obligation of any kind either to France or Russia to give them naval or military help.
  (2) The despatch of the Expeditionary force to help France at this moment is out of the question and wd. serve no object.
  (3) We mustn't forget the ties created by our long-standing and intimate friendship with France.
  (4) It is against British interests that France shd. be wiped out as a Great Power.
  (5) We cannot allow Germany to use the Channel as a hostile base.
  (6) We have obligations to Belgium to prevent her being utilised and absorbed by Germany.

Venetia was here being included in a discussion that was meant for the Cabinet alone. The idea that despatch of a force to France would serve no object is interesting. At this stage there were worries in Britain that if war should come, there would be an invasion threat, and it was thought that forces would be required for home defence. It was also still believed at this point that the British contribution might be largely naval. In the event, on 5 August 1914, the War Council decided to send the British Expeditionary Force to France.

The Germans were at this moment embarking on a massive military gamble. Their hope was that by attacking France through Belgium, they would be able to turn the French flank, march on Paris, and defeat France quickly. For this prize, Germany was prepared to risk the possibility of war with Belgium and Britain, believing that in a short war Britain's tiny standing army would not tilt the military balance. The government's divisions, and the problems in Ireland, must have encouraged this view.

In his letter to Venetia on Monday 3 August Asquith describes the Cabinet meeting of Sunday evening, and notes 'the large crowds perambulating the streets and cheering the King at Buckingham Palace … one could hear this distant roaring as late as 1 or 1.30 in the morning.' These were the bank holiday crowds whose activities have perhaps given a false impression of the popularity of the decision for war. Asquith was not taken in:

> You remember Sir R. Walpole's remark: 'Now they are ringing their bells; in a few weeks they'll be wringing their hands'. How one loathes such levity.

On Tuesday 4 August, the day that Britain declared war, Asquith was still holding out the possibility of a meeting with Venetia at the weekend, though in the circumstances he believed that this was 'the dimmest glimmer' of hope. He reported that they had learned in Cabinet of the German invasion of Belgium, and he felt that 'this simplifies matters'. An ultimatum was sent to Germany, to expire at midnight, requesting respect for Belgian neutrality:

> Winston, who has got on all his war-paint, is longing for a sea-fight in the early hours of tomorrow, resulting in the sinking of the 'Goeben' [a German battlecruiser in the Mediterranean]. The whole thing fills me with sadness.

At the end of the letter he wrote:

> We are on the eve of horrible things. I wish you were nearer my darling: wouldn't it be a joy if we could spend Sunday together? I love you more than I can say.

> *Letters from H.H. Asquith to Venetia Stanley, 1–4 August 1914*

'Dear dear Mrs Asquith can we not stop it?'

MARGOT ASQUITH AND THE GERMAN AMBASSADOR

Margot's account of the meeting with the German ambassador in London, Karl Max, Prince Lichnowsky (1860–1928) and his wife Mechthilde on the eve of the declaration of war paints a very emotional scene. The ambassador is portrayed as highly critical of the Kaiser and his advisers, laying the blame for the war at their door. This is interesting in view of the role Lichnowsky was subsequently to have in the arguments over blame for the war. In 1916 he wrote a pamphlet blaming German diplomacy for the outbreak of war, *My Mission to London 1912–1914*. It was printed privately, and having been published under several titles in Europe and the United States was used by the allies as a source for the evidence of German responsibility for the war. A British copy was published by Cassell and Co. in 1918 with a preface by Professor Gilbert Murray.

> Sunday 2nd Aug 1914
> Elizabeth and I and our married governess and her husband Fran and Herr Ruger went to St. Paul's Cathedral and all took the Holy Communion. I felt intensely sorry for her as I knew he wd. have to be called back to Germany to fight.
>
> After St. Paul's I went to see the German Ambassador and his dear wife Mechthilde Lichnowsky, friends of ours. I found them in a state of white despair. ...
>
> She was lying on a green sofa with her little Dachs hound who yapped drearily at me from habit, feeling no hostility only pity for his lady. Her eyes were starved from crying—he [Prince Lichnowsky] was walking up and down in silence. He caught me by the hands and said 'Oh! Say there is surely <u>not</u> going to be war (pronouncing it like far). Dear dear Mrs Asquith can we not stop it[?]' (wringing his hands). I put my arms round Mechthilde on the sofa while we both cried. She got up and pointed to the trees and sky and said 'To think that <u>we</u> sd. bring such sorrows to an innocent happy people! I have always hated and loathed our Kaiser have I not said so 1000 times dear little Margot he and his friends are all <u>brutes</u>! I will never cross his threshold again'

The Prince 'I do not understand what has happened! What it is all about'—

Margot 'I can only think his genius. . . .'

Prince L— 'The Kaiser is no genius! he is ill informed, <u>impulsive</u>, <u>mad</u>! Never listening or believing one word what I say—never answering telegrams!!'

M[echthilde]—'He treated Metternich just the same. He can't <u>bear</u> the truth. He is a <u>fiend</u> and a megolomaniac' (*sic*)

The P[rince] 'Some say it is not so much him. . . .' Mechthilde interupting [*sic*]

Princess—'They say what they like it is him and his idiot son and that horrible hard brutal war party that surrounds him'

I stayed on doing all I cd. but quite powerless to console them. The Prince had large tears rolling down his thin cheeks when I said good-bye.

On 4 August Margot and her daughter Violet Asquith visited the German embassy on the day war was declared, and she records that Lichnowsky said to her:

'So it is all over you will declare war tonight, and you knew we <u>must</u> go thro' Belgium, there is no other way, we never counted that old old treaty. Oh dear! Oh! dear don't. Don't go to war! Just wait!' holding my hands. I felt too sad to speak—we sat and cried on the green sofa.

Margot Asquith's diary, 2–4 August 1914

'Party begins tomorrow'

LIEUTENANT COLONEL MAKINS ON THE EVE OF WAR

Colonel Ernest Makins, soon to be a brigadier, was an alumnus of
Christ Church, Oxford, and a cavalry officer. His diary gives us an
insight into the attitude and reactions of a senior professional army
officer to an unprecedented military situation for the British Army.

As the European situation deteriorated, Makins was looking for
somewhere to live in Shropshire. On 30 July he was at a village fête
at the home of the Swire family, and noted that Admiral Thursby[12]
was present; while there Makins was ordered by telegraph to go to
Portsmouth. Returning to London on 31 July, Makins was forced to
'snatch a bun' at Wolverhampton as the railwaymen's strike meant there
was no restaurant car on his train. Dining at his brother Hugh's[13] club
in London that evening, he thought that 'the war news is worse'. On 1
August Makins noted that a customer at the bank had trouble cashing
a £100 cheque. Having gone to 'see about my uniform coming back
from Daniells, Tootles [his brother Hugh] and I catch the 2.10 train to
Ludgershall—awfully full with holiday people and officers etc rejoining
units. News could not be worse.' On Sunday 2 August he spoke to
another brother, 'Geof',[14] on the telephone, whose 'war news sounds
hopeless'. There were no mobilization orders on Monday 3 August, and
Makins went out for a horse ride round Sidbury Hill with Gilbert and
Bella, and played cricket with 'the boys' after tea. The Makins's guests,
Gilbert and Bella, were Brigadier-General Gilbert Mellor (1872–1947)
and his wife Isabella, Ernest's sister. The boys were his sons Roger,
later a diplomat and ambassador to the United States, and Guy. On
the day Britain declared war, Tuesday 4 August, Makins recorded that
he received a 'telegram from Gilbert to say "Party begins tomorrow"
which was to mean mobilization. So we are committed at last. We all
go for a stroll after tea.'

Diary of Lieutenant Colonel (later Brigadier) Ernest Makins,
30 July to 4 August 1914

'I can truthfully say that this has been the greatest moment of my life'

MARGOT ASQUITH'S ACCOUNT OF THE BRITISH DECLARATION OF WAR

Margot Asquith's description of the day war was declared reveals her excitement at being at the centre of British politics in such momentous times.

Tuesday August 4th 1914.
We declared war. It was an agonizing day and night. I asked H at night if he had had a bad day he said 'Six of my men have resigned—John Morley, Burns, Simon, Beauchamp and Trevellyan[15] [*sic*] ... I tried to persuade Morley to stay, this is his answer'. H gave the enclosed letter [not now present in the diary] to me and said ['Jone of the most distinguished men living and certainly the best talker. I shall miss him very much[']. He persuaded Simon and Beauchamp to stay on ....
WAR
We went to H of Commons. I sat breathless while Henry announced that an ultimatum had been sent to Germany on the question of the neutrality of Belgium. He spoke with xtraordinary gravity and in his most delicate tones. The house was packed......... 'We have asked that the reply to that request and a satisfactory answer to the telegram of this morning sd be given before midnight'.
These words called forth a roll of cheers from every part of the House.
Henry then got up and walked down to the bar of the House in a roar of cheers, was then called on the Speaker and announced 'a message from His Majesty signed by his own hand' his announcement was received with cheers wh went on as H walked up the floor of the House and handed his document to the Speaker.
I can truthfully say that this has been the greatest moment of my life and the greatest moment in British politics since Waterloo.
I was glad the Speaker's Gallery was dark and that no one cd hear my heart beat or see the thousand hammers in my brain. No one really at that time wd have turned a hair if we had all screamed

and fainted. Even the least imaginative was rivetted. I wasn't clearly aware of <u>myself</u> either, but I was quite clear that this final decision means 'a state of war xists between Great Britain and Germany as from 11 p.m. on August 4th 1914'.

Margot Asquith's diary, 4 August 1914

'There has been no Jingo-ism, but only a resolute determination not to be bullied'

THE RECTOR OF TICKENCOTE ASSESSES THE MOOD OF THE NATION

Lionel Cholmondeley, an alumnus of Oriel College, Oxford, was chaplain to the British embassy in Tokyo, Japan. Before that he had been a missionary in Japan, serving with the first Anglican Bishop of South Tokyo, Edward Bickersteth, the father of Burgon Bickersteth. As he was far removed from the unfolding drama in Europe, his correspondents kept him well informed with details of events and opinions at home. In this letter the rector of Tickencote gives his perception of the mood of the country just after the British declaration of war. The well-known accounts of crowds celebrating the onset of war may in reality be based on impressions of the activities of holiday crowds in central London. Christian's description emphasizes instead the seriousness of the resolution of the people and the lack of jingoism. In the early days of the war, Asquith's speeches and actions were very favourably received and he was seen as a model of firm resolve and quiet determination, and the writer acknowledges this though he was no Liberal. The letter indeed expresses another common idea among many churchmen, that the war would bring redemption through sacrifice to a nation that had lost its way, corrupted by secular and liberal values.

43

My dear Lionel,

The Country has been at War since Tuesday night. You will
hear from many Correspondents, better-informed than I,—that
the Temper of the people has been creditable. I see scarcely any
Newspaper except the Times, but its information may be relied on.
Both Houses of Parl. have behaved with dignity. Mr Redmond[16] in
generous terms assured Mr Asquith that England might count on
the loyalty of Ireland, which words apparently have had an excellent
effect.

Sir E. Grey's Despatches and Speeches shew a sincere desire of
Peace, and seem to be worthy of the occasion. And, so far as I can
judge, there has been no Jingo-ism, but only a resolute determination not to be bullied, and to stand to one's Engagements. In the
country generally there is practical unanimity. Men who have any
money, are willing to pay, and young Fellows are willing to serve.

The Archbishop spoke some wise words last Sunday, to which
I refer you, as expressing, much better than I cd have done, what
I feel. We must put our trust in God, and do our Duty. Personally,
I may say to you, without risk of being misunderstood, that I
dislike extremely the thought and the fact of our being at war with
Germans. They are our own Kinsmen, and though during forty
yrs of Prosperity they have been bumptious and overbearing, they
have nobler Ideals, and have more sense of Righteousness than
the French. It wd be silly to attempt to forecast the Result, but
one remembers that in 1870 the Prussians had only the French to
contend with, whereas now it is: N. Germany and Austria versus
Russia—France—and Eng.—with Servia, (for what it is worth). The
numbers appear to be against the Germans. In Eng. we have been
very much cheered by the Loyalty of the Colonies—Austr. N.Z.
Canada. and S. Afr and by the Kind Sympathy of Japan and U.S.A.
As I write—Aug. 8—the news comes in that Liège is still holding
out. May we all be preserved from being over-confident.

Monday. Aug. 10

We had special Prayers yesterday in our Church. There were
fairly good Congregations, and the people seemed to be impressed
with the gravity of the situation. Both in the morng and in the evng I
read some part of the Abp's Sermons. From all that I hear, the state
of Society in Eng. during the last twelve or thirteen years has been

very bad, and I do earnestly pray that, whatever may be the issue of this war, the next Generation may be more God-fearing than the present.

Letter from George Christian to Lionel Cholmondeley, 7 August 1914

'No woman dares to appear in the evening without a sock in her hand'

A LETTER TO ANDREW CLARK FROM SCOTLAND

Andrew Clark, rector of Great Leighs, was a Scotsman, born in Dollarfield, Clackmannanshire, in 1856. He married Mary Walker Paterson, daughter of the Provost of St Andrew's in 1886, and so had a number of Paterson in-laws who kept him supplied with information from Scotland. Into his diary of Great Leighs life he transcribed part of a letter from his brother-in-law, John Paterson, dated 14 August 1914:

We are having stirring times here. Cupar is just a big military camp. It is a base or a depot for this part. There are troops arriving and departing daily. There were seven special trains came in last night. Nearly every house has several officers billeted on them. The Gordon's have two. ...

The fields are full of horses tethered in rows, and the Guns are in the Public Park.

You can hardly get about the street for motors, wagons, and soldiers.

There are sentries all over the town. On all the country roads at night, even in this road I am in, there are four mounted men, all night. Every one out after 9 has to stop and give an account of himself.

In Cupar women are not to be out after 10.

Everyone is working for the soldiers. In this wee village I have every woman in it, knitting socks. I gave the wool for 30 pairs, all now in hand. I am hoping Mrs. Sharp will give me some more [Clark has added a footnote that this was Mrs Frederick Sharp, wife of a Fife landowner and Dundee mill-owner].

45

No woman dares to appear in the evening without a sock in her hand, or she has to explain to me why. I tell them it is Martial Law now! They are all very good and very willing. I make them wash the socks before they bring them.

Diary of the Revd Andrew Clark, rector of Great Leighs, Essex, 14 August 1914

'Unless position improves greatly in 24 hours it will be <u>very serious</u>'

THE BATTLE OF MONS AND THE CABINET

Lewis Harcourt's journal from 23 to 31 August 1914 allows us to trace the political and strategic impact of the first major action of the British army in the First World War, the battle of Mons (23 August), which was followed by a desperate two-week retreat to the outskirts of Paris. Harcourt's concise notes convey something of the panic that the retreat caused, and indicate some of the diplomatic and strategic options that were discussed as the allies sought to shore up their position at this critical moment. Among other concerns were the strain on Anglo-French relations and how to release bad news to the public.

Cab. 23.8.14
Sir J. French to Kitchener this morning: Namur fallen—our troops retreating to Valenciennes–Longueville–Maubeuge line as originally intended.

French says we must defend Havre now. Kitchener read letter from Sir J. French of Saturday—in good spirits then—hoped Namur would hold out 2 or 3 days.

Kitchener means to entrench if necessary at Cherbourg: he thinks the Germans will try to turn round Lille and give our men a very hot corner....

Sir J. French's general instructions were if necessary to retire towards the coast.

Long discussion as to warning we should issue to the Press as to fall of Namur and prepare public for bad news....

1 p.m. Sir J. French has just telegraphed for re-inforcements at the rate of 10%: this looks as if he had lost 10,000 men. ...

24.8.14
Dined tonight with Asquiths at 10 D. St. Played bridge—waiting for tel. from Gen. French as to our retreat from Mons. —only got it at 12.30 a.m.—on the whole more satisfactory than I expected, but no figures of casualties. ...

Cab. 25.8.14 ...
K. takes serious view of French retirement. We have now retreated to Cambrai.

We have asked Belgians to come out of Antwerp to cut German communications. K. says 'unless position improves greatly in 24 hours it will be <u>very serious</u>: we are going through 1870 again'.

We are not sending the 6th. div. now to Sir J. French: we may want it to seize Dunkirk in order to get him out of the country. ...

Winston trying to raise 'compulsory service'. P.M. trying to prevent him ('remote contingencies') ...

Telegram just in (1.15 p.m.) from Belgian Foreign Minister to say Namur forts have not fallen and will resist to the end: it looks as if the French had deserted them in their retreat!

Cab. 26th.8.14
Telegram from Sir J. French, still retiring, complains of hesitation of the French commanders. Kitchener telegraphs to Sir J.F. 'our present method of cooperation will soon be ineffective, if the French show no better morale'. ...

Churchill. We occupied Ostend with 3,000 marines this morning and will turn out some Uhlans there. ...

If we send 6th Div. it wd. only be to bring Sir J. French out and return here.

We may have to strengthen Dunkirk a little. Calais said to be indefensible but would be very bad for us if in German hands. ...

Cab. 27.8.14
... Gen. French retiring on Amiens and Rheims with Joffre[17] hopeful of better line. Gen. French followed by 250,000 Germans.

The French will have 1,200,000 men on Amiens Rheims line. ...

We shall have to move our sea base to La Rochelle and give up Havre and Cherbourg. ...

{The King wants us to vote in H. of C. £500,000 to Belgium for relief of distress—we don't agree it might fall into German hands} ...

Kitch. very much against <u>our</u> taking any initiative against Turkey.

Churchill talking again about offering Cyprus to Greece: I sd. you can't give it unless you are at war with Turkey. ...

I said 'you can buy Italy by giving her Malta'. This shocked Kitchener and Asquith, but Churchill agreed with me ...

Dined with Kitchener tonight at 2 Carlton Gdns. Ll. Geo. Sir __ Brade,[18] Sir G. Arthur and another W.O. man there.

Kitch sd. failure of the French 5th Army this week to cut in behind Germ line—northward from Namur—absolutely given away a position in which 150,000 German troops wd. have had to surrender.

Discovery that the French deserted Namur whilst forts still holding out is deep disgrace.

Kitch. thinks due to African Div. being placed on left of Namur. He told the French Military Attaché yesterday if he (Kitch) could get at the Gen. of the 5th French army he would shoot or hang him! ...

Cab. 28.8.14

... Bad news from Sir J. French: retired to Nogon on Amiens—Rheims line: very large further losses and probably 20 guns.

Sir J. French is now in a better position for defence: he got no support from the French for 2 days.

Winston very anxious to publish a great deal of our news: Kitchener bitterly opposed: we must not give away our present positions through the Press. ...

Cab. 29.8.14

... Another big battle is coming in 2 or 3 days: if it goes badly we must move our base from Havre southwards. ...

Cab. 31.8.14

Our and the French forces still retiring but doing well: Russian pressure increasing: we are retiring to the Seine or <u>behind it</u> with a base at Le Mans!

Our losses only 5,000–6,000 out of 148,000 men: we cannot understand this violent retirement.

Calais and Boulogne may now be occupied by Germans.

Crewe and Haldane think Sir J. French may be out of temper with Joffre. Kitchener does not think Joffre wrong: it looks like a quarrel between French and Joffre.

We are not kept properly informed by Sir J. French and staff.

Ll. Geo. very much upset: thinks Sir J. French has lost his nerve.

Kitchener is sending a stiff telegram to Sir J. French of surprise at his going so much behind the French line and telling him we expect him to cooperate fully with Joffre.

Cabinet journal of Lewis Harcourt, 23–31 August 1914

'Kitchener … issued an urgent appeal for 100,000 recruits'

BUTTERWORTH DESCRIBES THE RUSH TO ENLIST

George Butterworth, an alumnus of Trinity College, Oxford, was twenty-nine years old in August 1914. He was a composer, collector of folk music, a folk dancer, and a friend of and collaborator with Ralph Vaughan Williams, whom he had met at Oxford. His reaction to the outbreak of war was to attempt to join the army at once. With hindsight, this may seem surprising. His music, particularly the orchestral idyll *The Banks of Green Willow*, has often been seen as a musical equivalent of the war poetry of Rupert Brooke with its ruralist and elegiac quality, particularly as both men were killed in the war. This should warn us about over-simplifying our picture of the First World War. *The Banks of Green Willow* was written before the war in 1913, and its style epitomizes a vision that was prevalent in English music and poetry of the time. In retrospect, the war has provided a fixed end to the era, but *The Banks of Green Willow* would have been written, war or no war. This is emphasized by Butterworth's diary. Far from lamenting the war or regretting its necessity, Butterworth betrays no sign of any doubts about throwing himself into the conflict and clearly regards it as his duty. Indeed, he seems to have found a sense of purpose. He noted on 1 September that there was a rush of recruits, and explicitly states that the 'seriousness of the news from France' was one of the causes.

49

The first few weeks of the diary were written up retrospectively in September 1914 as Butterworth began to record his experiences, partly for the benefit of his father, with whom he kept up a continuous correspondence. Butterworth provides an account of the experiences of the ordinary soldier in the early months of the war, as for personal reasons he chose to join as a private together with some friends. The diary, however, illustrates the pressure that men of his education and background came under to become officers.

> War between England and Germany was declared early in August. At the time I was at Stratford-on-Avon for the session of the English Folk Dance Society. All the regulars and reserves were immediately mobilised, and Kitchener also issued an urgent appeal for 100,000 recruits. The creation of this new force would result in vacancies for some 2,000 officers, and my first idea was to apply for one of these. The wording of the manifesto suggested that previous experience was not essential, but this turned out to be illusory. I spent two days at Oxford making enquiries, and went so far as to send in my name—through the O.T.C.—but it was obvious that I had no chance, and I shortly heard from the Oxford authorities that they were unable to recommend me. After this I returned to Stratford, and remained there for the rest of the session.

A letter from R.O. Morris[9] informed him that a group of friends were joining up as privates, and as he had already thought that this would be 'the most practical and obvious way of serving the country, … I wired to Morris saying that I would like to meet him in London and discuss the proposal'.

> Sat. Aug. 29
> Returned to London and dined with Morris and Woodhead —found they had already made preliminary arrangements. They had been advised by Scotland Yard authorities to join the Duke of Cornwall's Light Infantry, as it had been decided to recruit for that regiment in large numbers, and this would give a better chance for parties of friends to join en bloc. …

Tues. Sep 1

Brown, the two Ellises and myself went early to Scotland Yard and got through the medical without difficulty. The filling in of papers took a considerable time, as there was a great crowd of applicants.

I ought to mention that just at this time there was a huge rush of recruits—on Tuesday over 4,000 joined in London alone, and in the next few days those that came in were probably as many as all those who joined during August. This was partly due to increased activity amongst recruiters, partly to the seriousness of the news from France, which during this week-end looked very bad.

Diary of George Butterworth, 4 August–1 September 1914

'Toeing the line to be off'

BRIGADIER MAKINS AND MOBILIZATION

Things moved quite slowly for Makins after war was declared. He went up to London on 7 August to get his uniform. The train was three hours late as 'all the ordinary service is distracted. The government has taken over all the railways'. He visited various shops to have boots repaired and to purchase a new jersey and a new pair of breeches, had a filling done at the dentist, and after tea at the United Services Club 'where the Cavalry Club is quartered' went to his parents' London residence at 180 Queen's Gate Kensington and dined with Gilbert and Bella there. That evening he wrote officially to the War Office to explain that he was unemployed for the next six months and wanted employment. On Saturday 8 August he watched the enlisting at Whitehall before returning to Wiltshire on the train, arriving over an hour late. On 10 August he received the bad news from the War Office that his 'appointment is in abeyance for the present'. He returned to London at once to try and sort things out, and on 11 August dined at the United Services Club:

the Kaiser's picture there has a large piece of paper stuck on it (apparently posted on the actual paint) saying that it had better be removed or it might be damaged and signed The Com[mi]ttee which is probably not a correct signature, and is at any rate very bad form.

On 2 September he heard that he was to be appointed to the 6th Cavalry Brigade, which was made up of the 'Royals [1st (Royal) Dragoons], 10th Hussars [10th (The Prince of Wales's Own) Royal Hussars], and 3rd D.G.s [3rd (Prince of Wales's) Dragoon Guards] from Egypt, a real good thing'. There followed a number of quiet days, some days shopping, and some inspection of horses. On 18 September he noted that there was not much news of the 'big battle along the Aisne', but later he received a wire that 'Geof', his brother, had been wounded. He headed to the War Office on the 19th where he met Kitchener, who was 'pleasant and … full of schemes to accelerate our division'. On 26 September he spent another morning at the War Office, seeing 'various people in connection with my mobilization'. Here he heard that '8000 bayonets have been wired for from France to equip the cavalry with'. On 27 September Makins inspected a draft of horses from Nottinghamshire and Derbyshire, 'not a very brilliant lot'. This was followed by an inspection of the regiment by the King on the 28th. On 1 October Makins was busy once again selecting horses for the brigade; he thought that a hundred horses brought in from Shropshire, Denbigh and Cheshire were 'quite a good lot', while the horses acquired by the 10th Hussars were 'unfit for mobilization'. On 2 October he took the train to London to arrange power of attorney for his wife, and to arrange his will, and then he did 'a lot of shopping'. More shopping followed the next day, and there was news that 'we may go tomorrow'. On Sunday 4 October he was 'absolutely toeing the line to be off', but the brigade's transport was blocked on the line. He motored over to the school at Winchester to say goodbye to Roger, but the journey back to Biddesden took two hours as the car's lights failed and the 'driver was an absolute amateur'. There was still 'no news of starting yet', but at last on 5 October the order came through:

the Div. is to move at 4.20 p.m. This order arrives at 3.30 p.m. The Royals are to go from Amesbury at 1 hour intervals, commencing at 12.30 a.m. tomorrow. The Xth Hussars and Brig. H.Q. from Tidworth at 1 hour intervals commencing at 11.40 p.m. tonight.

Diary of Brigadier Ernest Makins, 7 August to 5 October 1914

'We have crossed the Marne'

THE BATTLE OF THE MARNE AND THE CABINET

September 1914 began with the British and French armies still in retreat before the German advance, and the Cabinet contemplating the possibility of the fall of Paris, but from 5 to 12 September the allies counter-attacked at the battle of the Marne. The victory here proved to be a critical moment in the war: the Germans were denied the swift victory over France that their two-front strategy required. Kitchener's assessment that the Germans were beaten proved premature, but the scene was now set for a long war of military deadlock and naval blockade, where the superior manpower and resources of the allies would eventually tilt the balance in their favour. Harcourt records:

> Cab. 1.9.14
> Kitchener left this morning to see Sir J. French and clear up the situation.
>
> The President of the Fr. Republic asked Bertie [British ambassador to France] yesterday to telephone to Sir J. French asking for support.
>
> Sir J.F. now gives a bad account of the 'shattered condition of my small force' and now takes a poor view of the French Commanders.
>
> The casualty list contains Officers 36 killed 95 missing! In the 1st Battln. Cheshire Regt. all officers missing. Over 4,000 casualties in about ½ the force. It seems as if Sir J.F. was justified in his retreat. ...
>
> Paris will probably soon be invested and Turkey may then come out against us. Greece will probably then be in alliance with us and we might let them take Gallipoli. ...
>
> We must lay a new cable to La Rochelle if Havre, Dieppe and Calais fall. ...
>
> [2 September] 2nd Cabinet 7 p.m. ...
> Kitchener in regimentals arrived 7.10. Joffre and Sir J. French not quarrelled—but rather out of touch—great length of line. Kitch. talked over plans with Millerand [French War Minister]: Joffre not there. Paris will only be defended by Territorials, but will take a long time to fall. French army must be kept intact.

Sir J. French and his men now in the line again. We give him the 6th Div. now. ...

Our casualties 8,000 all told, including 6,000 missing—2,000 of these are known to be returning to the lines.

Rouen is being evacuated: we have 10,000 tons of petrol there.

Sir J. French did not like Kitchener coming to France.

Much discussion at Cabinet as to wisdom of sending 6th Div.

Asq. 'We must be sure we are safe here'.

Churchill 'I will guarantee you against anything even in the nature of a raid'. ...

Cab. 3.9.14

The French have got £160,000,000 of gold in Paris. ?we bring it over here for safety if we can get hold of it. Grey to speak to Cambon. ...

Sir J. French got everything he wants in France, but organization of communications has broken down and the stuff does not get up to the front.

Recruiting over 30,000 a day now.

We have got 270,000 men now to the new army: shall have 300,000 by tomorrow. Cannot deal with it: very short of field guns and rifles: Kitch hopes to get enough but is sure it will break down. ...

Cab. 4.9.14

We have crossed the Marne—now at Lamy. Germans pressing on 5th Army—we are now <u>East</u> of Paris. Many stragglers rejoining our troops.

But our casualties are now 15,000, though 12,200 of these are 'missing'.

The Germans are trying to engage the French Army before investing Paris: the Germans have moved 50,000 of their 2nd line troops from the West front to meet Russia. ...

Governor of Calais wants help from us to defend Calais (our Marines now returned from Ostend) but we declined to do this. ...

Cab. 7.9.14

Joffre and Sir J. French taking offensive. Joffre has sent many army corps <u>west</u> of Paris from behind and may cut off German army on the Marne where we are attacking. The French have 50 divisions to 44 Germans in this battle.

Kitch. wants to send the 6th Div. to France (Pulteney in command). We agreed. Churchill quite confident no danger of an effective German sea raid. ...

Cab. 8.9.14
Good account from Sir J. French on the Marne.
    We shall soon have 50 divisions all told: 12 mos. hence we might have 1½ million men on the continent—1 million in 6 months.
    Over 400,000 recruits now to new army. ...

Cab. 9.9.14
Good news from Sir J. French. ...

Cab. 10.9.14 ...
The British position on the Marne is very good. Kitch. says if we hold Germans tonight they will be in a very bad position.
    We are 8 miles north of the Marne. ...

Cab. 11.9.14
German armies I–V in rapid retreat: Kitch. says <u>practically a rout</u>.

Cabinet journal of Lewis Harcourt, 1–11 September 1914

'I don't know whether England or Germany brought on this war, and you don't'

W.B. YEATS REFUSES TO SIGN
THE DECLARATION BY BRITISH AUTHORS

Gilbert Murray, Professor of Greek at Oxford University, had developed a reputation as an anti-war campaigner during the Boer War, and was concerned with ethics and international law. Later he would be a significant figure in the League of Nations movement. But in 1914 and 1915, convinced that justice was on the side of the allies, he wrote a number of pamphlets in support of the British war position, including

Thoughts on the War (1914) and *How Can War Ever Be Right?* (1915), part of a series of 'Oxford pamphlets' produced by Oxford University Press to explain and justify the war to the public in Britain and beyond. In *How Can War Ever Be Right?* he wrote:

> I do not regret any word that I have spoken or written in the cause of Peace, nor have I changed, as far as I know, any opinion that I have previously held on this subject. Yet I believe firmly that we were right to declare war against Germany on August 4, 1914, and that to have remained neutral in that crisis would have been a failure in public duty.

He took on anti-war campaigners such as Bertrand Russell in another 1915 booklet, *The Foreign Policy of Sir Edward Grey, 1906–1915*. Murray's papers are full of reactions to the opinions expressed in his pamphlets, mostly in favour of his arguments.

This letter from the Irish poet W.B. Yeats was a reaction to a request from Murray to sign a declaration of British authors that was published in *The Times* on 18 September under the heading 'Britain's Destiny and Duty. Declaration by Authors. A Righteous War'. It was also published in the *New York Times*. Forty authors signed the declaration, including J.M. Barrie, Arthur Conan Doyle, H. Rider Haggard, Thomas Hardy, Jerome K. Jerome, Rudyard Kipling, John Masefield and H.G. Wells. Yeats's reply shows signs of having been dashed off quickly in the heat of the moment, the typescript being full of the author's manuscript corrections. Although doubtful about the causes of the war and the extent of the alleged outrages committed by the Germans, Yeats clearly accepted that atrocities had been committed. Both Germany and Britain had published diplomatic papers to justify their positions, the German 'White Book' arguing that Germany was fighting a defensive war against Russian aggression.

Yeats by this time had become well known in England as well as Ireland, spending much time in London where he socialized with, among others, the Asquiths.

W.B. Yeats, c. 1911. Photograph by George Charles Beresford

Coole Park, Gort, Co. Galway.

September 15

Dear Murray,

No. I am sorry, but No. I long for the defeat of the Germans but your manifesto reads like an extract from the newspapers, and newspapers are liars. What have we novelists, poets, whatever we are, to do with them? First: I don't know whether England or Germany brought on this war, and you don't. Diplomatic documents published in the White Book deal with matters of form. The question is whether Germany has as England believes been arming for years to wage war on England, or whether as Germany believes, England has surrounded her with hostile alliances waiting their moment to attack, through which she had to force her way at the first likely moment. That knowledge will be kept by secret diplomacy for a good many years to come. Second: I cannot see who this document is going to influence. It has every sign of its origin 'drawn up to include as many people as possible' that is to say to be something which nobody will wholeheartedly believe, and which looks all its insincerity. If a manifesto is to move anybody the man who made it must at least believe in it. I would gladly join with you if you would get up a declaration against secret diplomacy when the time comes, or get up now a manifesto demanding some responsible investigation of German outrages. The present campaign may result in reprisals that will make this war more shameful than that of the Balkans. There should be no anonymous charges, and when the war is over the whole question of atrocities by whatever nation committed should be sifted out by the Hague or some other tribunal. It doesn't seem possible to doubt the atrocities in many cases, but one hopes that investigation would prove that great numbers of German commanders and soldiers have behaved with humanity. I gather from stray allusions in the Press that the Germans also are carrying on an atrocity campaign not only against the Belgians but against the French and English.

Yours s[incerel]y
WB Yeats

Letter from W.B. Yeats to Gilbert Murray, 15 September 1914

'I frankly don't understand how so many men are expected to live in one tent'

GEORGE BUTTERWORTH ENDURES
ARMY HARDSHIPS AS A PRIVATE

George Butterworth's account of his spell in the ranks allows us to see the life of the ordinary recruit from the somewhat detached perspective of one who could afford to buy his way out of some of the hardships. One of the many misconceptions of the war is that troops were thrown into battle without any preparation for trench warfare. Although inevitably training could not re-create real conditions, Butterworth here notes, in the opening months of the war, that the recruits are being given more advanced training, and also that close-order drill is not given prominence as it would be 'almost useless in action'. The idea that troops were made to advance at a walking pace in close order has endured in many accounts of battles of the war, but in reality local commanders were given discretion to adapt tactics according to conditions (see also p. 197).

'First days in Camp, Sep 5–17.
As I am several days behind with this journal, it is impossible to give details of each day. I am now writing on Sunday, September 13th, and will try and give some sort of a summary of the intervening time. ...

Time-table—This is nominally as follows:–
6 a.m. Reveille, dress, clean up tent (a mug of tea is <u>sometimes</u> obtainable).
7 a.m. Parade—usually a short march along the road.
8 a.m. Breakfast.
9 a.m. Parade—various kinds of drill till 10 o'clock. Half-an-hour is always given to Swedish exercises.
1 p.m. Dinner.
2 p.m. Drill till 5-0 p.m.
5 p.m. Tea—After tea we are liable to be called upon for occasional extra work any time up to 7-0, but usually nothing particular happens.

7 p.m.–9.30 We are free to go anywhere, and usually go into the town for shopping and supper.

N.B.—The drill is never very continuous—there are occasional intervals for rest, and the easy things are sandwiched in with the more arduous movements. So far I have not once felt really tired, but no doubt they will increase the work by degrees. One thing which has kept us back badly has been the absence of boots and other equipment. The intention of the authorities is to take us on as fast as possible; comparatively little time will be given to close-order drill, which is almost useless in action. We have already touched on things which the ordinary recruit would not begin until he had done elementary drill for many months. At the same time a certain amount of 'smartness' is doubtless necessary, as it is the best and shortest way of getting men to respond to the word of command.

Tents—Owing to the general over-crowding we are sleeping 14 in a tent. We have been fairly lucky in our bed-fellows—for it was not possible to choose the extra ones; there are two splendid Birmingham chaps, young married working men, and two or three less desirable Londoners, of the shopkeeper class.

… I frankly don't understand how so many men are expected to live in one tent. The actual bulk of their bodies takes up most of the room, and in addition we must have—
14 rifles,
 " bayonets,
 " sets of clothing, etc.,
 " 14 blankets,
 " rugs,
 " plates, cups, knives, forks, etc., besides various odds and ends for general use.

In fine weather we manage fairly well, as we can expand into the open, but the less said about wet days the better. The effect of 14 wet people huddled together is bad for the temper.

Fortunately, when our organisation was at its worst, the weather was lovely, but now the equinoctial gales have set in.

Food.—The three daily meals supplied by the authorities are reasonably good—one expected rough fare—
Breakfast—Tea (so-called), bread and some tinned food.

<u>Dinner</u>—Stewed beef (invariable) and potatoes (ditto); for some
technical reason the cooks are unable to attempt roasting.

<u>Tea</u>—Bread, butter (sometimes), and jam or tinned fruit. Except that
there is never enough tea, these meals are fairly satisfactory,—
{N.B.—Nothing is supplied after 5-0 p.m.}

<u>Canteen</u>.—We are supposed to be able to fill up deficiencies at the
regimental canteens, of which there are three, one for beer only, and
two for food, tobacco, etc. All of these are very unsatisfactory, being
quite insufficiently equipped. The beer is simply not worth fighting
for; and there is no other way of getting it. The 'dry' canteens are
always running short of everything, and there is no way of getting
the cup of hot coffee or cocoa which would be so acceptable at
night. For our part, we have formed a habit of going into Farnbor-
ough every evening and getting a proper supper, but there are not
many who can afford that regularly.

<u>Clothing</u>—This is the chief grievance: every recruit on enlisting was
told that he would be provided with full kit <u>immediately</u>, and was
consequently advised to bring next to nothing with him.

As a fact, for many days nothing at all was supplied; undercloth-
ing and boots are now being gradually doled out, but no khaki
or overcoats; hence the men have no protection from wet and no
proper change of clothes, and every shower of rain means so many
more on the sick list. Here again, those with spare cash have been
able to supply deficiencies, but the majority are in a poor way.

<u>Provision for sickness</u>—This is practically non-existent. I believe
a few serious cases have been removed to hospital, but those with
ordinary complaints (chills, diarrhoea, etc.) can do nothing but
make themselves as comfortable as possible in their own tents—no
effort seems to be made to provide them with special food. There
are doctors, of course, but they can do little without proper help
and accommodation.

<u>Hospital arrangements</u> can only be written down as bad. There
should, of course, be a hospital tent for the sick. ...

<u>Wednesday</u> Sep 23—Sharp frost in early morning, followed by a
fine, warm day. We are getting on faster with our work now, even
if we don't know any of it very thoroughly. In the afternoon the

company carried out a sham attack. We advanced in a series of extended lines, alternating rushing forward about 50 yards, and then lying down and firing as fast as possible. Rapid fire is supposed to be the chief asset of English infantry. We have also been practising several movements which are quite new, the result of experience of the present War. These are chiefly defensive measures against sudden attacks by cavalry or artillery.

Diary of George Butterworth

'I don't believe class distinctions will be nearly as strong when it's over'

A CLASSICAL SCHOLAR BECOMES A MUSKETRY INSTRUCTOR

The complexity of the responses to the war among academics and thinkers is reflected in the attitude of Francis Macdonald Cornford (1874–1943), classical scholar and fellow of Trinity College, Cambridge. He had been a supporter of degrees for women and working-class education, and was active in the campaign to have Bertrand Russell restored to his Cambridge fellowship from which he had been removed for his stance on conscientious objection. Cornford surprised his friends, among them Rupert Brooke and Gilbert Murray, by becoming an instructor of musketry at Grantham at the outbreak of the war. He had been in the Cambridge University OTC before the war. This letter to Murray outlines several interesting points—such as the importance of training and of the lessons learned from the mistakes of the Boer War, and the value of practical instruction compared with academic teaching. Cornford felt that the war provided an opportunity to change the relationship between the classes because of the need for a broader interaction between them. The letter was written in response to Murray's pamphlet *Thoughts on the War*, reprinted from the *Hibbert Journal* and published as Oxford Pamphlet number 41.

Sunday gives me a moment to write and thank you for Hamlet, and indirectly for your Hibbert paper which J.S.H[aldane][20] sent me. I liked it and felt very glad you had written it. Your work is to go on writing that kind of thing and keep down the bitterness and the vengefulness. It is more important than mine, and much harder.

Teaching musketry makes it possible to leave the papers unread and forget the horror. It keeps me hard at work all day teaching subalterns and N.C.O's the elements of things. I am amazed at the intelligence with which the present Hythe course has been planned and worked out. It is the best bit of elementary education for the untrained mind I have ever struck. All new to me, and new to everyone since S. Africa. That war will save us now, and has already saved France,—if France is saved.

I live in a pleasant commercial inn with 5 other Musketry In-structors and a gymnast—all uncertain in the use of the letter H and excellent fellows. It is a comfort to live with non-dons for a bit. That is one of the great things this war has done for us: I don't believe class distinctions will be nearly as strong when it's over.

We have a whole infantry division (about 20,000 odd) under canvas while the huts are being built to hold us when the weather breaks. This is a bit of the First Army, and they are beginning to get into shape. All, or nearly all, are North-countrymen: my battalion is the 6th York and Lancasters. My dialect is the only difficulty I have, except complete lack of all appliances, which I have to make for myself in spare time. ...

I have learnt a great deal this last month and been more happy than I could have thought possible.

Letter from Francis Macdonald Cornford to Gilbert Murray,
11 October 1914

'There are a lot of odd Uhlans about'

MAKINS DESCRIBES THE FIGHTING NEAR YPRES

14 October was Makins's forty-fifth birthday. It was certainly eventful, and his diary of the day's events provides a clear illustration of the chaotic situation in the early stages of the war. Allied and German forces were still trying to outflank each other in the autumn of 1914,

moving north in the so-called 'race for the sea'. Ypres became a key German objective in their attempt to outflank the allied line to the north, but in desperate fighting in October and November the allies clung on. Ypres became a keystone of the British line once the war had become a stalemate and the trenches had formed all along the Western Front. Cavalry were called upon regularly during this mobile phase of the war. Uhlans were lancers, but in 1914 the British referred to all German cavalry regiments as Uhlans because the various branches—cuirassiers, dragoons and hussars, as well as lancers—all carried lances.

March to Ypres, and move out just beyond. Soon after we get there towards Kemmel a Taube aeroplane comes over us and we start firing at it, and it begins to drop and we see it dip down and fall just beyond the town—a very good beginning. I ride back to Ypres for orders, and am ordered on to Kemmel—ask for a section of guns and get them. Finally push on to Kemmel and then to Neuf Eglise, where the armed motors bag 2 German dead and wound another, and get 5 horses. The Xth Hussars capture a Uhlan near Mt. Kemmel and think they wounded another—a wounded German is found in a house, but is too bad to move. Get in touch at La Clytte with the 4th Hussars and presently John Vaughan comes along. The whole cavalry is hereabouts. ... There are a lot of odd Uhlans about. De Knoop empties his revolver at 7 of them as they cross the road just by him. The Xth H[ussars] then go after them and have a great hunt, bagging 5 of them. Miles thinks he bags a couple and Peto the same. The baggage kill one and capture another—the man of the Xth H who was there says 'the Dook (Teck) took his 'orse and his 'elmet, and the man was hit right through the 'eart'. We lose 3 horses killed and one was missing.

All this took place just six days after the brigade had landed at Ostend. The tone of the diary was to change dramatically within a few days.

Diary of Brigadier Ernest Makins, 14 October 1914

'You can see the French advancing in long extended lines'

WAR DIARY OF ERNST STADLER, POET AND OFFICER IN THE GERMAN ARTILLERY

Oxford graduates were not only to be found in the British army. The German expressionist poet Ernst Stadler (1883–1914) was one of more than fifty German Rhodes scholars who fought in the German army in the First World War. He provides a link between several of the belligerent nations. He was born in Alsace, which had been part of the German Empire since 1871 but was to be returned to France after the war. He studied in Strasbourg and Oxford and was a senior lecturer in Brussels until mid-1914. One of his early influences was the French poet, essayist and socialist Charles Péguy (1873–1914), but later his poetry moved in the direction of the avant-garde. His 1914 poem *Der Aufbruch* (The Beginning, or Departure), is now seen as an important work of early expressionism. Expressionists emphasized originality, intensity and modernity, and *Der Aufbruch* ironically celebrates the thrill of a cavalry charge, the imagery reflecting romantic ideas of a pre-modern war. When war was declared Stadler was about to take up a professorship in Toronto, but instead as a lieutenant in the reserve, he was called up to serve with the 80th Field Artillery Regiment in his native Colmar. His diary reflects his literary style, full of short and striking sentences and vivid imagery. As he entered France, all thoughts of the war seemed to vanish as he greeted the soil of a country he loved. On 30 October 1914 Stadler was killed by a British shell at Zandvoorde in the very action described by Brigadier Makins (see pp. 71–2).

Monday 10 August

> In the morning the final entrenchments on the heights. Midday —we had just finished eating—the order comes to advance immediately. We harness up immediately. The Captain ahead in the car. We advance via Trimbach–Weiler–Bassemberg–Grube to Urbeis. Here we fell out. In Urbeis we meet up with the light infantry, a battalion

of which is taking part in our mission. It is a boiling hot August day. We advance further via the Col d'Urbeis, past Mount Climont heights, up a magnificent mountain road, past the customs house to the frontier. At 7.30 we cross the frontier and advance down the pass. It is a wonderful evening. Clear view far into the French mountains. I greet France with almost the same sense of shock as seven years ago when I saw Paris for the first time. I'm hardly thinking that there's a war on. I salute you, sweet soil of France. At the front of the column the light infantry are striking up a song: *Die Wacht am Rhein*. Everybody joins in as we move down the mountain. A weeping beggar by the side of the road. We hear the enemy fire. Then the artillery is ordered forward. We trot past the infantry. People are calling out to us. The forwards movement of a dark decision. In Lubines all the houses are either empty or locked. Then onto some high ground at Colroy. Once again we hear the sound of guns. Then all is quiet. We unhooked the guns from their limbers but did not fire a shot. Dusk is falling. We limber up and ride into the village of Colroy. By now it's night. We have to get emergency billets. We bang on doors....

Saturday 26 September

We harness up the horses at 2.30 in the morning. We advance through Corbeny towards the junction of the Bouconville–Corbeny/ Bouconville–Chevreux roads. Cold, clear night. We stand in readiness in the woods. Above us and in front of us the shells are howling past. Day is breaking. We are sent forward to Craonne. No. 1 Troop takes up position under the Captain's orders. The rest of the Battery stays on the main road of the completely destroyed village. From 9 a.m. till two in the afternoon. Wounded men. Emptied shops.

Just before 2, I move up into position. One of our guns is positioned on some high ground at the upper exit of the village, commanding the plain and the heights opposite, and fires in the direction of the Bois de Beau-Marais which has now been shelled for so many days and to no good purpose. I am with the Captain and Ney at the observation post. Then we sit against the back wall of the neighbouring house and drink coffee. The village comes under enemy artillery fire. Pieces of shrapnel whistle past above us. One shell hits a roof three yards away from us, hurling dust and rubble over the horses of the limber that is standing in front of the house. The Captain has the foremost Troop of the Battery go back down into the lower village. The shell-fire on the village continues. We go into the room that is the dressing station. Conversation with the doctors. The wounded are carried into the basement, where blankets and mattresses from the houses are piled up. An improvised operating table. More and more wounded arrive. Artillery and serious infantry wounds. One whose brain has been completely exposed. He is still alive. They don't bother carrying him into the dressing station but into a house opposite: after all, he's only got a few more moments to live. The horror of war. I feel sick. ...

Monday 12 October

From early in the morning, Craonne and the adjacent heights come under heavy artillery fire. With particular intensity from three in the afternoon. We are listening out of the courtyard basement. Suddenly around 4 heavy rifle and machine-gun fire. One of the riflemen alerts us: 'The French are attacking'. I rush to No. 3 Troop, into the other part of the village, while all around in the street heavy artillery shells crash into the houses. Once I take refuge for a few moments in a basement. In it are a couple of riflemen with completely soot-blackened faces and injuries: they were buried when a shell hit the house and smashed down into the basement. Some of their comrades are still lying buried under the rubble. Another shell smashed into the light infantry trenches near the park wall and completely filled it with rubble: 3 dead, 8 wounded. I hurry on. To my right, a pioneer officer and three to four men with picks and shovels are running down to the trench in order to free the buried men. Onwards. The road is blocked by the rubble of the collapsed houses. Past the open bit onwards to the house where No. 3 Troop is positioned. It's on fire. A shell has hit the roof. Bits of the explosive warhead flew all the way down into the basement. The gun-crew isn't there. The guns are out in the street. I rush into the emergency shelter on the far side of the street. The men are there. I get them to man the guns and bring No. 6 gun into position. Then off with Flath to observe and through the gap in the wall through which No. 5 gun is supposed to shoot, out onto the slope in front of the wall. A few paces to the right of the gap we lie down in the grass, barely covered by the wall of the house on our right. 50 metres to the left of us the shells of the heavy artillery are exploding. We can look out over the entire valley floor. The French

infantry is advancing from the Beau Marais. We have been told to
fire only when they're in a range of 800 metres. Across the field,
past a long line of trees, you can see the French advancing in long
extended lines. Clearly they've not been spotted by our artillery, or
at least not fired upon. We open up at range 800. Too short. 1100.
Still too short. 1400. The light infantry bring heavy fire to bear
on the French. It appears that the infantry attack is halting. One
rifleman reports that 2 enemy guns have been brought up very close,
to the edge of Beau Marais wood. I have this information passed on
to the Captain. The guns are shelled by our No. 1 Troop, which is
positioned to the right near trenches 132, and silenced. Meanwhile,
their large-calibre shells are whistling past over us and close to us
and striking the ground. But the infantry assault seems to have
been halted. I have No. 6 gun brought out onto the street and
moved back into cover, and the men withdraw for the time being
into the emergency shelter while we carry on observing. (Trachte)
and (Hodam) gun-layers. Around 6.30 things quieten down. The
Captain arrives. I go back with him to our cellar. Post has arrived.
A letter from Fanny. As though from a distant, wonderful world. A
little parcel has arrived with it. I don't open it yet. Accompany the
Captain up to Brigade. Then a short, hurried supper. I go back to
No. 3 Troop, through the pitch-black village into which the odd
shell is still dropping. I spend the night sleeping in No. 3 Troop's
cellar, next to Flath. Highest possible state of alert.

I open the parcel from Fanny. A little almanach for the month
of October containing rhyming aphorisms by Angelus Silesius. On
the back of the envelope, pasted on by her, is a Madonna with baby
Jesus. The little book is like a magic charm for me. I read only the
first aphorism:

> Man, turn inwards on thyself.
> For if thou willst find the wise men's stone
> Thou mayst not travel first
> To foreign lands.
> [*Der Cherubinischer Wandersmann*, Book III: 118]

I am nervously excited. Can hardly grasp the meaning of the words.
Repeat them to myself incessantly. Finally I begin to calm down.
Why has she written down these lines for me? Outside several times
in the night to listen whether an attack is imminent. The night is lit
up by the fire of distant guns. Every now and again a flare goes up
and lights up the whole mountain and valley floor. Just before four

a report comes in: a French runner has been captured, the French will attack at 4.50. On the previous night a report had already come in via a listening post that a French officer had given a speech to his men, in which he had urged them to fight bravely.

Wednesday 21 October

March off at 6 in the morning. I have a headache. We pull back through Laon, Besny, up to the exit from Vivaise. Where there is a regimental and divisional conference. I meet Forster. We move on through … to B… where we arrive at around 4. Billets. Friendly people as everywhere in this area. While riding through Mayot, I saw how the villagers were looking after the infantrymen who had 'keeled over', poured wine into them. In the billet I am given eggs, and a fire is lit for me, a gesture whose good intentions outstripped the good it did me: I wake up in the night with a dreadful headache which is still there when I get up in the morning. Before that, in the evening, we had dinner with the Captain again: three requisitioned chickens.

Thursday 22 October

After the dismal, rainy weather of the last few days, a brighter, almost cheerful day. We leave at 8.20. Wonderful autumn landscape with water, the Oise Canal, brightly lit meadows with groups of yellowing trees. The tops of some have already lost all their leaves. On one occasion low chestnut saplings, reddish yellow in front of yellowish green lime trees. Later it gets more dismal.

We march on via V… to Castres. There we are accommodated in the village. We arrive at 2 o'clock. The village lies hidden in the valley, concealed by autumnally coloured trees. Difficulty with our quarters. Unkell, Ney and I move in with the Captain on straw.[21]

Diary of Ernst Stadler, 10 August to 22 October 1914

'An agitating day'

BRIGADIER MAKINS AND THE
CONFUSED FIGHTING AROUND YPRES

Brigadier Makins's diary describes the fighting known as the 1st battle of Ypres (19 October to 22 November 1914), a crucial phase in the 'Race to the Sea', from the point of view of a brigade commander. British forces began to move to Artois and Flanders to operate on the left flank of the French army to stop the German attempt to outflank the allies. The role of the British 3rd Cavalry Division was to help to cover the withdrawal of the Belgian Army from Antwerp, and then to move east of Ypres to defend a line between Langemarck and Zandvoorde. German attempts to capture Ypres were repulsed with heavy losses on both sides. By 22 November the immediate threat had been averted and the allied lines settled east of Ypres forming the Ypres Salient.

The trenches have become so much a part of the image of the Great War that it is easy to forget that the more open warfare of the early stages of the war left men even more exposed to shot and shell. Even officers of Makins's rank were exposed to great dangers, with no HQ being safe in the rapidly changing conditions. Between 19 October and 7 November when he was forced home with sickness, Makins recorded the fluctuating fortunes of the 6th Cavalry Brigade.

Wednesday 21 October was 'an awful night'. There was news that 'the Germans had rushed Langemarck', and the brigade remained saddled up all night. Makins 'got a lie down after midnight' but was woken at 3.45 a.m. with orders to retire to Ypres. Expecting a rest in Ypres, which they had reached at 8.30 a.m., they were instead ordered at midday to plug a gap in the line, followed by

> a desperate order—namely to take over the line and trenches of the Scots Guards from Zandvoorde to the chateau on the canal east of Hollebeke. The Germans are in the chateau and we do not get them out in the evening.

Taking over trenches from the Scots Guards between 11 p.m. and 3 a.m. was 'a most desperate job in the dark'.

Makins had a narrow escape on 23 October when retiring from the trenches:

> the fire is too hot from the shells for the Xth H[ussars] to do so, and Jorrocks, and Col. Fergusson and others are all wounded by a shell. As I ride back a Jack Johnson bursts well within 15 yards of me.

Several officers were wounded. Things got worse on 26 October:

> Have an agitating day. About midday am ordered to go and see Byng. He says there is to be a grand advance by the whole Cav. Corps, the 1st A.C. and the 7th Div. We are [to] remain in our trenches and cover the advance towards Kartewilch by the 7th Cav. Brig.—which is to take place at 3 p.m. However before that time the 7th Div. are in such difficulties that their advance is suspended, and the 7th Cav. Brig. are sent up to our support. The centre of the 7th Div. has been driven back and the Gordons on the left of the Xth Hussars have their left in the air. Everything is in confusion and nobody knows where anybody else is. One of our aeroplanes falls just in front of us, shot down by our own men. I am nervous about our left if the Gordons go, but Capper comes round and says they will not go unless we are told. The Blues make a most futile demonstration up to the German trenches—do no good and lose some horses and men.

Diary of Brigadier Ernest Makins, 19–26 October 1914

'A bad day'

BRIGADIER MAKINS DESCRIBES
THE INTENSE FIGHTING AROUND YPRES

On Tuesday 27 October Makins was up most of the night. A report that the Gordons had left the trenches, leaving his left exposed, was a 'facer'. Colonel Montgomery had to collect up men of the 7th Division and 'stuff them into the trenches' to rectify the situation.

The Germans attacked on the 29th after a furious cannonading. Makins was ordered to support the 7th infantry division in a counter-attack. Things became desperate on Friday 30 October. It was on this very day that a young German poet and alumnus of Magdalen College, Ernst Stadler, was killed at Zandvoorde by a British shell (see p. 65). His artillery regiment had perhaps even fired some of the shells now causing such carnage. Makins records several days of intense fighting before he was forced to retire from the battle through illness on 7 November.

Friday October 30th
A bad day. The 7th C.B. are driven in off the Zamvoorde [he means Zandvoorde] ridge and have 2 squadrons cut off. We occupy the reserve trenches with Xth H. A fearful hell of shelling and we fairly catch it. A 'Jack Johnson' lands just by us in the middle of H.Q., showers me with mud, kills poor Charles instantaneously, wounds Peyton, kills my orderly (Corp Vanson), the trumpeter and several horses, and wounds Susan [his horse]. Tommy has a bad time in the chateau, and is finally driven out of it. Arthur Brown is killed, Henry Jump is badly wounded and left to the Germans. Parkin and Swire are wounded later on. We hang on and the Greys and 3rd Hussars come up in support. Finally the 4th Guards Brigade come up and take over our trenches, but the troops cannot retire until their new trenches are dug, which is not till the early hours of the morning. Get Charles body taken to Ypres in an ambulance with the senior chaplain (Ensor) and buried there.

The next day, Saturday 31 October, was just as intense:

Zillebeke is badly shelled—several French are blown to pieces in the streets. A shell bursts in the wood in front of our house and one in the garden. We hurriedly leave and get the brigade about some woods to the East. Move to Hooge. In the afternoon move out under orders of Sir D. Haig to support Bulfin.[22] Put in nearly the whole brigade and support and carry on the infantry. Finally retire to Hooge with the H.Q. and the regts spend the night in the woods. The staff of the 1st Division have 6 off[icer]s killed and Lomax[23] wounded by a shell into the Chateau of Hooge. Col. Perceval[24] was blown to pieces—only his boots left. Gen. Lomax and Whigham had just gone to the next room otherwise they would have been killed.

Diary of Brigadier Ernest Makins, 27–31 October 1914

'I suppose it's all for somebody's good'

HAROLD MACMILLAN'S EARLY IMPRESSIONS OF ARMY LIFE

Harold Macmillan's correspondence chronicles the transformation of an Oxford Classics scholar into a diligent and highly motivated soldier. In the summer of 1914 the Balliol don F.F. Urquhart, known as 'Slig' or 'Sligger', planned a summer jaunt to his chalet in the Savoyard Alps, with a group of students, Macmillan among them. He was recovering from an operation for appendicitis, and wrote to Urquhart that he would leave the planning to him as 'I never can remember where places are in Europe.'

The outbreak of war brought very mixed emotions for Macmillan, an intense frustration at not being able to take part being mixed with confusion about exactly what the war was about and what his role should be. On 9 August he announced to Urquhart that he was 'physically as well as morally incapable of bearing arms', but at the same time wished he was able-bodied and was clearly envious of friends who were joining up. His feeling of helplessness in the face of his physical unfitness after his operation was only alleviated by the thought that he would not really be needed. His brother had been told by Lord Donoughmore and Lord Brassey that they had recruited the 100,000 men asked for many times over, and of course 'one can do much more good with one's intelligence in many other ways.' His remarks still betray a certain confusion about the war and its causes: 'How damnable it all is. But I suppose we had to join in in honour and we must put up with this punishment for our sins, as no doubt it is.' In an undated letter shortly afterwards he remarked:

> I'm afraid I've kept rather calm about it all, because I'm so vague about reality etc yet. And then I've a vague feeling that we must win in the end.

By September Macmillan had decided to join up. His earliest encounters with military life were by no means positive. He told 'Slig' of his depression at visiting Humphrey Sumner in camp at Sheerness in a letter probably written in September 1914:

The gloom of the place and the pitiless philistinism of military things made me very sad.

In this letter he announced that he too had 'deserted civil life' and joined the Inns of Court OTC.

In November 1914 Macmillan was with the 14th battalion of the King's Royal Rifle Corps, in Westcliff-on-Sea near Southend. The tone of resignation and sadness continued as the war began to take over Macmillan's life. Asking 'Slig' when he might come over to Southend to visit, he exclaimed:

> Oh, dear Slig, how I wish it were all over. But I suppose it's all for somebody's good. And things next year ought to see us either beneath 3 good feet of French earth or happily home again to civilian life.

A letter to his father of 20 November concludes with observations about fellow officers whom he finds dull. Betraying his classical education, he puts them in three categories using Greek letters:

(α) Dingy
(β) 'Tat rugger blues
(γ) (only one) a bounder—he is however much sat upon.

The company commander, a first cousin of Steel-Maitland, he thought 'quite a good fellow. He fought in S. Africa'. This reveals the respect that a novice would feel towards an experienced officer (and likewise the contempt for those who appear frivolous or amateur). This was all part of the process of initiation, and the transformation of an Oxford student into an army officer. This particular officer earns further respect because he had been out of the army, farming in the United States, and in consequence 'has a rough manner and a great knowledge of cocktails. I think he will be very good on active service.'

Macmillan's views on his fellow officers are expanded in a letter to 'Slig' around this time. Again expressing disappointment with the 'rather dingy' subalterns, he says he finds them 'tolerable' but not when they talk about women. He mused, 'why do young men think obscenity a sign of manhood, and confuse the bold with the amusing?'

Harold Macmillan was to say later in life that his experience fighting alongside ordinary working-class men had a profound influence on his outlook and political philosophy. In this letter he records his first impression of the men, and compares them favourably with the officers: 'How jolly the men are! I think them so much nicer than the officers.'

As they as yet had no rifles, there was very little to do. The colonel he described as an 'old dear—just what an old-fashioned Huntingdon-shire baronet ought to be, but he's perfectly useless'.

Letters from Harold Macmillan to F.F. 'Slig' Urquhart,
and to his father, July to November 1914

'In the trenches, under a hell of a fire'

GILBERT MURRAY RECEIVES
A LETTER FROM THE FRONT

This letter, sitting among Murray's correspondence with politicians and intellectuals about the rights and wrongs of the war and the British cause, must have brought the reality of the conflict very much to the fore. Gibson, an alumnus of Balliol College, had been mobilized on 4 August 1914. He was promoted to captain in the 2nd battalion of the King's Own Scottish Borderers, but was killed in action at Hill 60, Belgium, 5 May 1915. The letter epitomizes the ironic style fashionable among Oxford men, the gallows humour perhaps part of a more or less conscious coping strategy in extreme conditions.

Nov. 10. 1914
In the trenches under a hell of a fire. 1 pm. 2/Lt. 2 K.O.S.B.

Dear Professor Murray,
    The German Black Marias seem to have the range of the wood in wh. I am lying 'dug in' in a 'dugout' with our reserves, with two other officers, each speculating if the next whizz is not to clear us off entirely. One shattering fellow dropped very near us and not a few men have skedaddled. They are shouting that some people

are buried and must be dug out and I have not yet summoned up enough courage to go out and see what is happening—My hat, as a Canadian friend of mine used to swear, I've been out helping to exhume the man, one of my own platoon 15 yards away. The shell burst between his hole and that of another soldier of my platoon. He is not dead, but arm and leg broken: we've laid him out on the ground with some protection against splinters and sent for the ambulance.

There is a stain on the page here, which Gibson has indicated with an arrow, pointing from the following text: 'rum, of which I've just had a mouthful, don't tell Lady Mary [Murray's wife].'

Another one as close as I want it; all the earth in the world is coming about my ears, filling my hair and nostrils. I've ordered half of my men, on the suggestion of my platoon sergeant a smart little man to find shelter on the right a little further from the zone of fire. I wonder how much money the enemy has blazed off this morning. It would pay the pensions of a few dons, and may possibly withdraw one of them from the pension list altogether. Well, I set out to thank you for yr letter which came to me this morning, not to make a display a piece of bravado, but the shells began to fall close, as I was beginning.

I would much rather be in the fire trenches. The Germans are really trying for our artillery wh. of course is in the rear and the reserve often comes in for what the artillery should receive. I fear lunch is entirely spoilt. I had a rattling breakfast. Ham sandwich, a portion of Maconochie—ie preserved beef and vegetables all in the one tin heated tea with sugar and Nestle's milk, bread biscuit and army jam besides a great many cream chocolates wh. came this morning from Miss Lewis. Please tell her what a godsend they were. I must hurry up and finish them in case the next shell gets our little hole. I think however their bombs are wandering further astray and we may have a quiet afternoon. We learn from newspapers a week old that we are taking part in an important battle. 'My hat', as my Canadian friend says.

Letter from R. Gibson to Gilbert Murray, 10 November 1914

'The W.O. people are very easily to be deceived into a respect for special knowledge loudly declared'

T.E. LAWRENCE JOINS THE WAR OFFICE

Lawrence had undertaken archaeological work at Carchemish from 1912 until the spring of 1914 under the direction of C.L. Woolley. In January and February 1914 he carried out a survey of Sinai, which resulted in an archaeological report, co-written with Woolley, *The Wilderness of Zin*, written in Oxford and London during the summer of 1914. His knowledge of the Middle East, and his work on the Sinai survey, took him to the War Office, first as a civilian, but from 26 October 1914 as a second lieutenant, with no regimental affiliation.

I was to have gone to Egypt on Sat last: only the G.O.C. there wired to the W.O. and asked for a road-report on Sinai that they were supposed to have.

Well of course they hadn't got it—not a bit of it, so they came to me and said 'write it.'

I thought to kill two or three birds with my stone, so I offered them the wilderness of Sin ... they took it and asked for more. So I'm writing a report from the military point of view of a country I don't know, and haven't visited yet. One of the minor terrors is, that later on I'm to get my own book, and guide myself over the country with it. It will be a lesson in humility I hope.

It's rather hard luck though, to have devilled my way all over Sinai, and then to have to write two books about it, gratis. And this second one is an awful sweat, for it has to be done against time, and the maps are not yet drawn. So I have to oversee them also, and try and correlate the two. It will not astonish you to hear that I have found a grey hair on my pillow this morning.

The W.O. people are very easily to be deceived into a respect for special knowledge loudly declared aren't they?

I'm to go out on Sat. next, I am told. I don't care, but I am sure somebody will ask the W.O. for an epic poem on Sinai about next Friday, and I'll be turned onto that, gratis.

Letter from T.E. Lawrence to E.T. Leeds, from the War Office, 16 November 1914

'The Ypres cemetery will haunt me till I die'

MARGOT ASQUITH'S ACCOUNT OF HER VISIT TO THE WESTERN FRONT, DECEMBER 1914

Despite criticism from Sir Edward Grey, who told her she was being self-indulgent, Margot Asquith decided to visit troops and hospitals in Belgium. On 10 December 1914 she crossed to Dunkirk on the Admiralty ship *Princess Victoria*, though she was too sick to see anything. Her only fellow travellers were her escort Major Gordon, and an English airman.

> It was arctic cold but I had very sensible clothes—leather breeches, waist coat and coat, a silk jersey over silk blouse a blue serge skirt little black Belgian soldier hat (huge motor hood if I needed it) and civet cat spotted coat muff and boa high gaiters and St Moritz over shoes. All ugly but business-like.

She thought the French soldiers on the pier looked 'grotesque in their baggy red trousers and hard short black blue tunics'.

She was met by a chauffeur in the best Benz motor she had ever been in—smooth, powerful and fast. 'I really love going fast but had no idea anyone drove as fast as that man on such roads!' Major Gordon, 'a beautiful grey-haired Scot about 45 years of age', had bought £40,000-worth of things for the Belgian soldiers at Harrod's.

She paid a quick visit to Milly Sutherland's Hospital[25] to see the nurses there, among whom were family friends and relatives Diana Wyndham, Rosemary Leveson Gower, Rosabelle Bingham and Dinah Tennant. The hospital was crowded with wounded, including some 'beautiful Arabs and Moors'.

They moved on the Furnes, the Belgian army headquarters, and after a 'disgusting lunch in foul restaurant' went on to the King's household at La Panne. On 12 December she visited the King's villa. Here she noticed a youngish man poring over a map, not recognizing

Margot Asquith beside a ruined church in Flanders, December 1914, dressed in her 'ugly but business-like' clothes for her visit to the front

him as the King of Belgium. He congratulated her on her 'remarkable husband'. Margot thought he was 'absolutely real, no sort of swagger: keen, interested and asking every sort of question'. The King was 'extremely bitter' about the French, but full of praise for the English.

After lunch Margot Asquith travelled with Major Gordon by car to visit the Belgian trenches, and 'heard the guns on the Niewport [*sic*] road—the 1st I had heard—they gave me a thrill'; she visited a Belgian trench, and handed out cigarettes and matches to the 'Belgian tommies', whom she described as 'nice fellows, simple and unruffled'. She remarked that the 'Belgian trenches look very amateur to my unaccustomed eye', and noted the ruinous and shelled landscape.

She was very keen to meet her old friend Sir John French, but he was not able to see her owing to pressure of work. She confided her disappointment to her diary: 'Perhaps Sir John French is not as fond of me as I think! … perhaps Sir John thinks I am old. Henry likes very young females.'

Margot set off for Merville via Ypres and Bailleul on 13 December, the 'big 6 cylinder Benz motor was full of our biscuits, brandy, beef jelly, Malvern water, cigarettes, match boxes, small shawls, pillows etc etc.' She was struck by the 'tragic ruin' of Ypres, but it was the cemetery that really affected her:

> The Ypres cemetery will haunt me till I die. No hospital ward full of wounded ever gave me such an insight into war as that damp crowded quiet church yard. Most of the names scrawled in pencil on bits of wood were English—where the names had been washed off their little forage caps hung on a stick.

Her contemplation was broken when 'suddenly there burst on our ears a perfect fussilade [*sic*] of firing—I never heard such a noise'; several aeroplanes hovered above. Major Gordon, who had been digging, motioned Margot to stand on a bit of raised ground and look at the German line:

> I felt so xcited that I was stunned—if there had not been a faint haze in the sky I cd easily have seen the bombs. As it was I heard criack!! criawk!! BOOM!!! in 4s and saw white poplar lines of thin smoke and the flash quite clear.

Some French soldiers warned her to take shelter, asking if she was afraid. No more than them, she replied. They explained that the Germans were not shelling them, or the shells would have gone over their heads.

Margot wanted to go with Major Gordon to a cemetery nearer the German lines where he was to plant another cross, but he refused. French and Belgian soldiers gave her cashmere belts. She left in the car, 'and write my diary listening to the guns shaking the glass of the Hospital windows'.

On the drive to Bailleul she noted the sight of a dead horse in a pool of blood. At Bailleul she met her beloved nephew Edward Tennant:[26]

> He looked as if he had been dressed in Bond St, a beautiful beaver flapped cap tied under his chin leather coat breeches and gaiters and a beautiful khaki hand-knitted soft wide muffler. ... My heart warmed to the little hero (he has done wonders, had 3 machines crack up under him and his goggles shot off by German revolver) so sage and sweet and young standing in the middle of the road. I wonder if I shall ever see him again.

She was struck by the wonderful high spirits of the marching men, and tried to imagine what war must be like, recalling her hunting days as 'a very feeble comparison'.

As she dined at the house of Major Gordon's brother, '4 Jack Johnstones' landed 30 yards away. An officer, Nicholson, jumped up and said: 'My dear Gordon what will the Prime Minister say. ... I can assure you Mrs Asquith we've not had a shell or a shot for 2 weeks.'

Margot met General Henry Rawlinson[27] at his 'magnificent and hideous villa'. She dined with twenty men, all soldiers, and a liaison officer called Poniatowski, whom she describes as 'an awful rotter' who once asked her to marry him. Rawlinson she thought had a 'certain charm—simplicity, v nice but no mind'. She could see that he wanted to talk about his difficulties, but Poniatowski was in the way. She observed:

> I can see Rawly blames Haig for not coming up in time when the 7th Div. caught it so terribly. French blames Rawly.

Diary of Margot Asquith, 10–13 December 1914

'We speak hopefully to each other of "next year at Oxford"'

CAPTAIN GODFREY ELTON ON HIS PASSAGE TO INDIA

Godfrey Elton was an alumnus of Balliol College, and a captain in the 4th Battalion of the Hampshire Regiment sent to the North West frontier in India, and later to Mesopotamia. He was wounded and captured by the Turks after the fall of Kut al-Amara in April 1916, and remained their prisoner until 1918. After the war Elton was a fellow of Queen's College, Oxford, and lecturer in modern history 1919 to 1939. Not long after the war he joined the Labour Party. In 1934 he was raised to the peerage by Ramsay Macdonald as Baron Elton of Headington. His letter to Murray takes a typically ironic perspective, contrasting the new military life with the old Oxford ways. A later letter to Murray indicates that the account he mentions of his army life was published in the *Westminster Gazette*. Many officers managed to read a good deal on active service, one of the privileges of holding a commission being access to an officers' mess or a dugout with at least some personal space. *Sinister Street* was a novel by Compton Mackenzie, published in two volumes, 1913–14.

The fortunes of life military have taken me Indiawards, to hold the gorgeous East in fee; and now on one of six transports I am ploughing through the wonderful blue wine coloured sea of the Mediterranean. There are several Oxford men here and we speak hopefully to each other of 'next year at Oxford' and so on. It is no use treating the gigantic tragedy of this war as anything but a joke —until it is over. Inside the envelope is a first sketch of life with the Territorials and I should like to send it to the Westminster or Daily News, but I do not know where your word is most potent, and that is more important still.

I often wonder what kind of a life the Oxford Colleges are having now; some life I trust will remain until all the gallant fellows who have commanded double-companies under heavy fire return to be gated for not wearing gowns.

At present we are having as jolly a time as exiles can expect; we have even got an officers' library—of cheap editions presented by my father, varying from Light Freights [a work by W.W. Jacobs, a writer of usually humorous short stories and novels] to your Euripides in the Home University Library. I pass at intervals through agonies of homesickness, but I hope that by becoming gradually resolute to face the future I may do myself more good at the last than even I could by Greats—to which, in fact, I hope to return.

I have read Sinister Street II which appears to me to be very nearly, not quite, a work of genius, but assuredly not a work of art.

I do not like to ask how you have been treated by the war…

Yrs v. sincerely

  Godfrey Elton

Letter from Godfrey Elton of the 2/4th Battalion Hampshire Regiment to Professor Gilbert Murray, 18 December 1914

'He takes the whole job as a splendid joke'

T.E. LAWRENCE DESCRIBES HIS COLLEAGUES AT THE INTELLIGENCE OFFICE IN CAIRO

In this letter a bored and frustrated T.E. Lawrence paints a picture of the assortment of military men and intellectuals, like himself, with an expertise in Middle Eastern languages and culture, that made up the personnel of the Intelligence Office in Cairo. The tone is typically ironic.

Intelligence Office, War Office, Cairo, 12 February 1915

Well, here goes for another empty letter: my bicycle is here: very many thanks for getting it out so quickly: I wish the W.O. would send out maps equally promptly.

You ask about the other people in the office: well Newcombe and Woolley you have heard of. There is Hough ex-consul at Jaffa—pleasant and nothing more: there is Lloyd, an M.P. (I should think probably Conservative, but you never know) who is the director of a bank, and used to be attaché at Constantinople. He is Welsh, but sorry for it: small, dark, very amusing—speaks Turkish well, and French, German and Italian: some Spanish, Arabic and Hindustani—also Russian. He is quite pleasant but exceedingly noisy. Then there is Aubrey Herbert, who is a joke, but a very nice one: he is too short-sighted to read or recognise anyone: speaks Turkish well, Albanian, French, Italian, Arabic, German—was for a time chairman of the Balkan League, of the committee of Union and Progress, and of the Albanian Revolution Committee. He fought through the Yemen wars, and the Balkan wars with the Turks, and is friends with them all. Then there is Pere Janssen, a French Dominican Monk, of Jerusalem. He speaks Arabic wonderfully well, and preceeded [sic] us in wanderings in Sinai. We praise his work very highly in the 'Wilderness of Sin'.

There is also Graves, Times correspondent, and very learned in the Turkish army organization. I think that is about all. We meet very few other people, except officers on business—see a good deal of them, from General Maxwell downwards. He is a very queer person: almost weirdly good-natured, very cheerful, with a mysterious gift of prophesying what will happen, and a marvellous carelessness about what might happen. There couldn't be a better person to command in Egypt. He takes the whole job as a splendid joke.

Letter from T.E. Lawrence to his mother, from the
Intelligence Office, Cairo, 12 February 1915

'A good example of our English way of doing things'

BICKERSTETH ON SPORT, AND FRENCH AND ENGLISH ATTITUDES TO THE WAR

In these letters, Bickersteth highlights sporting and political aspects of British life that seem to have perplexed the French. The story of Walter Long looking for examples of maladministration in the army highlights the connections between the worlds of politicians and army officers, and the possibility for intrigue that this might create (see p. 187). Long, later first Viscount Long (1854–1924), was a Conservative MP in 1915, and in May, when the Coalition was formed, became president of the Local Government Board where he had responsibility for Belgian refugees. He was also asked to draw up plans for conscription, which was adopted in 1916. Like Bickersteth, he was an alumnus of Christ Church, Oxford. Bickersteth's opinions in the letter of 28 February epitomize the ethos of the late-Victorian and Edwardian public school. The schools, and universities, put great emphasis on sport, both to encourage 'manliness' and, as suggested here, to promote social bonds. In Bickersteth's mind this marks the major difference between the voluntary (and amateur) British army and the professional French army. The description of the football match occurs just after Bickersteth has commented on an article in *The Times* about the improving French army, which he believed to have been 'extremely badly officered' in some branches at the beginning of the war because it was a conscript army. Bickersteth himself won Oxford blues at association football, and had captained the Oxford University team to victory in the 1911 varsity match.

20 February 1915

Francis Hill[28] (on his way up to join the regiment (i.e. Scots Greys) dined with Joffre and some staff officers. … Hill gathered that there is considerable friction between ourselves and the French. The French cannot realise that we are taking the war seriously. They hear of racing and football going on, and were astonished when hounds were brought over and hunting went on just behind the firing line. This has now been stopped by order from our headquarters—which was entirely due to the objections of the French. Apparently they also think it is remarkable that we have not formed a coalition govt. comprising All the Talents —such as they themselves have in France. Of course it is true that party govt. as such is practically at an end for the time being in England—yet the French do not understand there being even the least criticism of those responsible for carrying on the war. As a matter of fact I suppose it is certain that the Unionists have not dropped party warfare to such an extent that they are not always on the look out for false moves on the part of the govt. Not long ago Walter Long (whose son Toby Long is in the Greys) wrote to Fordyce (one of our majors at York and in the Greys) to ask for any points with regard to army administration in which the Govt. were making mistakes—so that such mistakes could be brought up against them directly the war was over.

28 February 1915

The Royals draft came over and shot on Friday morning – and in the afternoon we had a game of football, the officers of the draft against the men of the draft—the horses unsaddled, all tethered by the side of the field behind the goal posts. I refereed as my knee did not allow me to play. During the match there was a great deal of fun—men yelling at their friends, or shouting encouragement to the officers, and officers and men alike charging into each other with the utmost freedom and good will. Directly after the match the order to on-saddle and move off was given—ordinary discipline immediately returned. I could not help thinking it was a good example of our English way of doing things, both in the army and as a nation.

Letters from Burgon Bickersteth to his mother from York, 20 and 28 February 1915

'Very full of terrors from spies prowling about to blow up bridges and cut down telegraph poles'

SPY SCARES

In the years leading up to the First World War 'invasion literature' became immensely popular and influential. William Le Queux epitomized the genre, producing *The Great War in England in 1897* (1894), followed by many more novels often serialized in newspapers. His most popular novel was *The Invasion of 1910*, which first appeared as a serial in the *Daily Mail* in 1906. Its aim was to warn the British public of the threat of invasion (from France and Russia in his early work, from Germany by 1906), and it had an enormous influence on the popular imagination. One result was that at the beginning of the war a 'spy mania' took hold of Britain, owing more to the imagination than reality. The truth was that just twenty-one real German spies were arrested on 4 August, and their activities had already been discovered by British intelligence. However, the government received thousands of reports of imagined acts of espionage, with some local authorities being only too willing to believe anything. Despite a lack of any real evidence of spying activities among Germans living in the United Kingdom, in May 1915 the government decided to intern 'enemy aliens' for the duration of the war.

Andrew Clark, rector of Great Leighs, recorded a number of incidents in and around the Essex village. On 26 September 1914 he recorded that

> Sir Richard Pennefather, of Little Waltham Hall [he was chief of the Special Constables] plumes himself that he has caught a spy. An elderly woman, with a strong German accent, selling lace at Little Waltham was arrested by his order. ... This is probably the lace seller who caused great alarm to the Tufnell household at Langleys, Great Waltham. She made ... most minute enquiry as to the number and character of the rooms in the mansion and as to the age and habits of all its inmates. The Langley people imagined she was a militant suffragette, planning an incendiary outrage.

On 20 October Mrs Sargeant, wife of the gardener at Lyons Hall, told of a German spy at the Boreham end of the village. One Harry Brown had seen him drawing plans of the roads, and reported this to two troopers of the Bedfordshire Yeomanry from the camp at Terling. They cantered over and asked the 'spy' the way to Terling, and noted that he had a foreign accent. Two soldiers were sent out on bicycles and arrested the man. It transpired that he was an Ordinance Survey reviser (they were very active during this period of planning for large-scale military manoeuvres), but no villagers could be made to believe that he was not a spy, and that his OS map was not a 'blind', until 'the Little Waltham policeman passed and certified his honesty and official status'.

Sir Richard Pennefather's enthusiasm eventually brought him some ridicule. On 29 October Clark notes that Pennefather had the Special Constables of Little Waltham, the 'grocer, butcher, baker and other comfort-loving citizens ... out as patrols, night by night'. He describes Pennefather as an 'amicable but fussy, ex-Paymaster of the Metropolitan Police, very full of terrors from spies prowling about to blow up bridges and cut down telegraph poles.' Le Queux's invasion novel had imagined a battle of Chelmsford, and even mentions fierce fighting around Little Waltham and Great Leighs![29]

The spy scare was not confined to the localities. Indeed, some of the activities of the Special Constables were clearly directed from the central government. At the Cabinet meeting on 4 August 1914, the day war was declared, Lewis Harcourt noted in his journal that 'there are many German spies here now and have been for a long time: we have full evidence against them and shall seize them at once.' On the 29th the Cabinet discussed the spy problem: 'Churchill says carrier pigeons being much used for spy purposes: we shall have a compulsory release of them all on one day.'[30]

George Butterworth recorded the arrest of his friend the composer Ralph Vaughan Williams in his diary on 29 August 1914:

After dinner visited Vaughan Williams, who was in great form. He had taken his family for a holiday to Margate, where he was arrested by a boy-scout while writing a lecture on Purcell; he then returned to London and became a sergeant in the Special Constabulary.[31]

Burgon Bickersteth, while still recovering from a knee injury at York cavalry barracks, related a story to his mother that seems to have the ingredients of a classic 'urban myth'. In March 1915 he claimed that following the capture of German codes found on a U-boat (this was true), it was decided to send 'one or two wireless messages to the British coast'. These

> were immediately answered by scores of spies. Three years ago 40 Germans came to Lincolnshire and the East coast, and worked with the farmers ostensibly as students of agriculture. When at work in the fields they are supposed to have laid any amount of underground cable.[32]

References to spy scares in the diaries of Andrew Clark,
Lewis Harcourt and George Butterworth, and the letters
of Burgon Bickersteth, August 1914 to March 1915

'Churchill wants to stop every ship to and from neutrals'

CABINET DISCUSSIONS

Harcourt's brief notes of the Cabinet deliberations of 2 March 1915 illustrate the range of topics under discussion at a single meeting. The constant stream of information, and misinformation, from all fronts and from home, and the interplay of social, economic, military and political factors constantly formed and reformed government policy. Radical proposals were regularly mooted, and ideas that in peace time would have been unthinkable were brought to the table.

2.3.15 Cab. noon
    absent Ll. Geo.
    Kitch. Russian news much better. Germans on that front said to be in g[rea]t disorder.
        Dardanelles bombardment probably resumed this morning
        Situation there very good.

If weather good we may get through in 4 or 5 days.

Winston 'We should take and occupy all Turkey in Europe'.

We are going to smash Smyrna.

Australians and New Zealanders now on their way to Dardanelles.

39,000 men ready at Alexandria to be despatched.

We may send a div. of territorial cavalry from here—about 8,000 men.

Bulgarians said to be mobilising 2 divisions to attack Turkey!

Greeks send us 3 divisions to Gallipoli and their fleet flotilla (at least this is offered by Venezelos[33])

German blockade. 1850 ships entered and left our ports—only 8 ships torpedoed.

We have over 1,000 vessels patrolling for submarines.

We are issuing a retaliatory proclamation by the King on stoppage of German trade—some difficulty in wording and provision as to disposal of cargoes.

Churchill wants to stop every ship to and from neutrals—Grey anxious not to act excessively.

Question of whether we should now confiscate all detained German ships here and in Dominions and Colonies. We decided against this.

? Should we take over by the State all armaments firms and take over all their extra profits and make the men feel they are working for the State and not for private profit.

Grey very emphatic for this and Runciman. Churchill and Kitchener opposed to it.

At the end of Harcourt's journal entry there is an exasperated note in pencil in Asquith's hand (see Plate 7), written on a small envelope and evidently passed to Harcourt at the meeting:

I shall some day keep a Cabinet time table.

I roughly estimate that about one-half of the whole is taken up by one person.

In case there should be any doubt as to who that person was, Harcourt has added the initials 'W.S.C.' [Winston Spencer Churchill].

Cabinet journal of Lewis Harcourt, 2 March 1915

'We are a set of Buccaneers sitting round a table'

HARCOURT ATTENDS THE WAR COUNCIL

In a letter to Asquith dated 3 March 1915 Harcourt asked to attend the meetings of the War Council. This body was created by Asquith and first sat in November 1914. It was intended as an advisory committee, able to assist the Cabinet. Originally it comprised eight members: five Cabinet members, Asquith, Churchill (first lord of the Admiralty), Kitchener (war secretary), Lloyd George (chancellor of the exchequer) and Grey (foreign secretary); the chief of imperial general staff, General Wolfe-Murray; the first sea lord, Lord Fisher; and A.J. Balfour, the former prime minister, from the Opposition. It soon expanded to thirteen members as other ministries such as the Colonial Office were seen to have an interest in its deliberations. It was not a very effective body as it was not intended to direct the war, having no executive function. Much of what it discussed was referred to the Cabinet, so decisions were delayed. As colonial secretary Harcourt felt he ought to attend the War Council as his office had interests across the globe, with responsibility for British African and Far Eastern possessions, Cyprus, Gibraltar and Malta, territories which had a bearing on Britain's relationships with other colonial powers such as France and Portugal, and with allies such as Japan. Harcourt attended his first meetings of the War Council on 10 and 19 March 1915. The meetings included much discussion of the post-war settlement, and the seeds of future disputes once the war was over are clearly present. The discussions illustrate the wheeling and dealing between the allies over the future distribution of territories not yet under their control. The Council was also concerned about the increasing expenditure of munitions and the regulation of labour for the war effort.

10 March 1915

> Balfour 'We must give Russia Constantinople but I don't like it—let us get the best we can in exchange.'
> Asq. and Kitch. mentioned Alexandretta.

Bonar Law and Lansdowne rather inclined to give Russia no pledge as to Constantinople at present, but in the end agreed to our views.

Ll. Geo. still pressing for a meeting of the 3 Foreign secretaries at Lemnos.

Grey nervous of possible squabbles amongst allies over the division of the spoils. ...

Churchill [—] we must have the surrender of the German Fleet and the neutralisation of the Kiel Canal.

McKenna says they cd. build another fleet in less than 10 yrs.

Asq 'We are a set of Buccaneers sitting round a table'.

19 March 1915

At Neuve Chapelle our expenditure of ammunition very great. 114,000 shells. Kitchener not pleased. 1,286,000 rounds of 18lbr. ammunition expended since the war began by us.

... Lloyd George doing well with the labour representatives as to relaxation of union restrictions and greater output of work.

Drink—we propose to close all publics [public houses] and clubs in military districts except from 12 to 2 and 7 to 9.

The employers press for this and the labour leaders will support it. ...

We shall push on with the Dardanelles operation at almost any cost.

Italy demanding too much on Dalmatian Coast to cut off Serbia from the sea.

French ambass. at Petrograd has demanded all Syria and Cilician Taurus for France. We discussing future distribution of Turkey in Asia. Haldane not in favour of our acquiring further territory in Asia.

Asq. agst. acquisition but says we are not free agents. Asia Minor must be cut up and we cannot put France, Greece, Italy, Russia there and we hold nothing.

Cabinet journal of Lewis Harcourt, 10 and 19 March 1915

'This life so different
from that of Nuneham Park'

A BELGIAN OFFICER RETURNS TO THE FRONT AFTER CONVALESCING IN THE HARCOURTS' HOME IN OXFORDSHIRE

Many owners of large country houses allowed them to be used for convalescent soldiers during the war. The Harcourts took in wounded Belgian officers at Nuneham Courtenay, and later Canadian officers were accommodated there. As a result there are a number of grateful letters to the Harcourts among their papers, such as this one to Lewis Harcourt's wife Mary, providing a very different source of information about the war for a Cabinet minister. It is notable that Giron expects the Harcourts to be familiar with the layout of a German trench from the many illustrated magazines available.

Furtham, le 28 mars 1915
Chère Madame,
    Pendant mes heures de loisir, ma pensée retourne souvent à Nuneham Park ou j'ai fait un si aimable séjour dont je vous garde une bien sincère reconnaissance. Je circule de mémoire dans votre splendide propriété et j'imagine que maintenant les mimosas sont en fleurs ainsi que bien d'autres plantes qui n'attendaient que le premier beau jour pour prendre leur parure du printemps. Je me rappelle les détails de la vie charmante que l'on menait chez vous et surtout de votre amabilité si cordiale et de celle de tous les votres.
    La vie que je mène ici est bien différente à tous les points de vue mais ne manque pas d'intérêt. J'avais soif d'être en première ligne et je constate que mon moral y est excellent. Naturellement il a fallu payer mon tribut pour m'acclimater à cette vie d'un confort si différent de celui de Nuneham Park mais depuis un mois que j'y suis après une forte grippe et une indisposition générale, j'ai retrouvé mon équilibre physique. L'existence dans les cantonnements est très supportable car on dispose d'un lit et que la nourriture est saine. Sur la partie du front que nous occupons face à face aux allemands de part et d'autre de l'Yser l'attitude est defensive [sic] des deux cotés. A travers les meurtrières les adversaires se fusillent à trente

mètres de distance et l'on fait des deux cotés un usage fréquent des bombes. Mon bataillon a été chargé d'en inventer de puissantes et nous avons réussi à lancer à des distances variant de 50 à 200 mètres des charges d'explosifs entourées de mitraille de fer qui semblent particulièrement désagréables aux allemands. Bien que nous ayons beaucoup de monde dans les tranchées et de nombreux travailleurs organisant et renforçant la nuit les 2<u>eme</u> et 3<u>eme</u> lignes souvent canonnées, nos pertes quotidiennes sont faibles. Les allemands ne font pas d'attaque sur notre front et se contentent de bombarder nos lignes et nos cantonnements les plus proches assez fréquemment. Je fais toujours mes visites de première ligne, pour l'examen des travaux en cours, pendant la journée et rien n'est plus curieux que cette zone de mort vide de tout être vivant aussi loin que l'on voit. On n'aperçoit que des fermes et des églises en ruine, des cadavres d'animaux en putréfaction. L'auto file à toute allure mais les observateurs l'ont vue et les shrapnells éclatent devant et derrière. La chance nous sourit car de tous les officiers de mon bataillon je continue à être le seul blessé depuis le début de la guerre. Quant aux tranchées allemandes vous les connaissez par les nombreux illustrés mais à cote de leur aspect pittoresque on en voit parfois l'aspect tragique quand on rencontre dans un de ces boyaux étroits un transport de blessé ou de cadavre. Le retour au cantonnement est intéressant par le contraste car dès qu'on sort de la zone de mort on apercoit [sic] les paysans au labeur, les enfants jouant sur la route et les chantiers de travail animés.

Les nouvelles générales de la guerre semblent meilleures et nous sommes ici tous confiants et de bonne humeur. ...

Paul Giron
Cdt le bataillon des P
de la 5<u>eme</u> D.A.

[In my leisure hours, my thoughts often return to Nuneham Park where I had a pleasant stay for which I remain sincerely grateful. In memory I walk in your beautiful place and I suppose that now the mimosas are in bloom and many other plants that are waiting for the first fine day to put on their spring finery. I remember the details of the charming life we led at your house, and especially the kindness of you and your family which was so cordial.

The life I lead here is very different in every way but is not without interest. I wanted to be on the front line and I find that my morale is excellent there. Naturally I had to pay my dues to acclimatize to this life so different from that of Nuneham Park but after a month of being here [and] after a bad influenza and general indisposition, I have once again found my physical balance. Life in cantonments is very bearable as one has a bed and the food is healthy. On the part of the front that we occupy opposite the Germans on either side of the Yser the attitude is defensive on both sides. Through loop-holes the adversaries shoot one another from 30 metres away and both sides frequently use bombs. My battalion has been tasked with inventing powerful ones and we have managed to launch explosive charges wrapped in iron shot to distances of 50 to 200 metres which seem particularly unpleasant to the Germans. Although we have a lot of people in the trenches and many workers organizing and reinforcing the often-bombed 2nd and 3rd lines during the night, our daily losses are few. The German do not attack our front and content themselves with bombing our lines and closest cantonments quite frequently. I continue my visits to the front line, to examine the ongoing work, during the day and nothing is stranger than this dead zone devoid of any living being for as far as one can see. One only glimpses ruined farms and churches, putrefying animal corpses. The car zips through but the observers have seen it and shrapnel bursts in front and behind it. Luck is with us as of all the officers in my battalion I am the only one to have been wounded since the start of the war. As for the German trenches, you know them from the many illustrated magazines but aside from their picturesque side sometimes their tragic side is seen when one meets in one of these narrow passageways a transport of wounded or dead. The return to cantonments is interesting for the contrast because as soon as one exits the dead zone one sees peasants at work, children playing on the road and animated work sites.

The general news from the war seems better and we here are all confident and in good spirits.][34]

Letter from Commandant Paul Giron to Mrs Mary Harcourt, 28 March 1915

'Hullo, ugly!'

THE DANGERS OF PATROLLING

As a result of spy scares (see p. 87), the cavalry in York barracks found themselves on patrol on the roads into the city, looking for suspicious motorists. On 16 April Burgon wrote to his mother:

> We have been out <u>all</u> night stopping motors on all the roads into York within a radius of 5 to 10 miles. ... They have been giving information to Zeppelins by motors with powerful headlights, and we have power to arrest anyone we think in the least suspicious.

He elaborates further in a letter to his parents on 18 April:

> It has been quite amusing work, and the men enjoyed the change enormously. We rode out to our posts every evening about 5.30 and immediately on arrival commandeered carts, barrels, ladders or anything else suitable for barring up the road .... I was in command of a picket on the main London road—between York and Selby—and from 6.0. o'clock onwards we stopped every car, no matter who was in it. We had some really very amusing experiences—the two funniest were those of young Baillie Hamilton, who was posted on the Harrogate side of York. Late at night he stopped the General (General Lawson O.C. Northern Command) who in plain clothes was returning home with a staff officer also in plain clothes. Baillie did not know the General by sight—made him get out, and the other officer, and searched the car. The General who is not much of a sportsman was furious—not at Baillie doing his job but at the fact that he, the General, was not known. He stamped and swore—D_d impertinence. Baillie saluted saying nothing. I say it is d_d impertinence young fellow. Baillie saluted again. Do you hear me you infernal little fool, it's damned impertinence I tell you. Baillie saluted a third time, told the General he might get [in] and allowed his men to let the car pass.
>
> Shortly afterwards a large grey car drove up precisely like the one owned by one of our subalterns here. Baillie put his head in (it was a dark night) and yelled 'Hullo, ugly!'—inside was a girl. Rapid retreat on the part of Baillie —the car was allowed to proceed at once.

> *Letters from Burgon Bickersteth to his mother and father,*
> *16 and 18 April 1915*

'We would like our own girls to wait on us, and not any of them toffs'

ANDREW CLARK DESCRIBES SOCIAL AND GENERATIONAL DIVISIONS

Despite the bringing together of the classes that the war entailed, social divisions could not easily be bridged, as the episode of the Cheltenham ladies' tea huts illustrates. Clark goes on to describe his problems fulfilling the training requirements of a Special Constable, the description of his infirmities bringing to mind scenes from *Dad's Army*.

Frid. 16 Apr. 1915
... A lady, visiting Mrs Vickers, told [how] ... at Cheltenham, ladies of the town had got up huts for the soldiers in which tea and coffee were served and also suppers. The ladies took turns in waiting at supper. After a few days the lady in chief charge asked a group of the soldiers she found in the hut, whether they had any complaint to make. They hummed and hawed, and required some pressure to make them speak out what was in their minds. They had two requests (a) We want spittoons; (b) We would like our own girls to wait on us, and not any of them toffs. ...

Su 18 Apr. 1915
... Mr Stoddart [the churchwarden] told me that Mr Caldwell, drill instructor of the Great Leighs Special Constables, had persuaded him not to attend the drill tomorrow (at 6.30 pm). He is elderly and finds it difficult to make out the commands quickly enough to be in the place, or facing in the direction he is intended to be. Being deeply conscious that, from physical failings, I myself hinder the drill, I made the same request to Mr Caldwell. I am at times very deaf, and do not hear the command distinctly enough to make it out. Being crippled with rheumatism, I cannot step out as the men thirty years younger than myself do. I judged from Mr Caldwell's readiness to grant my request that he was not sorry to drill the company with me not in it. But three at least of the company will miss the joy of shoving me into my place.

Diary of the Revd Andrew Clark, rector of Great Leighs, Essex, 16 and 18 April 1915

'What a strange being! He really likes war'

MARGOT ASQUITH AND LLOYD GEORGE DISCUSS WINSTON CHURCHILL

In a diary entry of January 1915, Margot had noted a conversation with Winston Churchill in which he overstepped the mark in his enthusiasm for the war. The incident took place at Walmer Castle, the residence of Lord Beauchamp as the Lord Warden of the Cinque Ports. Churchill reportedly said to her:

> My God! This <u>this</u> is living History. Everything we are doing and saying is thrilling—it will be read by 1000 generations—think of <u>that</u>!!
>
> Why I would not be out of this glorious delicious war for anything the world cd give me (eyes glowing hot with a slight anxiety lest the word 'delicious' s[houl]d jar on me)—I say—don't repeat that I said the word '<u>delicious</u>'—you know what I mean.

A few months later, on Sunday 8 May H.H. Asquith and Margot were at The Wharf, their home in Sutton Courtenay. They were joined by Lloyd George, Lord Reading and Sylvia Henley. Margot expected Lloyd George to be depressed over his recent defeat in the House 'over his Drink',[35] but instead she had never seen him in better form. He enthused about her home, and then they had a private discussion in her sitting room, 'The Burn'. The discussion turned to the subject of Winston Churchill, and Margot noted in her diary some of the observations that were made, beginning with Lloyd George's comment on Winston's lack of judgement and ending with an account of his joyous reaction to the outbreak of war on 4 August 1914.

> Winston is a difficult fellow: he has not merely <u>bad</u> judgement but he has <u>none</u>. His Dardanelles xpedition gave the Turks a fearful long start. He quarrelled with Enver and got us at war with the Turk wh. he need never have done. The Turk is a formidable fellow and I don't believe we shall get through this thing with less than 200 000 men. ...
>
> M[argot]. Winston has a good war temperament if good spirits and unruffledness is what is wanted—He also has a lot of suggestions

The two wartime prime ministers, H.H. Asquith and the man who ousted him, David Lloyd George, at The Wharf in Sutton Courtenay, 1915 or 1916

and many ideas, elastic vital youthful military ideas but he is very dangerous because he has no imagination in the sense of seeing deeply into events and probabilities. I've seen it all through his life—when he was a little navyite and intrigued against McKenna, how wicked and above all how <u>foolish</u> and short sighted! ... He muddled his Antwerp and he will again muddle this I fear. What a strange being! He really likes war. He wd. be quite damped if he were told now 'The war is over'—He has no imagination of the heart.

Ll George[.] <u>He has none</u>. I shall never forget that night—that 4th August 1914 when war was declared. I dined alone—I was sent for to see the P.M. about 10.30. I found McKenna and Grey in the Cabinet room with the P.M. We were all very serious, very anxious. The P.M. said midnight abroad is 11 here—we all looked at the clock and Grey said 'it's not all over yet.' He then told us that a wire from Japan had been intercepted by our Post Office saying Goschen in Berlin had sent for his passports—I (Ll. G.) said it's all over then and we sat in complete silence——. Big Ben struck 11. Very slowly came the Boom—Boom—Boom. We sat in complete silence I sd say for

10 minutes after the last Boom. ——Winston dashed into the room radiant his face bright his manner keen and he told us one word pouring out on the other how he was going to send telegrams to the Mediterranean! The North Sea, God knows where. You cd see he was a really happy man.

Diary of Margot Asquith, 8 May 1915

'On Sunday night came the War Office telegram'

BICKERSTETH'S ACCOUNT OF THE LAST FEW DAYS IN BARRACKS

In this long letter, Bickersteth describes the charged atmosphere in the cavalry barracks at York as news arrives of the need for officers to go to the front.

About 12.0. Bill Browne a regular Royal subaltern ... came into the stable and told me that a telegram had just arrived from the War Office saying eleven officers were wanted for the Royals ... and that I was to hold myself in readiness to go any time and not leave barracks. We knew absolutely nothing about the reason why these officers were so suddenly wanted, but evidently the regiment had been in the trenches (or possibly all the cavalry had attempted to break through, as planned at Neuve Chapelle) and had suffered severe casualties.

The excitement was of course considerable ....

The day before yesterday word had been sent for a draft of 100 men ... but if this was due to the same hard fighting it seemed a small percentage of men in proportion to so many officers—so all was speculation. Who had been killed? How had it happened? When should we go? Instead of going to the Knavesmire to play polo, we had to be content with a scratch game on the Low Moor ... within the precinct of the barracks.

... About 6. pm. a telegram came from Colonel Steel—the C.O. of the Royal Dragoons—giving 10 names of those subalterns whom he wanted. Mine was not among them. ...

Mess instead of being somewhat dull was an exciting meal that evening. Wires kept arriving—but not the long looked for W.O. wire. ...

On Sunday May 16 we ... marched to the Minster for the annual military Sunday service. There were several thousand troops—nine or ten bands—and the Minster full of khaki clad figures. ...

Frayling the Greys bandmaster conducted 'The Entry into Valhalla' which was simply magnificent. But the most moving moment was when the drums and trumpets played the fanfare and then the National Anthem crashed out, every man rigidly at attention. The sun shone through the windows of the old Minster—and hanging from the great columns were the war-stained standards of famous regiments. One felt the inspiration of worshipping in a place so full of great memories—and not a few of us felt that if this was to be the last great service we should attend before we set off to the war, it could not have a [more] perfect setting.

In the afternoon Bickersteth had tea with the Archbishop of York at Bishopthorpe Palace.

Edward Gibbs had just returned from Wimereux where he had been looking after 2 base hospitals for a month.

He says it is rather depressing work—as one only sees the sick and wounded—and they are all rather broken and downhearted after their experiences. The Monmouths and Cheshires ran like hares the other day from the oncoming gas. We don't mind shot or shell or a hail of bullets, they told Edward Gibbs, but why stay and be poisoned ... to wait is to be either asphyxiated or bayoneted while temporarily unconscious. ...

On Sunday night came the War office telegram—seven officers were to go to the Royals at once. ...

Neither Cubitt[,] Ripley or myself were on the list to go—but we hope to go with a draft which will assuredly be wanted. The Royals casualties occured [*sic*] in the trenches—or rather in the open, because the trenches occupied by the infantry had been absolutely blown away by the German bombardment. ...

Steele (Colonel of the Royals) was wounded badly—also Julian Grenfell (Desborough's eldest son) .... (see pp. 120 & 207)

Letter from Burgon Bickersteth to his mother, 16 May 1915

'I am in charge of 240 men, scarcely one of whom I know by sight!'

GEORGE BUTTERWORTH AT ASHFORD

Having recently decided to take a commission, George Butterworth found himself rather suddenly taking on extra responsibility in the absence of the company commander who was called to the front. It is curious to read Butterworth's reaction to the strike on the North Eastern Railway (where his father was a general manager). Butterworth the composer is known for lyrical and reflective music, but here we see a thoroughly hard-edged side to his personality in his call for drastic measures to stop the strikes. He lays the blame firstly at the door of the employers, attacking alleged profiteers, a popular target for resentment in a country that saw itself as pulling together to face the crisis. He then attacks the unions for organizing strikes. Although this passage is good-humoured and probably not meant to be taken literally, Butterworth has clearly identified himself with a soldier's way of thinking, believing that only full support for the army and the prosecution of the war is the way for the government to act. In another context, this could be seen as the very 'Prussianism' that many felt the war to be trying to bring down, and liberal consciences were always troubled by the means needed to bring about the ends. The tone of anti-parliamentarianism, and the call for perceived enemies of the state to be suppressed, looks forward to the troubled interwar years in most belligerent countries.

The 13th (Service) Battalion of the Durham Light Infantry moved to Aldershot in November 1914, before moving to Ashford, Kent in February 1915, and on to Bramshott, Hampshire in May that year.

The move to Aldershot Monday, Nov 30

This was rather an interesting performance, as the whole brigade marched in as a body, 100 yards separating each battalion. Appropriately enough the weather was at its worst—a gale of wind and driving rain. This did not make the job of packing and loading any easier, but by mid-day we were all ready to move off. One got some idea from this of the vast scale on which army transportation has to be worked; a brigade is, of course, a comparatively small body, and we were certainly not over-stocked in any way, but it took something like 100 traction engines and motor lorries to move our stuff. These were ranged along the road in an apparently endless line, and made us feel very important. Owing to the wet we were, of course, unable to strike camp, and a party was left behind to do this as soon as the weather allowed.

After an early dinner had been served, we marched off triumphantly in drenching rain, and so, farewell to Bullswater, and at the other end comfortable barrack rooms, and fires in each!

Letter to 'm'Lady' (Dorothea Ionides, George's future step-mother) Ashford, 5 March 1915.

We are here for an indefinite time—billets very comfortable, other prospects poor. No progress whatsoever to report, except that we are now khaki clad.

These strikes are a nuisance, and I see there is a small one on the N.E.R. Personally I should do three things—

(1) Hang (or bayonet) all employers whose profits show an increase on previous year.

(2) Imprison for duration of war all who organize cessation of labour in important industries.

(3) Make Lord Robert Cecil[36] dictator for duration of war, as being the only man in Parliament who has anything useful to say. ...

Ashford, 20 May, 1915[37]
We move on Sunday to huts near Liphook. Address 13th D.L.I., Bramshott, Hants. Since returning I have been rather hustled—it is bad enough being transferred to a strange company, but, in addition, owing to the absence of the junior captain, I found myself temporarily second in command—then a further shock last night; the company-commander, an excellent man, is suddenly summoned to join the Expeditionary Force in France at 24 hours' notice, so now I am in charge of 240 men, scarcely one of whom I know by sight! This is likely to continue for perhaps a fortnight, and involves immensely complicated accounts and considerably more responsibility than is good for any one at such short notice.

However, I hope to pull through!

Diary and letters of George Butterworth, 30 November 1914 to 20 May 1915

'We shall set foot on French soil with hearts ready for anything'

BICKERSTETH LEAVES FOR THE FRONT

The first letter, written to his father, bears the printed address 'St James's Palace Hotel' in London, to which Bickersteth has added, in pencil, 'and in train to Southampton'. His longing to see action seems to be about to be fulfilled, and the letter is full of eager anticipation. The second letter, addressed to his parents, is written on Hotel Tortoni, Le Havre, headed paper, and gives an account of the voyage and Bickersteth's first impressions on landing in France. As with many such accounts, the juxtaposition of the ordinary and everyday with the effects of the war catch the writer's eye. In this case the situation was all the more strange as Bickersteth had known France before the war, having studied at the University of Paris at the Sorbonne, 1913 to 1914.

22 May 1915

> ... and now we are speeding towards Southampton. Thank Goodness at last! ...
>
> At this moment Buster Cubitt sits in one corner, I in another —and the other two corners are occupied by Ripley and Frank Brown—the latter is priceless and keeps us in fits of laughter. But it is all a little pathetic, as we know well enough that our hearts are really with those we have left behind. Tomorrow it will be different and we shall set foot on French soil with hearts ready for anything.

23 May 1915

> ... we received various tickets and proceeded on board the ordinary Southampton–Havre packet. On board there were about fifty other officers and a detachment of flying corps men, some marines, and a few Belgian and French officers. There were also a number of civilian passengers; about 200 passengers in all—and no crowd or rush. I had a first class berth with a flying corps officer from Farnborough. ... a score of transports were lying off the Isle of Wight, some with steam up, some without signs of life and shortly after gaining the open sea we passed a whole string of empty transports returning. ... I then fell asleep and only awoke at 8.30 am ....

(*above*) A cart commandeered by Burgon Bickersteth's squadron, May 1915

(*centre*) 'The way the men fraternize with the peasants': Royal Dragoons near Rouen, May 1915

(*below*) 'Billets!' accommodation for the horses of the Royal Dragoons, May 1915

All from the Bickersteth photograph album

(*above*) The Royal Dragoons in trenches at Sanctuary Wood (near Hillebreke),
Ypres salient, 28 May to 4 June 1915

(*below*) C Squadron Royal Dragoons, May 1915

All from the Bickersteth photograph album

It was a brilliant morning, the sea sparkling in the sun and a brilliant blue sky. France looked very attractive. We landed at the ordinary quay where I have landed before many a time. A staff officer and a number of transport men took us in hand. We all signed our names in a book and arranged for our kit to be transported either to the station or to the base H.Qs according as we were going on to Rouen or not the same day.

Then an electric launch took as all across the harbour to the main part of the town. The first thing I noticed was a crowd of French people on the quay watching an Indian soldier (in khaki suit and khaki turban) bowling at a French boy who wielded a genuine English cricket bat—rather a curious sight we all thought. ...

It is a brilliant afternoon—and everybody out enjoying the sunshine and the Whitsuntide holiday. There is little to suggest war in the animated scene before me as I write. We sit in an open air café—flower girls and paper boys pester us—a soldier out with his maîtresse—a little girl in white dress and veil from her première communion—the open market with flowers and vegetables and people basking about in the sunshine. There are plenty of khaki-clad fellows in the street ... but they have long ceased to be out of the ordinary. Military motors with the flags of the countries they belong to and big numbers painted on their bonnets rush about—but really that is all—and it is difficult to realise Germans still occupy many square miles of la belle France.

Letters from Burgon Bickersteth to his father, 22–23 May 1915

'The world at present is full of horrors'

ASQUITH AND THE FORMATION OF THE COALITION

In the aftermath of the 'Shell Crisis' and the failure of the Gallipoli offensive, Asquith was forced to form a coalition, bringing Conservative ministers and the Labour leader Arthur Henderson into his Cabinet to form a national government. Returning from hearing a speech in the Guildhall, Asquith found his Liberal colleagues on the verge of revolt against the proposed coalition.

19 May 1915

> ... a regular mutiny was on foot among our people against the 'Coalition'. They got together a meeting in one of the Committee rooms wh. was attended by almost all the good men on the back benches ... and expressed themselves with the utmost freedom: 'duped by the Government', 'treated like dirty ciphers' etc etc, and proclaimed their intention to debate the whole matter in the House this evening. The situation looked serious and Gulland[38] implored me to go and beard them: which I promptly did. It was one of the most curious experiences I have ever had: a roomful of old and devoted friends, full of soreness and indignation, and in many cases of fury. I was of course unable to tell them the whole, or even half of the truth, so I had to go more for their affections than their reason. I can assure you it was a difficult job.... I suppose I spoke about 10 minutes or a quarter of an hour, and had good reason to be satisfied with the effect. Several of them were on the verge of tears, and they rose and cheered wildly and declared that they were absolutely satisfied!

Eight days later, the Coalition was about to hold its first Cabinet (see Plate 8), and in his letter to Sylvia we see the private and public worlds of the Prime Minister in sharp relief.

27 May 1915

> We are so sad to hear the news of poor Francis Grenfell's death.[39] Margot was devoted to him, and he was as fine an example of clean and unselfish manhood as was to be found in the country. We hear this morning that Julian—Ettie's eldest son—has succumbed to his head wound. The world at present is full of horrors, and we are all walking in the valley of the shadow of death.
>
> In an hour's time we shall have our first meeting of the new Cabinet: it will be a strange experience, and I can only hope that it may better my expectations.

> *Letters from H.H. Asquith to Sylvia Henley, 19-27 May 1915*

'It is disgusting bad luck being stuck in a place like Argungu'

THE GREAT WAR COMES TO WEST AFRICA

Harry James Graham Miller-Stirling was a colonial administrator in Nigeria. His reaction to the coming of war was much like that of many other young men of his class—he was eager to be involved and frustrated at his remoteness from the centre of events. His letters show the difficulties of keeping in touch in this outpost of northern Nigeria, and reflect the fear of the colonists about the effects on the African population. Miller-Stirling was eventually commissioned in the West African Frontier Force (WAFF). The WAFF was involved in the conquest of the German Kamerun (Cameroon) 1914–16, though Miller-Stirling was not involved directly with this campaign. However, with the prolongation of the campaign in East Africa due to the guerrilla campaign conducted by General Paul von Lettow-Vorbeck using German *Schutztruppe* (colonial troops), the WAFF was used there from 1916 to 1918. Harry Miller-Stirling was killed on 16 October 1917 and is commemorated in the Dar es Salaam War Cemetery, one of 1,500 officers and men who died in East Africa from January 1917, and who have no known grave. Miller-Stirling had two brothers who were officers in the army. The family illustrates the global commitments of the British Empire at war. Edward George Bradshaw Miller-Stirling was killed serving with the 2nd Battalion of the Black Watch in Mesopotamia, 14 March 1917. Lieutenant Arthur Eustace Stirling Miller-Stirling was in the Indian Army, but was attached to the 1st battalion of the Gordon Highlanders in the British Expeditionary Force in 1914.

> Wednesday 12 August, Argungu, Sokoto Province, Nigeria
>
> I got news of the war last Thursday and everyone has been very busy since then. Telegraph going night and day, everything in code and strictly censored. ... I see the Germans are being driven out of Belgium. Whether we shall do much here I can't say, but I understand we may occupy the German Kameruns as we already have Togoland. Troops withdrawn almost entirely from Sokoto probably for this purpose. It is disgusting bad luck being stuck in a place like

Argungu at this time. Everything quiet here and news of the war has not yet been told to natives, but it must come out very shortly. ... The Germans seem to have put their foot in it badly this time. So far I don't know cause of Germans war with France and Russia but suppose we joined in because of invasion of Belgium.

Miller-Stirling goes on to relate the effects of the war on Sokoto: all leave had been stopped; they had a German prisoner, a trader at Sokoto; there were likely to be difficulties with food supplies as he expected the government to commandeer all supplies in the stores. He was envious of his brother Arthur:

I suppose Arthur will have taken a commission in some Regt. by now and perhaps will get a chance in the Expeditionary Force if we send one over to the Continent. Splendid luck for him right at the start. Wish I was anywhere but here. News takes some time to come along but I have special mounted men on the road to bring in wires at any time.

The next letter in the collection was written from Sokoto several months later on Sunday 18 April 1915.

I arrived here last Monday and am off today for Argungu where I am to be for a month or so probably.... They have wired up from head quarters to say that I am probably to be attached to the W.A.F.F. and will have to take over the Company at Birnin Kibbi.... I shall be glad of a chance which may possibly lead to the Kameruns later, but it may only mean garrison duty up here....

I was very sorry to see about the Falaba [a British passenger-cargo ship bound for the Gold Coast, now Ghana, sunk by a submarine off the coast of Ireland 28 March 1915; there were 100 deaths]. The Germans seem to have made worse brutes of themselves than usual in her case. Only one man I know lost as far as we have yet heard. The Dakar also burnt I conclude near Lagos. ... This will upset the homeward mails as it leaves us two steamers short.

On 31 May 1915 he wrote another letter to his father describing a great storm that had damaged houses and taken away part of his roof. He had received a postcard from his brother, 'Eddie', posted at Port Said, and supposed he would be sent to the Dardanelles. For himself there was little action, but news of the formation of the Coalition government in Britain had reached him:

> No news of the Kameruns, and no chance of this Company moving at present, so one can only go on with routine and we are not allowed to do any musketry as we have only our reserve supply on hand. The new Cabinet sounds extraordinary but what on earth Haldane has got the O.M. for beats every one. The Iron Cross would be more suitable....
>
> ... we go on here with trivialities and polo and so on, all rather 'fiddling while Rome burns' but one can't do anything else and at any rate one does not want to arouse native suspicions by showing any anxiety.
>
> *Letters from Harry Miller-Stirling to his father, written from Argungu, Sokoto Province, Nigeria, 12 August 1914 to May 1915*

'Resolute, confident, imperturbable optimism'

ASQUITH MEETS THE GENERALS ON HIS VISIT TO FRANCE

The first letter is written in pencil, and the envelope bears a War Office postmark. The printed address 10 Downing Street is crossed out, and Asquith has written 'somewhere in France (as the correspondents say) ... Midnight 30 May 1915'. The letter conveys a very favourable impression of Sir Douglas Haig, at this time commanding the 1st Army Corps under Sir John French. In December Haig replaced French as commander-in-chief of the BEF.

30 May 1915

> We dined on board a special train and got before 9 to Dover, where we found the scout 'Attentive' waiting for us, and escorted by a destroyer on each side (the 'Cossack' and the 'Viking'—what names!). Crossed the Channel at high speed and arrived safely at Calais. There was a squadron of motors awaiting us, and in less than an hour I was shaking hands with Sir J. French. He is comfortably quartered in the house of a notary, and I am just across the

street in the room wh. he tells me the King occupied, with Bongie[40] next door. It is all very nice, but I can't help contrasting this hour (about 12.30) with the corresponding time the last 2 nights, when you sat and we talked in my raftered bedroom at the Wharf. What delightful hours we had—hadn't we?

Asquith complains of the long programme ahead of him, mainly visiting the 2nd Army, but one item on the agenda cheers him:

I am glad to see the item '4.0 p.m. to visit G.O.C. Cavalry Corps— (General Byng)', as I feel sure I shall then have sight of Anthony [Colonel Anthony Henley, Sylvia's husband].

Writing at midnight on 1 June, Asquith told Sylvia that 'during these 2 days I have longed that there was some telepathic or wireless mode of communication—quicker and less cumbrous than the post (even in a War Office bag!).' He then described his visit to Haig's headquarters at Merville, accompanied by Sir William Robertson,[41] 'whom I increasingly like and respect'. In this and the next letter Asquith gave his impressions of British and French generals:

Haig is our big commander, and has steadily gained reputation since the 1st days of the War. He has a certain amount of personality and authority and great knowledge both of the science and practice of war, but he is curiously inarticulate. All the same, motoring through his country which is the terrain of the First Army one felt how superior in every way it is to the Second, in whose sphere I spent yesterday. The second and third and even fourth line trenches and points d'appui carefully thought out and constructed during the wet winter and spring, are masterpieces of forethought and organisation; and whatever else happens Haig can never be driven back from the ground wh. he occupies. We passed (Haig and I) thro' long lines of troops, Indians, Canadians (under Seely) Highlanders and the rest, of the best appearance and quality. We ended up with tea (of wh. I tasted half a cup) at a pleasant little château, as the guest of the peccant Gen. Gough, of Curragh notoriety. As I said to French afterwards at dinner—what (a year ago) could have seemed more paradoxical: he (Sir J.F.) (then in more or less disgrace) commanding in chief the largest army ever put in the field, Seely a Canadian brigadier, and myself the more or less honoured guest of Gough?[42]

General Headquarters, British Army in the Field [printed address]

2 June 1915 <u>Midnight</u>

... I have had a great blow to-day: no letter from you! ... the post arrived (about 2 p.m.) and the beastly thing brought me a pouch-full of telegrams from Bulgaria and Rumania ...

He had chaired a 'curious conclave' with French, Robertson, Foch,[43] Joffre, Millerand, with General Huguet acting as interpreter. They discussed a lot of 'more or less technical things, and I was glad to see how well Sir J.F. held his own.' After the formal conference Asquith spoke to Joffre and Foch:

> Joffre is a big heavy man, stooping at the shoulders, with a shock of hay-coloured hair, eye-brows and moustache: blueish grey eyes, a broad pallid jowl, and a soft low voice. I thought him more intelligent and impressive than the lean-faced, mercurial Foch. But the curious thing about both was their resolute, confident, imperturbable optimism. They are absolutely convinced that we have the Germans in the hollow of our hands. Once break through (wh. they are sure we shall, and that before long) and all is over! What a contrast to the unrest and forebodings of London. I cross-examined them to ascertain the grounds of their opinion, and in return got little but generalities. But it is a fact that they and Sir J.F., and all the best men in responsible positions here, are quite <u>unshakeable</u> in their sanguine forecast of the near future.

Letters from H.H. Asquith to Sylvia Henley, 30 May to 2 June 1915

'Regimental life is beginning to tell on my nerves'

MACMILLAN JOINS THE GUARDS

Rather like George Butterworth, Macmillan was unsettled in the battalion he had joined, and found a new lease of life on transfer to a more congenial one, in this case the prestigious Grenadier Guards. It was Macmillan's mother who helped this to happen. In this undated letter to his father, probably of May or June 1915, he outlines his reasons for wanting to move:

(i) The 14th K.R.R. is not to go out as a unit ... if there had been any chance of our going out as a battalion, I should not think of moving.
(ii) We are to supply drafts to 1st New Army and Regular Army if necessary.
(iii) We are going to be under all the most unpleasant conditions here of a draft battalion. About 30 or 40 officers or more in this rather crowded place. To tell the truth regimental life is beginning to tell on my nerves. I don't think I can go on living without a break in the atmosphere.
(iv) If I'm in the Guards, I can live at home, change into mufti at 3 p.m. every day, and just drill at Chelsea in the day time. I also know several of the subalterns there now, and lots who are in the regiment in France. ... I don't think it's ungrateful to my battalion, since anyway we shall be split up and may go to <u>any regiment</u> or battalion.

Letter from Harold Macmillan to his father, May or June 1915

'To die for one's country is a sort of privilege'

T.E. LAWRENCE TELLS HIS PARENTS
NOT TO MOURN THE DEATH OF HIS BROTHER

In these letters on the death of his brother Frank, Lawrence almost seems to be indifferent to the anguish of his family, though he may have been trying to deal with his own grief by finding a deeper meaning for their loss. Frank Helier Lawrence (1893–1915) was an alumnus of Jesus College, Oxford. He served as a second lieutenant in the Gloucestershire Regiment. He was killed at the age of twenty-two leading his men up to the front line before an attack in the battle of Aubers Ridge, 9 May 1915.

I haven't written since I got your wire as I was waiting for details. Today I got Father's two letters. They are very comfortable reading:— and I hope that when I die there will be nothing more to regret. The only thing I feel a little is, that there was no need surely to go into mourning for him? I cannot see any cause at all—in any case to die for one's country is a sort of privilege: Mother and you will find it more painful and harder to live for it, than he did to die: but I think that at this time it is one's duty to show no signs that would distress others: and to appear bereaved is surely under this condemnation.

So please, keep a brave face to the world: we cannot all go fighting: but we can do that, which is in the same kind.

His attitude clearly upset his mother, and a little later he wrote to her:

Poor dear mother

I got your letter this morning and it has grieved me very much. You <u>will</u> never never understand us after we are grown up a little. <u>Don't</u> you ever feel that we love you without our telling you so? —I feel such a contemptible worm for having to write this way about things. If you only knew that if one thinks deeply about anything one would rather die than say anything about it. You know nearly all men die laughing because they know death is very terrible and a thing to be forgotten till after it has come. ...

In a time of such fearful stress in our country it is our duty to watch very carefully lest one of the weaker ones be offended: and you know we were always the stronger, and if they see you broken down they will all grow fearful about their ones at the front.

Letters from T.E. Lawrence in Cairo to his parents, 4 June 1915, and to his mother, undated, later in June 1915

'I shall <u>never</u> write to you again from a Cabinet or War Council'

ASQUITH, THE BURDEN OF LEADERSHIP AND THE BALKANS

In the summer of 1915 Asquith became increasingly dependent on his relationship with his new confidante. His letters are full of expressions of love and devotion, though there is no evidence that the relationship went any further than this. Asquith was quite happy to divulge major state secrets to Sylvia, even on occasions sending her important letters from politicians enclosed with his own. The letters reveal a man struggling with the burdens of state, and we see glimpses of personal opinions and feelings which would never be found in the official record.

On 12 June Asquith wrote a ten-page letter to Sylvia, written from Easton Grey, Malmesbury, Asquith's summer retreat. He sent her a chronicle of the 'experiences of last week':

> a chaos of munitions, and Dardanelles, and reactions about the Campbell appointment, and infinite gossip as to Lloyd George, fate of the coalition, leadership of party and Government, the campaign in France, the wavering possibilities of Romania and Bulgaria, Bryce's resignation, the future attitude of the United States, and about 199 other things—what (I say) emerges as <u>to me</u> the salient and dominant factor of the week? Can you guess? I know you don't need to guess. Of course, it is <u>you</u>.

He admitted that he might have given the impression a week ago that he was losing his nerve, and although he is not in anything like high spirits now, he is 'collected and tranquil' and feels he has the strings in his hands, thanks to her.

In a letter of 14 June we gain some insight into the somewhat dangerous game that Asquith was playing, politically and emotionally. He had been on another 'heavenly drive' with Sylvia, but mentions her 'criticisms (about writing letters at War Councils) and your warnings (about limits!)'. Later he added that she had given him a good deal of good advice that day, 'and I shall <u>never</u> write to you again from a

Cabinet or War Council!' In a postscript he reminded her to 'always put ("personal") on your envelope'.

The next few letters dwell on Asquith's growing love for, and dependence on, Sylvia. The next significant reference to the war came on 18 June:

> French's last telegram is not encouraging as to the actual progress made ... I am afraid it is in all quarters a very bloody operation. Did you see that Rupert Brooke's only brother was killed in this latest fighting?

And in a later part of the same letter, Asquith gave full vent to his feelings about dealings with the Balkan states:

> I have been hoeing one or two rows [he has been using an extended gardening metaphor for some weeks, inspired by reading Voltaire's *Candide*], my fellow labourers being Crewe and Lansdowne: a nice gentlemanly team. The scene of our operations this morning was the Balkan peninsula—an 'unweeded garden' indeed, of wh. one may say with Hamlet 'things rank and gross in nature possess it merely'. All these cunning half-civilised and wholly greedy little States are waiting on their respective fences, playing for time, and holding out for exorbitant terms. Every day is of importance just now, and the co-operation of any of them becomes less and less valuable as the weeks roll on. ... you have to bargain with each behind the backs of the others.

A 'turbulent' discussion of the Dardanelles had followed at the Cabinet: 'an odd lot, Carson,[44] Winston, and Lloyd George, very nearly coming to blows'. The 'waves subsided', however, and they got through it, and war loans and even Lloyd George's munitions bill, without serious disagreement.

Letters of H.H. Asquith to Sylvia Henley, 12–18 June 1915

'I am enclosing ... a very interesting letter ... from Douglas Haig'

ASQUITH ENTRUSTS STATE SECRETS TO THE POST

The extent to which Sylvia Henley had access to the innermost corridors of power in the state is indicated in letters sent by Asquith at the end of June 1915. On 27 June he sent a letter from Munstead House, Godalming, containing a highly confidential enclosure:

> I am enclosing (wh. accounts for the size of the envelope) a very interesting letter I got this morning from Douglas Haig. The last paragraph is, I am sure, absolutely right. Please return it to me to-morrow or next day.

It is possible that this refers to a letter from Haig, 25 June 1915 (now MS. Asquith 14, fols. 70-74), in which he states that progress will be disappointing unless young officers who have shown ability are promoted to command larger units.

Two days later he was asking to have it back so that he could answer it! This was not the first or the last time Asquith enclosed documents of this kind. A week earlier he had enclosed a letter from the former first sea lord, Admiral 'Jackie' Fisher, in the aftermath of his row with Churchill over the Gallipoli campaign which had led them both to resign in May 1915.

The danger of such practices was highlighted by an alarm in July. On 9 July Asquith enclosed with his letter a highly unusual present from his latest visit to France:

> Dearest—This is the souvenir which I promised to send. It is rough-hewn, and just as it developed: not perhaps easy to follow. But historically it might have some interest: anyway it is yours.
> Yr ever lovg HHA.

The 'souvenir' was a set of scribbled notes taken at an Anglo-French conference in Calais on 6 July 1915, including a diagram of the seating arrangements. The notes are hard to decipher, but there are references to a deal over the Banat in the Balkans, and discussions, in French, about the aims of the allied 'offensive–defensive', where the idea that operations in the following months should be aimed at wearing down the enemy rather than territorial gain ('plutot tuer des hommes que gagner du terrain'—rather to kill men than to gain ground) was discussed. The words, written in Asquith's hand, are ascribed to Monsieur Millerand, the French minister of war, and Asquith has added 'M. Balfour a exprimé la même idée' (Mr Balfour expressed the same idea).

On 13 July a clearly relieved Asquith wrote to Sylvia:

> I was rather anxious when I heard that the 'souvenir' had not reached you: there might have been the devil to pay if it had by any mischance gone wrong. I am glad that you keep it in a safe but accessible seclusion.

Letters of H.H. Asquith to Sylvia Henley, 27 June to 13 July 1915

'These singularly fatuous operations at Hooge'

ASQUITH ON THE DEATH OF BILLY GRENFELL

On hearing of the death of another family friend near Ypres, Asquith lets the political mask fall for a moment and betrays a real anger at the seeming pointlessness of some military operations in Flanders. 'Billy' was the Hon. G.W. Grenfell, son of William Grenfell, later Baron Desborough, and Ethel Priscilla Fane (Ettie). He had entered Balliol College in 1909 along with Cyril 'Cys' Asquith, the prime minister's son. Having served in the OTC he joined up on 14 September 1914, and became 2nd lieutenant in the 8th Rifle Brigade. He was killed in action near Hooge on 30 July 1915. His older brother was the poet Julian Grenfell, a captain in the 1st Royal Dragoons. Also a Balliol man, he had served from the beginning of the war, and died at Boulogne 26 May 1915, of wounds received in action near Ypres. He seems to have relished soldiering, once writing 'I <u>adore</u> war. It's like a big picnic without the objectlessness of a picnic.[45] His most famous poem, 'Into Battle', glorifies war and is the antithesis of the later poetry of Wilfred Owen and Siegfried Sassoon.

> Isn't it terrible that Ettie's 2nd son Billy is also killed? He was an exact contemporary of Cys at Summerfields and Balliol, and we have known him ever since he was 3ft high: such a bright clever creature and with lots of character and oceans of promise. I hardly dare to think of her. I gather from K[itchener] (whom I saw before lunch) that the poor boy was killed straight off by a machine gun the first time he had ever been in action, in these singularly fatuous operations at Hooge. French (who has been here for 2 days) told K that he knew little or nothing about them. Some one ought to be heavily dropped upon.

The next day Asquith added a few further comments:

> I must write to Ettie about the death of poor Billy, but I cannot frame in my mind what to say. There is still one boy left, happily well under military age. ... Billy had a delightful nature, more so to my thinking than Julian: but they were rare and splendid boys, and her life henceforward will be a desert except for its memories.

Letters from H.H. Asquith to Sylvia Henley, 4–5 August 1915

'Quartered on the Commander-in-Chief's flag-ship'

THE PRIME MINISTER VISITS A BATTLESHIP SQUADRON AT INVERGORDON

The letter describes a visit to the fleet stationed at the naval base in Invergordon in the Cromarty Firth in August 1915. It is written on 10 Downing Street headed paper, the address crossed out and replaced in Asquith's hand with 'H.M.S. Iron Duke', Admiral Jellicoe's flagship. The rather odd episode relating to the supposed German mine, although a source of amusement, does highlight one of the key concerns of naval warfare in the Great War—the vulnerability of the great battle fleets to mines or torpedoes. It was for this reason that the capital ships of both Britain and Germany remained in harbour for most of the war.

> ... you will see from the above address that I am quartered on the Commander-in-Chief's flag-ship, which we reached after a fairly adventurous day at about 8.15 last night. We left Invergarry soon after 11 in the morning in our motors and had a wonderful drive in perfect weather through wild and beautiful glens to Loch Alsh .... There we lost a lot of time, as the motors had successively to be rowed across from one shore to the other in the most primitive of ferry boats.... we started afresh on another beautiful drive to Strome Ferry on Loch Carron. There the ferrying operations had to be renewed with even more primitive appliances and across a much wider passage. From first to last they consumed over 2 hours; but it was a lovely day and we watched the rather tedious process fitfully, basking on a bank in the sun. The sensation of irresponsible idling was quite worth enjoying. At last ... we were able to start on our last stage, straight thro' Ross-shire from W. to E.—some 70 or 80 miles, and just as we were nearing our destination at Invergordon the petrol gave out, and we came to a standstill. Luckily we were able to commandeer a supply from a passing motorist .... At Invergordon we parted from our ladies ... and boarded this ship, where we were hospitably entertained by a big dinner of Admirals, Captains, etc etc. How well one gets to know and recognise the naval cut and attitude! Better even than that of your military associates. I sat between Jellicoe and Sturdee. The former I like, and he inspires me with a good deal of confidence: a rare plant after the ravages of the last 12 months. Of the other, the 'hero' of the Falkland Islands fight, I will say nothing. He was in old days Charlie Beresford's right hand man, and bears traces of it.[46]
>
> ... There is a fine battle-ship squadron here of a rather mixed kind including the old original Dreadnought and the latest 'super's —Benbow etc—together with the newest comer, who has flitted back from the Dardanelles—the celebrated Queen Elizabeth. In a few minutes McKenna and I are going on board her to see what she is like. It is again a beautiful day. We have just had morning Church on deck: I read the lesson, Romans 8th .... The blue-jackets and marines were a fine muster, and sang well. ...

Later.

We have just been over the Queen Elizabeth—a beautiful ship—who carefully preserves the scars of the shell-wounds she received at the Dardanelles. She is driven entirely by oil—a great saving both in men and in dirt and discomfort. We are now going off in a destroyer to see the booms and defences. All the Admirals and Captains are absorbed in a double sub-marine hunt wh. is going on in the sea outside, and circumscribes the movement of the big ships. ...

Midnight

... We went out after lunch—the Admiral, Mckenna, Bluey and I—in a Destroyer called 'The Bat'—along the line of battle-ships and cruisers, right out to the open sea. ... the array of lethal monsters was in its way an exhilarating spectacle. As it happened, we came across a great yellow coloured object wh. the Admiral and his experts declared to be (possibly at any rate) a floating German mine. So we slowed, and circled round it, and fired a lot of shells from our small guns, without effect, for it bobbed up and down in the most elusive fashion among the waves. We got nearer and nearer, and as our destroyer possessed only one rifle, the Admiral himself took possession of it, and at pretty close quarters aimed again and again at the floating target. He hit it more than once, but alas! We came away with the melancholy conclusion that it was an empty mine-case of our own.

Letter from H.H. Asquith to Sylvia Henley, Sunday 8 August 1915

'The most sickening thing is the failure of the surprise landing'

THE PRIME MINISTER BLAMES HIS GENERALS AT SARI BAIR

In two letters, one written on Sunday morning at Sandwich, the other begun the same evening and finished the following day at Downing Street, Asquith shares some highly confidential military news with Sylvia, and vents his anger on his generals. The surprise landing refers to the Suvla Bay landing at the opening of the Battle of Sari Bair, also known as the August Offensive. This was the last British attempt to seize control of the Gallipoli peninsula which ended in failure. The 61-year-old General Sir Frederick William Stopford was sacked by General Hamilton after failing to press home the landing at Suvla Bay with enough vigour. Asquith had a personal stake in the matter since his third son Arthur 'Oc' Asquith was serving with the Naval Brigade in the campaign.

Sandwich, Sunday 15 Aug '15
… Yesterday was on the whole a beautiful day tho' diversified by thunderstorms, and I spent some hours not unprofitably on the links. While I was out in the afternoon K[itchener] arrived suddenly from Broome at our little villa. He was not able to find me but left behind his news, wh. was not good. Ian Hamilton wires bitter complaints of the incompetence of Stopford (commanding 9th Corps) and his Divisional generals, which has blocked his intended advance and compels further delay. K. replied telling him to send Stopford home at once and to supersede the other 2 if he can (Hammersley and Mahon[47]), adding 'this is a young man's war—if any generals fail, do not hesitate to act promptly: any generals I have available I will send you'. He proposes to send out Horne (Haig's man) to take Stopford's place. But it is a terrible nuisance to have to make these changes in the middle of a critical operation. 'Crosses' indeed! …

Monday 16th Aug
… I have come back into a welter of trouble. … But the most sickening thing is the failure of the surprise landing thro' the incompetence of the generals. It might have transformed in a day the whole fortunes of the campaign. If only you were here, I could tell you a lot that I dare not put down on paper. As you know, I am not apt to be downhearted, but A.J.B[alfour] (who has just been here) and I agree, that, in the whole 12 months of the war, nothing has happened comparable to this. Everything was perfectly conceived and admirably arranged: the Turks were wholly unprepared: and the presence of one man with any gift of leadership wd. have ensured a brilliant and resounding success.

Letters from H.H. Asquith to Sylvia Henley, Sunday 15 August 1915

'We might be in England
for all the outward signs of war'

HAROLD MACMILLAN IN FRANCE

In these letters, Macmillan, now in the 4th battalion of the Grenadier Guards, describes his accommodation in the reserve area, and we are given an insight into the way officers tried to make themselves as much at home as possible. Reading was very important to Macmillan, and he asks for books to be sent out, although evidently there were limits to the size of a library that could be carried about on active service. Alert to his new experience, Macmillan was keen to convey every sight and sound that met him once he was in France. He noted in his letter of 18 August that it was more peaceful this far from the front than perhaps he had expected.

> Things are very quiet here—we might be in England for all the outward signs of war. But it is curious to see how completely we have taken over this part of France. Everything is under the control of the British Military authorities, and M. le Maire bows obsequiously to the C.O. as he gracefully relinquishes all but the name of office into English hands.

In his next letter of 21 August he reports no news, but asks his mother to send more soap, and reading matter:

> If you are writing again, will you please also send me my edition of the Iliad? Bks 1–12. It is one of the brown Oxford texts, and is in the smoking room at Birch Grove. ... PS Only send Bks 1–12 to start with and then I'll send it back.

We get a fuller picture of his accommodation in his next letter of 23 August.

> I hope my letters arrive all right. I have written nearly every day; but I was not sure till I got your letter the other day whether to write to London or Birch Grove.

My room? It is large, and shared now with one Leigh-Pemberton.[48] My bed is comfortable and (with a free use of Keating's Powder) even sanitary. The walls are covered with

1) an exceedingly ugly portrait of the family of the King of Italy, in oleograph.

2) several crucifixes.

3) a print of Rafael's Madonna Granduca.

4) a picture in colours from a 'Tatler' of last years shewing an English Tommy embracing a French housemaid; this drawn with the vulgarity of the English unredeemed by the wit of French 'comic journalism'.

The mantlepiece contains (and in this resembles the mantlepiece of every French house I have ever seen) 2 bronze figures, very ugly, holding vast candelabra or cornucopias or something of the sort. These plastic marvels are firmly set at either end. In the middle there is a gigantic clock, which I cannot imagine even the most plunderous Hun being able to remove. The floor has rather a nice Turkey carpet. The windows are large and open like the ordinary French window. We are on the first floor.

The chateau (I believe I so called it in a previous letter) is only so termed by euphemism. It is a delightfully musical comedy sort of affair, in the most baronial of styles, with spires, and stucco, and all the rest. The owner is a wine-merchant, named Bélanger —he has a daughter who is young and quite pretty, a son, who was yesterday 'permissionaire'—(i.e. on short leave from the front) and a most amusing old wife, who is perpetually trying to explain that it is only she who is really bourgeois, while Leon (the husband) is very comme il faut.

They are really most kind and delightful people. The daughter plays the piano very well, and M. Bélanger sings with a vast basso voice, rich with the liquor of 60 years. A length of black beard —curiously curled—and the most extravagant taste in waistcoats —can you picture my home life a little?

A little more colour is added later, with further details about the eating arrangements in his new life:

I find I still have time to write a little more before the post goes.

We have very good food here. Each company messes by itself, in some little inn, near its own quarters. We are too much spread over the village to have a Battalion mess, but one is always having guests

126

from another Company or going to dine with them. The food comes partly from the Govt. 'rations', partly from the country, and partly from Fortnum & Mason. I will give you the menu of the dinner we are giving tonight—with 5 or 6 guests and a concert for the men of our company after it.

Cantelupe Melon

—

Creme Tortue

—

Bloater Anglais à la Belle-Mère

—

Dindon Roti
Saucisses

—

Poulet Froid
Salade

—

Peches. Poires. Fraises sauvages.

—

Sardines on Toast

—

Fruit—Cigars etc.

Such are—at present—the hardships of active service.

Letters from Harold Macmillan to his mother, 20 to 23 August 1915

'A fine "Grenadierly" noise'

THE GRENADIERS HOLD A CONCERT PARTY

Macmillan exercises his writing skills in this colourful description of an entertainment for the soldiers. Although he recognizes the sentimental nature of the evening, he is clearly impressed and moved by the occasion and shows that he is developing a strong bond with the men of his battalion.

> The concert which we had in our company was a great success. Imagine an old, draughty barn, about 100 ft. long and 30 wide —with straw on the brick floor of it, and for all illumination 3 oil lamps, hung round the wall, burning rather gloomily, moody, ill-omened.
>
> Into this barn (where 5 platoons would ordinarily be asleep) 5 strong men introduce a cottage piano. This is gala night. On the piano 5 bottles stand, a candle in each. Then a sturdy corporal, with more bottles and more candles—and soon the place is (to our eyes) as well lit as any West End theatre.
>
> So the evening begins. A recitation, very pathetic this, about the poor lad who slept at his post, and how the colonel sentenced him to death, and how his widowed mother pleaded for him, her only son, and how his pal, a hero of some 17 years, did so noble a deed in battle as to win the Victoria Cross—and the 'pal' chooses to refuse his decoration and asks instead a favour of the colonel. 'And what my lad is this, I pray' 'Pardon Bill Williams, Sir' the hero said (Bill is the delinquent) He is but young. Give him his head! So Bill's alive whom all gave up for dead!'
>
> And then wild and vociferous applause—almost tears in some eyes. Quite wonderful.

A rousing rendition of 'The British Grenadiers' and 'God save the King' finish a 'not unenjoyable evening. And not unimpressive either. For in a barn like this 250 voices make a fine "Grenadierly" noise.'

There is a reminder of another duty that fell upon officers, that of censoring the letters that their men sent home: 'Well (all the soldiers in their letters always say well...) well—I really must stop now.'

Letter from Harold Macmillan to his mother, 25 August 1915

'I have heard further details
of the show on the 7th and 8th'

A FUTURE PRIME MINISTER REFLECTS
ON GALLIPOLI AND LABOUR POLITICS

Clement Attlee (1883–1967), the future leader of the Labour Party and prime minister 1945–51 following his defeat of Churchill in the 1945 general election, was a captain (later major) in the South Lancashire Regiment in 1915. In April 1915 British and French forces had invaded Gallipoli, part of a strategy largely formed by the first lord of the Admiralty, Winston Churchill, as an attempt to knock Turkey out of the war and so offset the stalemate that had emerged on the Western Front. Three months later the Gallipoli campaign had also become a bloody stalemate, and in August the British command tried to seize the initiative by attempting to capture the Sari Bair ridge, the high ground overlooking the Anzac landing. The Australian and New Zealand Army Corps (ANZAC) were to attack towards the ridge while British forces would land at Suvla Bay in support. In the event, neither attack made progress. When the Anzac thrust failed, the Suvla Bay force became the focus of the offensive, but this too, after initially securing the local hills, found itself under attack from higher ground and suffered heavy casualties. The ageing and inexperienced General Stopford was blamed for not acting with enough decisiveness and was relieved of his command (see pp. 123–4).

Attlee was among the forces sent to Gallipoli, but at the time of the Suvla Bay attack he was ill with dysentery. Later his regiment was sent to cover the evacuation of Gallipoli, and he was one of the very last men to leave Suvla Bay. His letter to his brother Tom was sent from a hospital at Dragonara Villa, near St George's Bay, Malta, lent by the Marchesa Scicluna as a convalescent home for twenty officers. His political opinions are clear from the letter. He had been educated at Haileybury College and University College, Oxford, but his encounters with East End poverty through work with a boys' club in Stepney (a mission organized by Haileybury) from 1905 led him towards socialist views and he became a member of the Independent Labour Party in

1908. Here he anticipated some aspects of the experiences of public-school-educated officers during the war, taking a commission in a junior section of the Territorial Army which members of the Stepney Boys Club had to join, and learning about the way of life of a different class. Indeed Attlee's path to a commission in the war in many ways reflects the public-school ethos of the era, with strong elements of paternalism, and a sense of public duty informing his socialist values. This perhaps made Attlee's mental world more complex than that of many of his fellow officers, especially as his brother Tom held pacifist views and was imprisoned as a conscientious objector. The obscure reference to the Labour leader and E.D. Morel may relate to Arthur Henderson's inclusion in the Coalition Cabinet (May 1915), or perhaps more likely to the politics of the Union of Democratic Control. Morel, a Liberal, was secretary of the UDC, an organization opposing the government's war policy and advocating a negotiated settlement. Attlee was clearly unhappy about the 'anti Belgium' aspects of the arguments being put forward. Morel had been sympathetic to the German cause before the war and opposed intervention on the grounds of the violation of Belgian neutrality. Attlee also clearly identifies strongly with his regiment, a crucial factor in maintaining morale for officers and men.

Mse Scicluna, Dragonara, Malta, 27 August 1915

I have moved from hospital to this place a very fine house lent by one of the local nobility for convalescent officers with £100 per month to run it. It is on a little peninsula to the north of Valetta and consists of a courtyard surrounded by rooms with a broad pillared terrace all round, a walled garden below …. . Inside are selections of the worst possible Italian paintings of the 17th century in the style of the Caraccis [*sic*] tainted with Rubens. Fat goddesses and fawns etc.

The company changes constantly as people are sent to England or sent here from the hospitals. It is rather far from Valetta but the air is lovely and the view: the bathing also excellent to say nothing of the cuisine.

I hope to get away any day now but it is easier to get to England than back to Dardanelles. I have heard further details of the show on the 7th and 8th. We had 5 officers killed and a dozen or so wounded: there are only 5 officers and 280 men of the battalion still in the firing line. My company led the attack and so caught it worst of all. I doubt if there are 50 left though of course many were only slightly wounded. As usual in war the best men are among the killed. Major Wilkins and Longbottom one of my subalterns two awfully good chaps with whom I used to discuss psychology etc. and little Willis my greatest friend in the regt., Birch and Ray Faulkner wounded, the latter badly. I saw our C.O. last week down with dysentery or perhaps enteric. Our brigadier and brigade-major were both killed hence the casualties are coming out very slowly.

We were in the new landing and the attack on Saribair. I think our men did very well.

The papers as you say are vile, especially the Times who are bursting for conscription for all they're fit. They must know that at this stage conscription will not be of any service.

I had some discussion on the subject at Hamrun [a military hospital in Malta], one man quite openly saying how useful it would have been in the labour troubles railway strikes etc. When I took him on and told him how right the workers were to suspect 'the patriots' he was quite hurt and indignant but the rest of the room saw the point all right.

I see they have raided the labour leader. Isn't there a bit too much of E D Morel in it? I never care for having in these non socialists who have particular axes to grind in the case anti Belgium.

I feel a desire for more solid reading than I am getting. I bought and read Carlyle's Cromwell the other day and left it with an increased admiration for Cromwell and an added detestation of Carlyle. ...

There's a chance I may look you up soon as one can never tell what may happen. Some men who are quite fit have been sent to England. I'm trying to avoid it as it probably means being seconded to another regiment which I don't want at all.

Letter from Clement Attlee to his brother Thomas, Malta, 27 August 1915

'The knowledge one gets
of the poorer classes'

HAROLD MACMILLAN AND HIS MEN

Macmillan discusses one of the many tasks allotted to the junior officer, that of censoring the letters of the men, a task he described in an earlier letter as 'very laborious and only occasionally amusing'. His reaction might seem to be patronizing, but working so closely with working-class men was a completely new experience for him. It was one which stayed with him for the rest of his life and informed some of his political values. In this letter we are left in no doubt of the genuine affection and sympathy he began to feel for them. This war was a war of poets, and Macmillan feels that he is in the presence of a poetry every bit as valid and meaningful as that of the literary kind:

One of my men (whose letters I censor) wrote to his mother saying—
'We are none of us downhearted: I don't think—<u>even the officers</u>!'
Rather delightful, don't you think! ...
Dear Mother—do not worry about me. I am very happy; it is
a great experience, psychologically so interesting as to fill one's
thoughts. A company has just past [sic] my house, back from a long
route march, singing wonderfully the dear soldier songs, with silly
words and silly tunes, but which somehow seem, sung by their great
childish voices from the depth of their very lovable hearts, the most
delicate music and the most sublime poetry. Indeed, of all the war,
I think the most interesting (and humbling too) experience is the
knowledge one gets of the poorer classes. They have big hearts,
these soldiers, and it is a very pathetic task to have to read all their
letters home. Some of the older men, with wives and families who
write every day, have in their style a wonderful simplicity which is
almost great literature. And the comic intermixture of official or
journalistic phrases—the kisses for baby or little Anne; or the 'tell
Georgie from his daddy to be a good boy and not forget him'—it is
all very touching. ... Indeed, I think there is much to be learnt from
soldier's [sic] letters.

Letter from Harold Macmillan to his mother, 30 August 1915

1 Parliamentary Recruiting Committee Poster no. 60, 1915

2 Parliamentary Recruiting Committee Poster no. 104, 1915

3 Parliamentary Recruiting Committee Poster no. 80, 1915

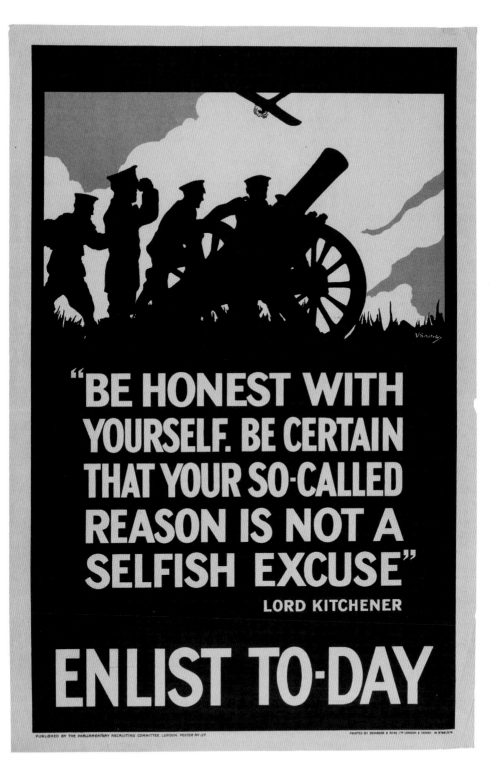

4 Parliamentary Recruiting Committee Poster no. 127, 1915

No. 5.—THE SECRETARY OF STATE FOR THE COLONIES.

.11665.]

TELEGRAMS.

[Thursday and Friday, July 30 and 31.

CONFIDENTIAL.

The time of despatch of telegrams to the Foreign Office shown in brackets is the time given by the telegraph operator.

No. 1.

Mr. Crackanthorpe to Sir Edward Grey.—(Received July 30, 11 A.M.)

Nish, July 30, 1914.
(No. 66.) R. (July 30.)

INFORMATION received here this morning is to the effect that Austrians recommenced bombardment of Belgrade yesterday evening. Servians replied from forts, and bombardment ceased. Minister for War states that Servian frontier has not yet been violated.

No. 2.

Sir M. de Bunsen to Sir Edward Grey.—(Received July 30, 11 A.M.)

Vienna, July 29, 1914.
(No. 124.) (July 29, 11·30 P.M.)

RUSSIAN Ambassador informs me that Russia has ordered mobilisation of corps destined for operations on Austrian frontier. Military attaché learns from his Russian colleague that thirty-one divisions will be mobilised, namely, those of Wilna, Warsaw, Kieff, and Odessa army corps. News is not yet generally known in Vienna this evening, but I believe it will not be a surprise to Ministry for Foreign Affairs, which has tardily realised that Russia will not remain indifferent. In present temper of this country irrevocable steps may be taken unless mediation which German Ambassador declared its [*sic*] readiness in principle to offer in concert with three other Great Powers not immediately interested be rapidly brought to bear. Both Russian and French Ambassadors have spoken to-day to German Ambassador, who feigns surprise that Russia should take so much interest in fate of Servia. Russian Ambassador explained impossibility of her doing otherwise, and expressed hope that matters might yet be arranged. He said that Russia had already used her influence to secure compliance of Servian Government with principal demands of Austria. She would probably go further still in this direction if approached in a proper manner. But she could not consent to be excluded from the settlement, and she was justly offended at having been completely ignored in the matter. Interview with French Ambassador was disagreeable, but German Ambassador in the end said that personally he thought German Government might consent to act as a mediator with other three Powers, provided that proposals could still be formulated which would have any prospect of acceptance on both sides. From what Russian Ambassador tells me, I gather that Russia would go a long way to meet Austrian demands on Servia, but his Excellency greatly fears effect on Russian public opinion if a serious engagement takes place before an agreement is reached.

Italian Ambassador fears that Austro-Hungarian Government would decline mediation if offered before Austrian arms had obtained at least one decisive victory over the Servians.

706—27]

2.8.14 Belgian neutral – Winston "If the Germans violate
" Belg I want to go to war " & if not resign

– J. Morley will resign if we do go to war

– J Burns & Beauchamp on — Grey wires to Cambon
this afternoon.

– Mobilisation 3rd fleet proclamation
– Lunch Beauchamp no 2
6.30 Grey, talk with Cambon. Winston seen Fr. Naval
Attache. Morley very angry

– Our fleet views not intimated to Germany
– No decision on Belgian violation of country
by Germany

(Germans crossed Fr frontier tire (Luxembourg)

– New Zealand offered expeditionary force. I thanked
them but sd. no necessity at present.

– No orders given to our fleet to attack Germans fleet
if they come out tonight.

– J.B. nothing to change his position – must resign
Asq. asked to see him after.

Walt.
C.
Su.

6 Sketch of a camouflaged warship, drawn by Joseph Pease and passed to Lewis Harcourt during the Cabinet meeting of 18 February 1915

From Asquith at Cabinet
2.3.15

I shall some day
keep a Cabinet
time table.

I roughly estimate
that about one-half
of the whole is
taken up by one person
(W. S. C.)

7 Note passed by H.H. Asquith to Lewis Harcourt at the Cabinet meeting
of 2 March 1915, expressing exasperation at the amount of time taken up by
Winston Churchill

Position round
Table of Coalition
Cabinet
27.5.15

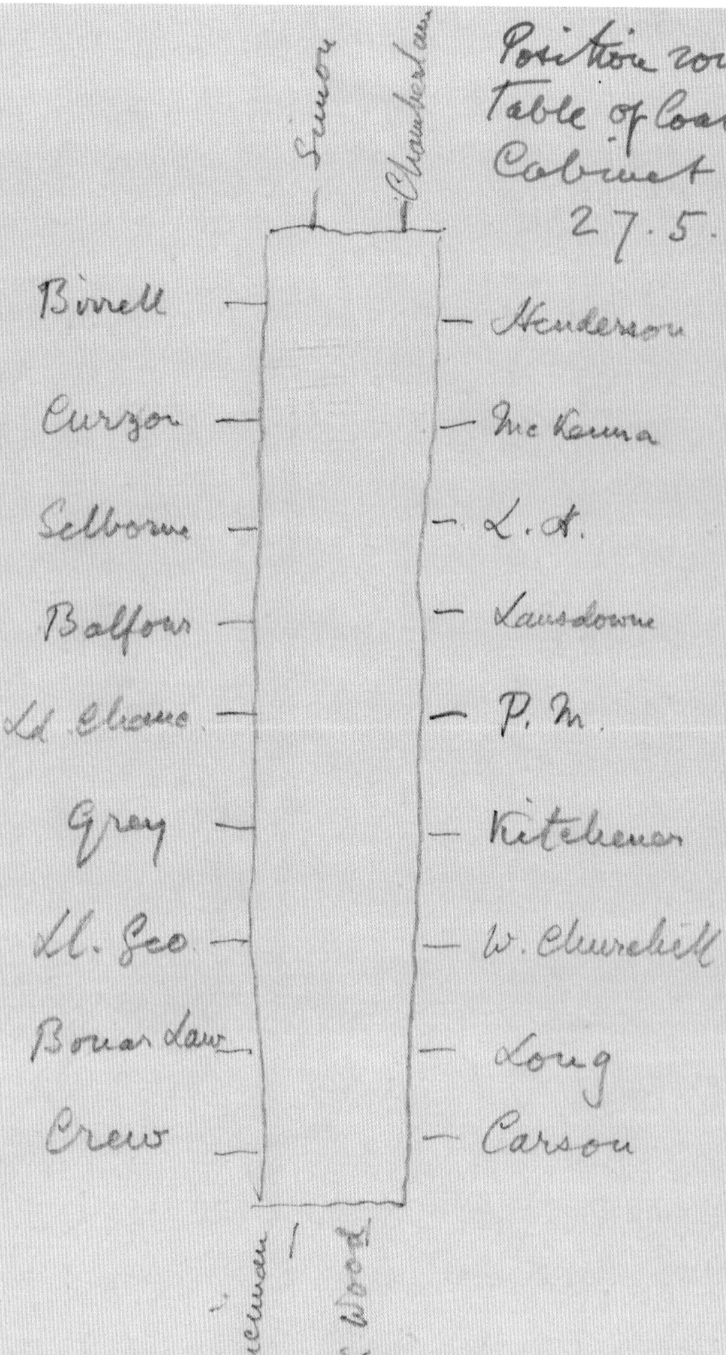

Simon — Chamberlain (top)

Left side	Right side
Birrell	Henderson
Curzon	McKenna
Selborne	L. A.
Balfour	Lansdowne
Ld. Crewe	P. M.
Grey	Kitchener
Ll. Geo.	W. Churchill
Bonar Law	Long
Crewe	Carson

Runciman — McK Wood (bottom)

27.5.15   Cab. noon.
[I gave up my seats at Buck Pal
at 10.45 a.m. King very pleased]

C.O
10. Downing Street,
Whitehall. SW.

First Coalition Cab.

Lansdowne between P.M. & me
P.M. sd. we joined for national purposes
& must be self forgetful
— We holding on well at Ypres, but position
is unpleasant.
— Russian losses lately in Galicia 300,000
men and all their rifles!
They have got only 2 or 3 rounds per gun left.
— Russia has 900,000 men ready to put in the
field if they can get rifles for them.
We are trying to get them for Russia from
Japan.
— We started this war with 700,000 men
We have today 2,300,000
(601,000 now in France)
— Our ammunition has never dropped below
5 28 rounds per gun (18 brs). The French
has been down below 300.
— Bonar Law wants more information from
Kitchener.

8 Sketch by Lewis Harcourt from his journal, showing the positions round the
table of the first coalition cabinet, 27 May 1915, together with his notes of the
discussions

Apple Trees

One Tree Hill

The Bowery

Auchonvillers

Mailly-Maillet

Cemetery

Hawthorn Ridge

Vitermont Mill (Site of)

Vitermont

Englebelmer

Hill 142

Mesnil

Cemetery

Avéluy Wood

Han

Baillescourt Farm

Bois d' Hollande

Beaucourt
sur Ancre

Grandcourt

Cemetery

Square **R**

St Pierre
Division

The Mound

Crucifix

Cemetery

Thiepval
Wood

Thiepval

Line of Apple
Trees

Farm du
Mouquet

DIAGRAM

Minor corrections to detail 28-4-16.

Ordnance Survey 1916.

SECRET. Number 7

NOT TO BE TAKEN BEYOND BRIGADE HEADQUARTERS.

LUFTTORPEDO   WALD VON THIEPVAL ALBERT

ANCRETAL

KAMPF UM THIEPVAL –

9 (*previous spread*) British trench map, Beaumont edition 2.B. Detail showing the British (blue) and German (red) trenches around Thiépval on the eve of the Somme offensive, June 1916

10 (*above*) 'The Battle for Thiépval'. Watercolour and gouache by Albert Heim, 1916, showing, Lieutenant General von Wundt, commander of the Württembergers of the 51 Reserve Infantry Brigade, observing the British bombardment, probably from the Beaucourt Redoubt

11 (*right*) T.E. Lawrence as Aircraftsman Shaw by William Patrick Roberts, 1923

...or leaves its trench, the next edges along to the part of the trench it occupied, so that the attack may all be made on the same frontage.

A-B = our line
E-D = enemy line
E.F. = enemy 2nd line with seven communication trenches between.
(1 (2 (3 (4 = dug-outs etc.

Distance from A-B to C-D abt 300 yds.

(not drawn to scale)

Distance from C-D to E.F. abt 100 yds.

trenches & dug-outs were the
most formidable that have yet
been seen. The fighting is still
going on, & the last report shows
that we are making steady way.
The casualties are naturally very
heavy: so far, 1300 Officers and
41,000 men. The Adjutant General
has just been here with the returns.
Some battalions of Manchester &
Lanc^s. Fusiliers are practically
wiped out. On the other hand he
says that of the total casualties
only 5% are killed, and 25%

12 (*left*) Harold Macmillan's sketch of a training trench showing the plan for a
trench attack described in his letter of 7 September 1915

13 (*above*) Letter of Asquith to his confidante Sylvia Henley reporting early
news from the battle of the Somme, 3 July 1916

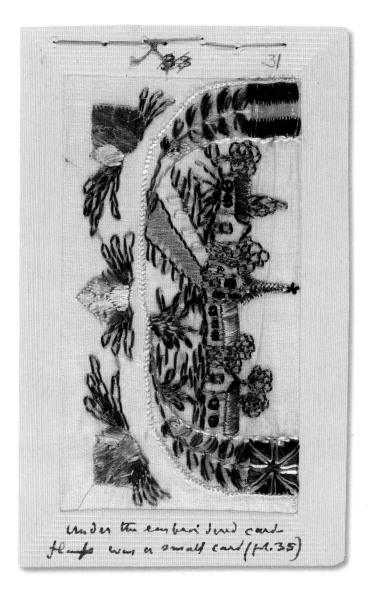

14 Embroidered souvenir card pasted into Andrew Clark's diary, July 1916:
'the soldiers buy these cards for what they call a "shilling" – no doubt a franc.'

'I spent the morning with No. 3 Coy. in a practice attack'

HAROLD MACMILLAN DESCRIBES TRAINING FOR AN ATTACK ON A TRENCH

This letter includes a detailed description of training for a frontal attack on an enemy trench, and shows that Macmillan was becoming a conscientious officer with an eye for detail.

> Your letters reach me every day, and are so welcome! Today there is no more news. I spent the morning with No. 3 Coy. in a practice attack. My duty was to organise (or devise rather) a system for bringing up parties of bomb-throwers in a frontal attack.
>
> They are to come (I think) in the second line. In the fourth or fifth line (after the trench is taken) come men with sand-bags (empty) and shovels.
>
> The attack will then be something like in the diagram [see Plate 12]. We did it today with one platoon at a time (the bombers going with the second platoon. Only the frontage of one platoon is attacked, and as each platoon leaves its trench, the next edges along to the part of the trench it occupied, so that the attack may all be made on the same frontage.

He goes on to explain the nature of such an attack:

> When the bombers get in to the trench, they must immediately begin to work, each party separately. One party goes along the main fire trench to the right, one to the left. Others go down the communication trenches leading to the enemy second line—they get well 60 or 80 yards down and then build two barricades in the trenches with sandbags, about 20–30 yards apart.
>
> The idea is that the main body of the infantry will thus be able unmolested to consolidate the line which has been won. When night comes, a communication trench (or several trenches) would be dug back to the line A–B, so that we can next day safely bring up reinforcements of men and ammunition.
>
> If the bombers who are working along the trench laterally are successful, they will be supported by infantry, who will at once

consolidate all ground which is won. All communication trenches have to be blocked, otherwise the Germans will work down them and bomb our men out. If a single communication trench is missed it may spoil the whole attack and the ground won, prob. at great expense, may be entirely lost.

   This was the scheme which we worked on this morning. The G.O. was watching, and considering that it was the first time it went quite well.

After all this explanation, Macmillan rather belatedly wonders if this can really be of interest to his reader, though he mentions in earlier letters that he would like his letters to be sent on to his brother too:

> I do not know whether the military operations interest you. But I think this is quite a good system and I am rather proud of it. Not that I invented it, but Capt. Ridley and I worked it out together.

Letter from Harold Macmillan to his mother, 7 September 1915

'The big guns from the cricket ground was fired'

ACCOUNTS OF A ZEPPELIN RAID ON NORTH LONDON

The first Zeppelin attacks on England came in January 1915, with the first raid on London in May. The intensity of Zeppelin activity increased in late 1915 and 1916, though their rate of loss was very high. As a terror weapon, airships had preyed on the public mind even before the war, and their appearance caused a great deal of excitement. However, as these accounts in letters to Andrew Clark suggest, fascination seems to have outweighed fear, with people running out into the street to see the great airships.

   The two accounts below are extracts by Clark from letters sent to him by Mrs. A. Brown of Hornsey, North London. He has highlighted some words and phrases with speech-marks.

5/9/15 we had an awful shock one night when we were going to bed about 10.45 P.M. It was the Germans. They followed up an express train from Southend. They knew they were following them. So they stopped at Leyton Station instead of going to St Pancras where they were due a little after 11 P.M., and did not arrive until after 4 A.M. When I heard the first three bombs, I called out 'Did you hear' to the people upstairs. They were in bed. We all dressed again and ran in the street. Every one was out, some in 'there night clothes' and some with a jacket over a shirt. I did not stop to take off my 'nighty' and I put on all my things on over it, and jacket on the top of them. The big guns from the cricket ground was fired. ...

I saw houses and the almshouses without roofs. Also the glass out of the station windows blown out. There are rows of houses all dilapidated. There were a lot of people injured and 15 killed. The brewer's man that used to take the beer to Mr. Fluner had just taken in his van and opened the door as a bomb 'droped.' He was blown to pieces—Poor man! He told Mrs Fluner he had 7 children—Holes in the ground were made that a cart would go in—also where a van would go in. I do hope and trust that we shall not have them again.

14/9/15. The very evening I posted your letter we had the Zepps over here. I was getting ready for bed and just washing when I heard the bombs going off. I got dressed as well as I could, and the zepps were in front of our door. Everyone in the road, and streets, were out. Some were dressed; some were in their night dresses only. It was all but over our house. We thought our time was very near. We saw the flames, sparks and firing fly. Oh dear, it was a grand sight. It was quite 'facinating' to watch, but we never want to see it again. ... the poor 'Belgian' were nearly beside them selves. They said they had been through it once. They did not think they would see it again.

Diary of the Revd Andrew Clark, rector of Great Leighs, Essex: copies of letters of 5 and 14 September 1915

'"The realities of life" are little but the extravagant visions of a fleeting nightmare'

HAROLD MACMILLAN MUSES
ON WAR AND CIVILIZATION

On 10 September Macmillan described his practice bomb-making activities, and then lists his library, which he thinks is 'wide and liberal'. It included:

The Bible
The Imitation of Christ
The Confessions of S. Augustine
The Iliad
Theocritus
Horace. Odes and Epodes.
Poet's Walk
Henry IV
Twelfth Night
The Winter's Tale
The Poems of Emily Bronte
Maxim Gorky's 'Les Vagabonds'
The Shaving of Shagput (Meredith)
Lalage's Lovers (G. Birmingham)
The Ring and the Book
Ruskin's Sesame & Lilies & Crown of Wild Olive

I shall try to send back some which I have read and should like to preserve. I have written inside

France. Sept. 1915.

and they will be curious and (I hope) interesting tomes in the library which I trust will one day astonish Europe for its rare combination of elegance and learning.

The role of this library in keeping him 'civilized' has taken on a great significance, and is an example of ways in which young officers, faced with the dangers and discomforts of war, found ways of linking back to their former lives. Correspondence with home, having books, favourite foods or other home comforts sent out, all helped an officer to maintain that link physically, and more importantly, emotionally. Macmillan emphasizes a favourite theme, the unreality of his present military world:

> I have a friend who was said to have read the Iliad 'to make him fierce'. I confess that I prefer to do so to keep myself civilized. For the more I live in these warlike surroundings, the more thankful I am for all the traditions of the classic culture compared to which these which journalists would have us call 'the realities of life' are little but the extravagant visions of a fleeting nightmare, lacking true value or permanency.

This theme is picked up once more on 17 September when he pictures his mother at home in Birch Grove:

> I can imagine you so easily, sitting in the summer house on the lawn; with the Sussex downs in the distance, —very familiar now, dear hills we know and have watched in every changing mood.
>   In the hot sultry days which we are having now I can see the mist in the valley at home—a great haze overhanging the range. Then (as today) a shower of rain gladdens us in France. And I can see that shower in Sussex—coming up from the South-West, up the valley. The sun soon follows; the hills are very clear now and very close. You can see the great Jubilee 'V' perhaps,[49] or the glint of the sun's refracted rays on a green-house—oh—it's all most present to 'that inward eye which is the bliss of solitude'.

The contrast with his present reality is clear, but this reality itself is only a sham as is evident from the slightly bizarre attempt to recreate battle conditions:

> Last night we spent in making wire entanglements from 7.30–9.30. It was a very instructive and useful operation, but it is very annoying to be obliged to take it all down again when it is finished. We succeeded in making a most formidable obstacle in quite a short time. Of course all unnecessary noise is forbidden and if the Germans fire a place or open rifle fire, the men have to lie down at once. We practised this with electric lamps to represent the flares and whistle blasts as equivalent to rifle fire.

Letters from Harold Macmillan to his mother, 10 and 17 September 1915

'Every gun within miles
had its turn at the evening "hate"'

The tone of Butterworth's diary during the last few months of training in England was one of frustration at the slowness with which his battalion was being prepared for the front. Indeed, he allowed his diary to lapse for several months, and only maintained a regular record from August 1915 once he was in France. Even here he remarked that 'during this period we went on training exactly as in England, and quickly relapsed into our dull and monotonous habits.' Then in September his platoon was sent up to the front line, being informed that this was 'for "instructional purposes," 24 hours at a stretch, being attached to the units actually on duty there.' For the junior officer, this was the defining experience; all the waiting, all the training had been for this moment, and an officer could only feel that he had become a real soldier in his own estimation once he had experienced the front line. Butterworth very self-consciously describes his own reactions, affecting an air of ironic detachment which, in his own mind, would be the attitude expected of a young officer. Despite their iconic status with soldiers and civilians however, front line trenches in reality varied considerably; Butterworth points out that this was a quiet trench, and also that the real dangers lay beyond the trench's comparative safety.

> September 18th.
> We have been in the fire-trenches three times—twenty-four hours at a stretch. This was just a preliminary canter, and we none of us had any real responsibility, merely assisting those already in possession. Naturally enough we were not put into any of the dangerous sections, but it may be of some interest to describe what a normal day on a quiet part of the front is like. The first day we started from a point some miles in rear, and timed our march so as to get up after dark. As we got nearer and twilight set in, the artillery noises grew more and more insistent; ours seemed to predominate, and

every gun within miles had its turn at the evening 'hate,' which is an affair of regular occurence [*sic*]. As night set in the artillery fire ceased, but the rifles went on cracking continuously with every now and then a splutter of machine guns. We reached the entrance of the communication trench safely; it is about 600 yards long, and as our guide lost his way several times, we spent quite a long time in it; stray bullets were now flying all about, and the explosive sound they cause as they pass overhead was new to most of us; the depth of the trench, however, made things quite safe. At last we filed into the fire-trench, and immediately opposite the entrance I found, to my astonishment, a little wooden shanty, and the officers of the company having dinner; so just at the moment when I felt braced up for a vigorous onslaught on the Hun, I was hauled off to roast beef and beer, while a sergeant posted my men.

Later on I went along the line with the officer of the watch. Every minute or so a flare went up, and then the enemy position was plainly visible, about a quarter of a mile away (the trenches here are really breastworks, built up high with sandbags).

The sentries and snipers on either side exchange compliments pretty frequently, though there is rarely anything to fire at (I have not seen a German yet). In the trench, one is perfectly safe from them; it is the working parties behind who are worried by the stray bullets. And so it goes on all night, and every night; occasionally a machine gun gets on to a target (real or imaginary) and then there is half-a-minute's concentrated fury, after which comparative peace again.

It is extraordinary how soon one gets accustomed to all this rattle. I slept excellently each night I was in, and as I was not on any special duty I was able to get a decent amount of rest.

By day there is very little rifle fire, the sentries are fewer in number and work by periscope; the German snipers make it dangerous for anyone to expose his head above the parapet by day for more than a second or two (even at 500 yards).

In this respect they are all over us—and in fact we are still well behind the Hun in all the tricks of trench warfare; as regards machine guns we have pretty well caught up, and our artillery distinctly has superiority.

As far as my platoon was concerned, we had a very quiet time each day we were up; only one shell fell anywhere near us and we have not had anyone hit. Others have not been quite so lucky; one platoon was caught by a machine gun on its way home the very first night (presumably through the guide's fault), and had five wounded. Another lot narrowly escaped destruction by a mine explosion, but the battalion has lost less than twelve wounded altogether and none killed.

So much for our period of instruction; we are now in divisional reserve four miles behind the front, and expect to take up duty in our own allotted section in about a week's time.

There is not much excitement here, but we hear the artillery at work practically all the time; usually it is simply a gun or two trying to annoy somebody, but occasionally there is a concentrated 'strafe' for half-an-hour or so, and then we all sit up and wonder if someone is trying an attack; and of course there is always a chance that we may be shelled ourselves. But no one minds that.

Diary of George Butterworth, 18 September 1915

'A queer life and one of complete comfort after Flanders'

CHARLES FISHER SETTLES IN TO NAVY LIFE

Charles Dennis Fisher (1887–1916) served as Senior Censor at Christ Church, Oxford, 1910–1914. At the outbreak of the First World War he joined the Red Cross and served in Flanders. He transferred to the Navy in September 1915, and this letter appears to date from this time as he is clearly adjusting to his new shipboard life. HMS *Invincible* was a battlecruiser and with HMS *Inflexible* had sunk the armoured cruisers *Scharnhorst* and *Gneisenau* at the battle of the Falkland Islands in September 1914. At the battle of Jutland she was the 3rd Battlecruiser Squadron's flagship. Fisher as Temporary Lieutenant RNVR was killed at the battle on 31 May 1916, along with 1,026 officers and men, when the ship's magazine exploded after she had been hit by shells fired by the German battlecruisers *Lützow* and *Derfflinger*.

My dear Waddle,
    Still flourishing and I hope learning a little more every day. On watch tonight 8.30 to 12 wh is one of the most favoured for it gives

you a night in bed. The morning I generally spend studying some devilish instrument or other after the ordinary divisions are over.

... It's a queer life and one of complete comfort after Flanders, though of course the procedures in Flanders are much more simple and direct. A ship is a floating laboratory, with a foreign language of its own, as difficult as Greek. However stout is still called stout and we have a very good tap on board. Nothing could be jollier than my companions and the dinners in the evening are very gay parties, and so is the after-dinner, which alas I shall miss tonight. The penguin on the paper [the headed paper incorporates a small picture of a penguin] indicates Falkland Islands and is a new device to celebrate the part played by Invincible in that battle. Malvinas the old Spanish name for the islands or for the penguin I don't quite know which. There may be some leave soon and I will let you know as soon as things are fixed up. Life however is uncertain. If I don't go ashore there are plenty of ways of getting exercise. We start the morning by running round the ship with the men for five minutes with the band playing. There is a medicine ball too and that gives one all one wants in about ½ hour. There is also a crude kind of Lawn Tennis on the quarter-deck. The Captn is a great man.

Yrs CDF

Letter from Charles Fisher to Waddle, from H.M.S. Invincible, Monday 20 [September 1915?]

'On the events of the next few weeks— even the next week—the whole destinies of Europe do most certainly turn'

HAROLD MACMILLAN FINDS BILLETS FOR HIS MEN ON THE WAY TO THE FRONT

In this letter Macmillan describes his task, as billeting officer, of finding accommodation for his men, as the battalion moved towards the front in the week before the battle of Loos began. The letter ends with an extraordinary leap from the minutiae of military life to a sense of the grand historical drama.

We left the village where we have been for five weeks at 7.48 p.m. on Wednesday night. We marched 3 miles only to another village, rather smaller. This I will call 2, our original village I will henceforward call 1. I will give a number in this way to each stopping-place and keep a key which can be shewn you later.

We found quite comfortable billets at 2. I had a room to myself; my platoon was in a barn of the same farm. You will see that I have a platoon in my Coy. (no 4) and do the ordinary work of a platoon-commander in a Company. I am only called upon to act as 'Battalion Bombing Officer' should need for grenade warfare happen to arise.

Thursday morning we breakfasted quietly at 9 a.m. Five of us — that is our Company officers—found a little Estaminet or Inn, where our Company Cook and servants got us a very good meal.

At 3 o'clock I went off with a sgt to the next village, where we now are. This I will call 3. 3 is about 9 miles from 2, one officer and one sgt. from each company are always sent on to see to the billets. Major Ponsonby (2nd in Command) also came with us.

We got to 3 at about 6 p.m. Here we found the Mayor and his entourage—all very friendly. I am given the 'area' for my company, a list of names, and a little boy. That is,—I am told that my company is to be between such and such a farm and such and such a road. Then I have a list of likely places and the names of the owners. The little boy directs me to each place in turn, and he is quite invaluable.

So I begin my task.
'M. Carron'
'M. Pierron'
'Mme. De Croix' …
and so it goes on.
M. Carron is old and testy. He is quite clearly the grandfather of the family. The son who now works the farm, is away at the wars. His young wife and family are left in charge—Secretly, of course, old M. Carron is not displeased, for he can resume a tyranny which it is clear he only unwillingly relinquished. And M. Carron will <u>not</u> give any straw.

20 men and no straw! 'But they cannot sleep on stone!' 'Mais pou'quoi non, m'sieur? C'est enco' mieux que la terre quand il pleut.' I look round to see that a storm has burst over us, and it is pouring in torrents. The discussion continues for a few minutes, and finally, after much coaxing, the old man produces the straw, and I continue my rounds, after profuse thanks.

Mme. Pierron is much more amicable. She has a beautiful barn, where she will take 60 men. She has also 2 rooms and 3 officers will be put in them. She is most obliging—'Estceque'il y aura de la place pour les ordonances (servants) tout pres des officiers?' I ask her. And she very kindly makes up beds for them out of old mattresses on the kitchen floor.

So, with varying success, I continue, till I have found billets of all my Coy. 201 men and 5 officers. Also of course a Coy. Hdqrs. has to be found; a place for the Coy. Sergeant-Major and the Coy. Quartermaster Sergeant to sleep; a place for the Captain's pony to be stabled—also 2 horses which draw the 'cooker' and 2 ammunition mules. The rain and the darkness made it more difficult, but by 8 p.m. I was finished. On each house one chalks up the no. of occupants and who they are to be. e.g.

16 platoon (45 men)

13 platoon (and Capt.'s horse)

and so on.

The Battalion arrived at about 9.30 p.m. I met my Coy.—and conducted each platoon to its billet (the sgt. assisting). Of course I had arranged it so that the platoon which was leading in the line of march should have the billet furthest up in the town in my area—the rear platoon has the last. Thus they can detach themselves easily and find their homes for the night without any fuss or trouble.

By 10 p.m. all the men were settled in, had been given their teas and biscuits, and turned in for the night.

This morning—Friday, it is still wet. I think we shall prob. move on again tonight, but I expect only about 6 miles. You could see the flash of the guns yesterday evening at dusk, and today the booming of them is terrific. But we are still several miles from the line of trenches and very quiet.

Except for the guns—and these mind you, are only like thunder in the distance, we could not imagine that there is war. And yet at this moment the greatest battle that the world has ever seen, is just begun. On the events of the next few weeks—even the next week—the whole destinies of Europe do most certainly turn.

Now the front is called for.

Goodbye—Love to all

   Your own

     Harold.

Letter from Harold Macmillan to his mother, 24 September 1915

'The wildest rumours were afloat'

TOWARDS THE BATTLE OF LOOS

In this letter Macmillan describes the slow and wearisome progress towards the reserve trenches as his brigade approached the battle of Loos, and conveys the sense of apprehension and anticipation of men approaching battle.

We left 3 not on Friday night, as we had expected, but at 8 a.m. Saturday morning (yesterday). We marched till 10 o'clock and halted at 4, where we were told we should be billeted for the night. At 1 p.m. however we received orders to move on, and at the same time we heard some good news of the advance in front of us. We then marched till 3.30 p.m., the whole Brigade (4 Battalions) being on the road altogether. We were the rear Battalion.

At 3.30 p.m. we were checked just outside a fairly large mining town, 5. We kept moving on 50–100 yds. and then stopping. Finally we reached a level crossing in the town. The first 3 Battalions of the Brigade got across the railway and the road, which ran parallel to the line and at right angles to our line of march. But as we were going to cross the railway line and road, we were suddenly halted. We were ordered to stop for two Cavalry Brigades to come through and one Battery. The cavalry were being rushed up to the front, where they are to be in waiting for a suitable opportunity. We waited at 5, from 3.30 p.m.—9.30 p.m. We were kept standing almost all the time; but every time we were about to move on, fresh orders came for us to wait. The line of troops passing in front of us seemed never-ending. To add to our discomfort it poured steadily all those six hours. We got a cup of tea while waiting, but otherwise no food, except chocolate.

A stream of motor-ambulances kept passing us, back from the firing line. Some of the wounded were very cheerful. One fellow I saw sitting up, nursing gleefully a German officer's helmet. 'They're running!' he shouted. The wildest rumours were afloat —I do not yet know whether there was any truth in them. I fear not. But our men were much encouraged, and we stood on that road from 3.30–9.30 and sang almost ceaselessly, 'Rag-time'—music-hall ditties, sentimental love-songs—anything and everything. It was really rather wonderful. At last, at 9.30 p.m. we were able to move.

Lieutenant Harold Macmillan (*far right*) and fellow officers in a playful mood before the battle of Loos in September 1915

The rest of the Brigade had gone ahead of us, with six hours start, and we were temporarily without any communication with them at all. This of course means shocking staff work and we were all most indignant. We had no idea where we were supposed to get to or what to do. The C.O. sent out signallers and bicyclists all over the place to find the rest of the Brigade, and we marched on in the direction which seemed most probably right. At 11 p.m. we halted in a field. Luckily the rain had now stopped. The stars were now shining in a clear sky, and the full moon gave us a splendid and most encouraging light. We halted then, in this field. The 'cookers' had been cooking the tea on the march, and we all got hot tea and bread and cheese. At 11.45 p.m. we set off again, having established communication meanwhile with our Brigadier. We marched till 1.15 a.m. to 6, the village where we now are. We found billets in some fine barns with plenty of straw. At 1.30 a.m. we sank into a blissful and well-deserved sleep.

I don't think I've ever realised before how comfortably one can sleep without a bed. A lovely pile of straw in an old cow-stall was to me then the softest of feather-mattresses. My woolly waistcoat was worth many a costly linen sheet. My 'Burberry' was more valued than all the 'eiderdowns' and quilts which I have enjoyed at home.

We were not allowed, however, to remove boots or puttees as we had to be ready to move at a moment's notice. But I think most of us would have been too tired to do so even had it been permitted.

6 is almost deserted and has suffered grievously from shell-fire at some time or another. At present, I should say it is out of the range of the German guns. At least, they haven't shelled us here yet.

We were woken up again at 4.30 a.m. this morning and breakfasted at 5 a.m. expecting to move immediately. But it is now 7.15 a.m. and no orders have yet arrived.

Letter from Harold Macmillan to his mother, Sunday 26 September 1915, 6.45 a.m.

'I do not feel frightened yet, only rather bewildered'

THE EVE OF THE BATTLE OF LOOS

Macmillan continues his account of the advance to Loos, creating a picture of the changing scene as the battalion moves ever closer to the firing line.

I hope my letter written from 6 reached you all right. I am doubtful about whether the post ever went from there.

We left 6 at 3 p.m. Sunday. The whole Brigade marched together. The 1st and 2nd Brigades were in front—having gone on some time before us.

We marched till 5 p.m. with one halt. At 5 p.m. we halted for half-an-hour just outside a big mining town. Here we struck one of the big main-roads. We were then about 3 miles behind the firing line. We went along this road till about 9 p.m. This road was more or less parallel to the line—S.E. in direction. We turned off N.E. at about 9, and at 9.30 halted, each company being given its line of trenches.

We (No. 4 Coy.) are in some trenches which run through a cemetery. We are only in support, but we expected to get shelled last night, and indeed we may get a little this morning.

Last night (after our 15 miles march) we slept pretty readily as you may imagine. Our guns are keeping up a tremendous bombardment from behind and on each side of us. We can hear the shells whizzing over our heads but one doesn't mind that; indeed the noise of one's own artillery is a very comfortable sound. The Germans are not doing much in the way of retaliation; they dropped a few shells short of us and some right over us last night.

We all slept in the open, beside the trenches. It is so uncomfortable to sleep in the trench and the men were so tired after these 2 hard days, that this was decided upon as the best system. We had sentries to watch; and if there had been any sign of shell-fire dangerously near us, we should have jumped down into the trench. There is of course no rifle fire, as we are at present in the support or 2nd line.

Lieutenant Harold Macmillan (*front left*) and fellow officers of the Grenadier Guards just before they entered the battle of Loos in September 1915

We do not know how the battle is going. There are bound to be fluctuations, and of course some of the New Army Divisions are rather shaky. My chief feeling at present is one of thankfulness that I am in the Brigade of Guards. All the way up on the road we were greeted with delight by the wounded and all other troops. And it is so much easier to command men who seem to obey orders with engrained and well disciplined alacrity as soon as they are given.

It is very curious to hear the different noises all night. There is the heavy boom of the 12 in. gun and 80-pounder—this shakes the earth with massy vastness. Then there are the field guns, with a less majestic but still very serviceable 'bang'. Finally the 'ping-ping' of the bullets.

I do not feel frightened yet, only rather bewildered. We are all in excellent spirits and health. Please don't worry at all about me. I hope you get good news in England—I expect you hear more than we do.

Love to all.
Your own
Harold.

Letter from Harold Macmillan to his mother, Monday 27 September 1915, 7.45 a.m.

'I rather dread Oxford and what it may be like if one comes back'

T.E. LAWRENCE BEGINS TO RESENT HIS INACTION AFTER THE DEATH OF ANOTHER BROTHER

William George (Will) Lawrence (1889–1915), an alumnus of St John's College, Oxford, served with the Oxfordshire and Buckinghamshire Light Infantry, and was attached to the Royal Flying Corps as an observer. He was shot down on 23 October 1915 near St Quentin after just a week in France. At twenty-six years of age, he was only a year younger than T.E. Lawrence. The loss of both his younger brothers unsettled Lawrence, and made him feel acutely his own lack of action.

> I have not written to you for ever so long ... I think really because there was nothing to say. It is partly being so busy here, that one's thoughts are all on the job one is doing, and one grudges doing anything else, and has no other interests, and partly because I am rather low because first one and now another of my brothers has been killed. Of course, I've been away a lot from them, and so it doesn't come on one like a shock at all ... but I rather dread Oxford and what it may be like if one comes back. Also they were both younger than I am, and it doesn't seem right, somehow, that I should go on living peacefully in Cairo.

Letter from T.E. Lawrence, Military Intelligence Office Cairo, to E.T. Leeds, 16 November 1915

'I am enjoying myself immensely'

BICKERSTETH ON THE FRONT LINE

Bickersteth describes his experience as part of a small party sent up to the front line to dig machine gun emplacements. He had volunteered to accompany the officer in charge, Birkbeck, who 'had never heard a shell or seen one go off in his life'. Bickersteth's description is positively lyrical, and he admits that he is enjoying his experiences. Many years later he annotated the copy of the account in the 'Bickersteth Diary' for the benefit of disbelieving readers, 'this was literally true'.[50]

It had been a glorious mellow afternoon—and now the sun was rapidly disappearing behind the slag-heaps of N——. The last golden rays lit up the red brick walls of the shattered houses and caught the tops of the trees bordering the roads. ... As the sun disappeared and the dusk rapidly came on, the flares began to go up, a long row of stars of greenish light, showing exactly where the line ran some 1700 yards from where we stood. ... I was to take my men up to the Q—— ['Quarry' appears to have been crossed out]. ... We had not gone more than 300 yds before we met the N. Somerset Coy Commander, who told us we were to go back and leave our tools, then go on to Clark's keep, pick up stores and then go up. So back we had to go, and flounder through mud and water to the keep. There in the dark I sorted out stores—each man carried either loop-hole plates, timber, corrugated iron, sand bags or something of the kind. ... The Q-Alley up which we went is a long communication trench at least a mile and a half long. The whole of it was floored with wood. Down this we tramped. Progress was very slow. The stuff we were carrying was heavy—frequent rests were necessary. We met various parties returning. The trench was narrow, and as we were a large party, we let them pass. It was a beautiful star lit night—with a young moon. Star shells followed each other incessantly, making the night day. In the burst of artificial greenish light the figures of the men and the heaped-up earth of the trench stood out clear cut against the sky. Every now and again the Huns swept the flat country on each side of us with machine-gun fire. One could hear them traversing from one side to the other. Machine-gun fire when high and at some distance sounds tremendously loud. Then there would come the occasional whistle of isolated rifle bullets—all of which is quite entertaining when one knows one is safe in the friendly earth. Finally our trench debouched into the quarry —like enough to any quarry except that the sides are not very high. All round the sides dug-outs had been dug right into the banks, and in each one was a little fire. As we crossed the quarry pretty quickly for fear of stray bullets, and dumped our stuff in the middle, the whole effect was most picturesque. The quarry itself shrouded in the dim silvery light of the moon—the fires all around at the mouth of each dug-out, throwing into relief the figures of the soldiers as they stood at the door way—the frequent burst of light due to the star shells. The deafening fire of our guns some few yards behind us, and the sound of trench mortar fire in front of us, added to the impressiveness of a little corner of this huge battle line, which I shall never forget. ...

Later
... We are about 40 yards from the Bosches, and I gather mines are the worst trouble. I am enjoying myself immensely.

Letter from Burgon Bickersteth to his mother and father, 9 January 1916

'To be so very near death is no slight shock'

BICKERSTETH'S SOBERING EXPERIENCE ON THE FRONT LINE

Having told his parents how he was enjoying his front line experience, Bickersteth's next two letters brought home the stark reality of war. Bickersteth's account of the loss of his comrades emphasizes the arbitrariness with which death could strike—here the little details of the mundane conversation and the mug of tea bring home the shocking sense of a sudden catastrophe despite Bickersteth's own apparent sangfroid. Many memoirs written after the war dwell on this theme.

15th Jan. 1916
… Personally I had a very trying time, as Waterhouse (a Capt), my troop sergeant, and one of my men were all killed by a 'whiz-bang' (shrapnel bursting on concussion) within three paces of me.

… The line was so close to the Huns that it was a life of continual strain—mining underneath and sapping in front of the trenches. We are midway between the Hohenzollern Redoubt and the Quarries[?]. The right part of my line rested on 'the Kink', a famous bit of the line. …

16th Jan. 1916. Sunday.
… On this particular morning, I was to stay on duty until about 9.0. am when I was to be relieved for breakfast. I was the only officer in the front line. … Since dawn we had been firing a number of rifle grenades—I should imagine with some effect— evidently the Huns were annoyed and they were replying with whiz-bangs. … Evidently the Hun thought the rifle which had been firing … was stuck up in the corner near the archway. They were not far wrong …. As I was standing there, up came Waterhouse cheerfully to relieve me. We stood talking a few moments. Then he said 'Have you a sentry posted round this corner?' I said, yes. 'All right' he answered, 'go off and get something to eat and I'll carry on till you come back.' He turned the corner. I walked about six paces away, which took me three or four seconds. I had hardly gone the six paces before there was a tremendous explosion in the trench just round the corner. The parapet just in front of where I had been standing had most of the sand bags carried away. I rushed round the corner, almost to stumble over the bodies of Waterhouse, my troop sergeant (Sergt Futcher) and the sentry, a man called Bowie. I saw at once the man was killed, and Sergeant Futcher though just breathing, was practically dead. Waterhouse was terribly wounded and by the look on his face I knew he could not live. I had seen that look before ….

Waterhouse's death is a terrible loss to the regiment. He was an Old Carthusian—we played in the same school XI in 1905. He was a good soldier—an exceptionally fine horseman and a very nice fellow. He was wounded at Hooge on May 13, and had only just rejoined the regiment. …

My troop sergeant, Sergt Futcher, is also a great loss. By common consent he was the most promising young sergeant in the regiment and was marked out to become a squadron sergeant-major. He was just my age, and a month ago I got him leave to go home and get married. I have written to his young wife. At the moment he was killed he had a mug of tea in his hand and a piece of bread and bacon.

Well, carry on, was the word. I got the trench cleaned up, posted another sentry and then at 10.0. am went down to get some breakfast, which I rather needed. The rest of the day was quiet and I was glad of it. To be so very near death is no slight shock.

Letters from Burgon Bickersteth to his mother and father, 15–16 January 1916

'The Germans dig out towards us and would bomb us out of [the] front line'

BICKERSTETH DESCRIBES SAPPING, MINING AND SNIPING AT THE FRONT

In the same 16-page letter of 16 January, Bickersteth provides a detailed description of trench warfare in his sector of the line in the Loos salient. The warfare he describes was typical of the period between the 'big pushes' at Loos in September 1915 and on the Somme in July 1916 as each side tried to weaken the other's defences and sap morale. The use of the terms 'company' and 'platoon' instead of squadron and company indicate that Bickersteth's unit was now acting entirely as infantry.

16th Jan. 1916. Sunday.
… The communication trenches are about 2000 yards long in this part of the line and feeling more like ferrets than men we nosed our way round bends and corners till we were almost dizzy … and it was over an hour later that we arrived within about 400 yards of the front line. … The trenches now became very complicated—many turnings led off from the communication trench—but everything was marked clearly with boards, for all the world like a town. …
The … last three [platoons] went straight on—past our Battn HQ dug-out, past our Company HQ dug-out, past the support lines, and

finally up to the front line. ... I was met by the platoon leader of the platoon I was relieving ... and I went straight round the line with him and saw exactly how he had his men posted. My men then came on, took up the same posts, and the 2nd Life Guards marched out.

Here, we were left to our own devices ... within about 50 yards of the Huns .... The whole part of the British line which has been handed over to the Cavalry is the most intricate sector which is held by us out here at all .... The intricate character of the line is due not so much to the maze of trenches immediately behind our front line (you must remember that all this part was held by the Hun before the Sept 25 push) as to the continual mining and sapping. We mine—the Germans mine. We blow up the mine: a crater is formed: and we rush forward to occupy it—the Germans immediately begin to sap towards it—that is dig a trench out from their own front line towards the crater. Every crater has many saps running out to it and embracing it on every side. Then again there are many saps quite apart from craters. We have to do this, as the Germans dig out towards us and would bomb us out of front line [*sic*] if we did not dig forward also to meet them. These saps which run out ten, twenty or thirty yards, or more (according to the distance the two lines are apart) are manned always by bombers. At the head of the sap sit two bombers day and night always on the alert with a pile of bombs at their elbow. ...Besides these complications <u>between</u> the two lines and <u>behind</u> them (saps <u>between</u> and supports, 2nd lines of defence, communication trenches <u>behind</u>) there are the mines under ground. The Huns begin to mine and we countermine—each of us dig listening posts. Sometimes the order would come round for absolute silence in our front line, no talking and no walking about —the sappers were 'listening'—and you knew that at the end of each tunnel three or four men were crouching in absolute stillness listening for the German pick and shovel. Often it is a race, with just a few hours in it, as to who blows up his mine first. ...

The Royals Company had a nasty bit of line ... our casualties were 20 (of whom 7 were killed) out of about 240 men—in four days. This I suppose constitutes about the average wastage.

... I had half my platoon left of the archway ... and the other half ... on the right .... I was the right platoon of the Royals. Where I joined the 3rd DGs the line became very complicated. It is called The Kink. There is no proper front line trench. <u>My</u> front line joined onto the line which is the 3rd DG support. The front line consisted of a collection of saps running round a crater and joined by small communication trenches. On the other side of the crater the front line began again. The trenches themselves were dry—floor boards along nearly the whole length—they were below the level of the ground but well lined with sand bags. There were very few places where one had ... to keep one's head down. In each firing bay there was a broad fire step, up to which one had to clamber to shoot by night <u>over</u> the parapet, by day through a loop hole or with a 'sniperscope'—a rifle attached to a frame .... There were very few proper dug-outs in the front line. The men when off duty slept at their posts. At intervals along the fire bays were hung gongs—generally empty shell cases. These ... were to be beaten in the case of gas attacks. My sector of trench was in pretty good order. Outside, both in front and behind were a fair number of dead lying—their bodies had been there since Sept 25. In one corner the boots of an English Tommy protruded through the back wall of the trench, which is called the parados—but I had him covered up at the first opportunity. About 30 yards in front of my trench was a German sniper's post—probably the head of some old sap. ... The sniping is a thing which I had entirely failed to realise till I saw it for myself. All day and night long the German snipers keep up continual firing—and I think the infantry have let them get the upper hand much too much in this part of the line. ... They have men lying out in all sorts of positions. Sometimes right out in the open behind some little rise, or behind a dead body—... sometimes behind the front line concealed in some cleverly constructed shelter on top of the parados or from a commanding position in the rear. ... We are always discovering and destroying these positions but they quickly find new ones. Plop, plop, plop go their bullets against our parapet incessantly. Before we left however we had several snipers' posts—I shot from one myself once or twice (though I don't think I did any damage!).

Letter from Burgon Bickersteth to his parents, 16 January 1916

'*Times* doing great harm to us in Germany by giving impression that the Govt. here is tottering'

HARCOURT RECORDS THE CABINET'S DIFFICULTIES

Harcourt's record of the Cabinet meetings early in 1916 reveal a government under immense strain. With continued stalemate on all fronts eating up more and more of the economic and human resources of the country, the British government found itself having to make increasingly difficult decisions about strategic alternatives while taking into consideration relations with its allies, the colonies and dominions of the Empire, and the workforce at home, all under the constant scrutiny of the newspapers and public opinion. At the same time it had to keep an eye on planning for the post-war world and be wary of the potential effect of decisions made in the heat of war on future industrial peace at home and diplomatic relations abroad.

> 2.3.16   11.30 Cab.
> Kitch[ener]. Question of using our German prisoners 8,000 on road making in France. Grey says we must be careful about reprisals.
>
> Asq. says 'this wd be good work for the conscientious objector of whom there are said to be 10,000'.
>
> Balf[our] sd he wd put them nearer the firing line and under shell fire.
>
> We agreed to use our German prisoners for quarrying road material in French Govt. quarries. ...
>
> Long[51] says too many young unmarried men have gone into mines and munition factories to avoid military service.
>
> Long says we must deal with the 'conscientious objector'. 25,000 men have been brought back from our front to work in controlled factories here.
>
> 9.3.16   Cab. 11.30
> ... Hughes (P.M. of Australia) here at Cabinet today.
>   Conferences at Paris
>   Strategic (Kitch. to attend)
>   Political

Commercial

Salandra [Italian foreign minister] comes from Italy; no one of importance from Russia.

We cannot lay down any hard and fast line as to post-war commercial policy. Our representatives must <u>discuss</u> but not commit us.

The Allies may have soon a serious shortage of corn and meat. We may have to dilute our flour with cereals, maize, peas, lentils etc.

Referred to Food Supply Committee.

We should acquire the whole of the shipping of neutrals which is acquirable. ...

Aylmer[52] on Euphrates has made an attack but was unable to penetrate Turk lines.

Nothing much happening at Verdun and French have still 10 new divisions they can bring in. ...

Ll. Geo. thinks the strategic Conference in Paris very premature, before Verdun result is known—and wants to postpone it. Kitch says the Conf. is mainly to support the French Govt. and Joffre both of whom wd. disappear if Verdun fell.

We have taken over 20 more miles of the French front.

Hughes (as an old Free Trader) says it is desirable to have an early declaration by the Brit. Govt. of their fiscal policy. I sd we must hear what Russia is prepared to do at the end of the war. I quoted views of Timiriazef (former Minister of Commerce in Russia) that on conclusion of Peace 'Germany cannot be deprived of most favoured nation treatment'. ...

The Allies require 13,000,000 additional [shipping] tonnage. ... Board of Trade only see their way to 4,000,000 ...

Proposal to import 2 battalions of lumber men from Canada to cut timber here. ...

16.3.16   Cab. 11.30

P.M. still in bed (bronchitis) ...

Mesopotamia going badly. Townshend cannot hold out beyond end of March. ...

Long. 'Times doing great harm to us in Germany by giving impression that the Govt. here is tottering['].

... Long wants Robinson (Ed. of Times) told to moderate his line.

Many of us said Robinson was helpless in Northcliffe's hands.

Kitch. sd. Times has done infinite harm to us throughout the war.

Long. Question of moratorium for rents etc of married men called up.

Long thinks impossible to do anything: would have to apply to <u>all</u> men married or single ....

Bonar Law is convinced we shall be <u>driven</u> to do something for the married men, as to rents, life insurance, Building Societies etc....

Balfour wanted to know what he might say (at a dinner in the City to Hughes) on the subject of the closer union of the Dominions and Gt. Brit.

We sd. he must use his own discretion.

Farm Colonies for disabled soldiers. Selborne[53] to set to work on this and a Cabinet Committee to consider the plan. ...

30.3.16   11.30 Cabinet

... Grey. Paris Conference

to back up French and support Briand[54]

to get Italians to declare war on Germany. Italians made an urgent demand for more munitions. ...

French very angry at idea of our withdrawing a Division from Salonika.

Robertson (Ch. of Staff) sd. if we cd. not bring this Div. home we cd. not take the offensive in France in the spring. Joffre sd. if this was so they wd. say we had deserted them.

The thing grew very hot, but Grey sd. 'it was put right at last and we fell on one another's necks but the Div. remains at Salonika'. ...

Strike on Clyde. Leaders deported to Edinbro'. The strike deprives us of 6 and 8 inch Howitzers and gun carriages which are in urgent need.

They are now striking in works on flat bottom boats urgently wanted for the Tigris.

Henderson [the leader of the Labour Party] complains he has been ignored in all these matters and not consulted. ...

A gt. mass meeting to be held at Glasgow tomorrow under impression that Govt. have decided that none of the low paid Clyde labour shall have increased wages. We have not decided this. Ll. G. and McK[innon] Wood say these men <u>are</u> underpaid.

Cabinet journal of Lewis Harcourt, 2–30 March 1916

'I carried half of the cake into the charge'

PRIVATE T. BARNES AND THE FUSILIERS' ATTACK

The 'charge' mentioned in this letter would appear to relate to the St Eloi Craters action of 27 March 1916, described by H.C. O'Neill in *The Royal Fusiliers in the Great War* (London, 1922). The operation began with the detonation of six very large mines; 30 seconds afterwards, an attack was launched, aiming at the German second line. While the Northumberland Fusiliers met little resistance, the 4th Royal Fusiliers met intense rifle, machine gun and artillery fire, and lost heavily. They nevertheless stormed the German wire, and captured the first German trench, but they could gain no further ground. The chaplain, the Rev. N. Mellish, repeatedly went out with volunteer parties to rescue wounded soldiers on 29 March, for which he was awarded the Victoria Cross, the first chaplain to receive it during the war. Private Barnes's account is however remarkably terse, and is just the kind of letter alluded to by Harold Macmillan when describing the letters he had to censor (see p. 128).

Dear Miss Acland

Just a line in answer to your parcel which I was very please to receive. I received it before I went into the charge which I suppose you read in the paper. Thank God I came out the same as I went in.

... Dear Miss Acland I am very please to say I am still in the best of health hope you and auntie[55] and all the housemaids are the same. I carried half of the cake into the charge and when I got into the German trench I went to eat a piece. I found it all got broke up but still it was very nice just the same. Being as I feel very tired after the charge you much [*sic*] excuse short letter.

Now I must close

From Your

Truly

Pte. J. Barnes

PS If you get the News of the World dated the 2nd of April you will see the Great Charge of the Royal Fusiliers.

Letter, Private T. Barnes, 4th Battalion Royal Fusiliers Machine Gun Section, B.E.F., to Sarah Angelina Acland, 3 April 1916

'To take no part ourselves in what we regard as a crime'

GILBERT MURRAY AND CONSCIENTIOUS OBJECTORS

Gilbert Murray's humanitarian and liberal sympathies led him to take an interest in conscientious objectors. He was not a pacifist, as his stance on the war shows. Murray could take a strong stand against the most extreme pacifist positions, and fell out with the philosopher and anti-war activist, Bertrand Russell, on the issue.

Conscientious objection, the moral objection to killing another human being, was not as widespread as certain notorious cases might suggest. It has been shown that appeals for exemption from compulsory military service that came before Military Service Tribunals, set up under the Act that brought in conscription in 1916, were overwhelming concerned with economic or domestic hardship. Appeals on moral grounds made up a tiny percentage of cases.[56] Those who did object on grounds of conscience could be very harshly treated, and Murray wanted to help such people if he could. The following extracts from Murray's correspondence give some sense of the emotions roused by the issue.

From a letter of R.W. Postgate, 21 March 1916:[57]

> When you were kind enough to give me my testimonial, you told me to tell you how I got on. I got non-combatant service at the first tribunal. This is interpreted by the War Office to mean trench-digging, fixing barbed wire, sewing on lines of communication etc. I appealed from this: my appeal was dismissed. I am called up tomorrow (Wednesday) there is nothing left but to resist.

From a copy of a letter of Daniel Huxstep, 15 April 1916:[58]

> Dear Bert [Bertrand Russell],
>   Some day I may be able to tell you the story of the past 3 days. I've been in a cell nearly all the time. Stripped naked twice; once for medical examination, and once because I refused khaki. I've been bullied and coaxed until I'm sick. I've disobeyed all orders; in spite of that I'm here in a labour battalion I understand, and I may be

Bertrand Russell, *c*.1910. *Photograph by Hugh Cecil*

in France in a few days. I hear there has been about 15 C.O's here, and they have been put to general service and such like, and packed off out; you may imagine the rest. It is a matter of death for me now I suppose, and I fear I cannot brave it out. I thought of hunger striking, but think it's too late now to be any use. If I fail don't think too hardly of me, the machine is tremendous. Can you send me a few handkerchiefs and razor. ... I feel only those who are really prepared for death will persevere.

Dan.

From a letter from Major A.K. Slessor,[59] 16 April 1916:[60]

Dear Murray,

Unfriendly is the last term I should dream of applying to any action you thought fit to take in the matter of these miserable creatures, whom I have to waste time over in the police court. ... I only regret that any man of yr distinction should be capable of what seems to me so lamentable a lack of judgment as to imagine that any possible result but a loss of regard for himself can arise from pestering public men, whose time and attention are already over occupied, on behalf of a misguided half hysterical boy, who simply needs to be let alone in order to fall in to line. It's the more senior fanatics, who pander to the pig-headed egotism of these contempt-ible youths and make them believe they are fine fellows, that I should like to administer a dose of gaol to ... .'

From a copy letter from Gilbert Murray to Bertrand Russell, 16 April 1916:[61]

I find in pleading for the C.Os. that the pitch is terribly queered by the resolution of the N.C.F.[62] Convention rejecting any form of alternative service. I did not know about this, but it cuts away the ground from my proposal to put the C.Os. under civil authority instead of military.

Have you any positive proposal to make by which the act could be administered or modified? Or are you merely out to break it by agitation? If (1), can you suggest any method by which a conscien-tious objector to military service can (a) Prove that his objection is a matter of conscience, and (b) Show that he is ready to make some sacrifice approximately comparable to that which his fellows are making. If you have any such plan please let me know quickly. If (2) you are out merely to break the act by agitation, I see nothing for it but for the C.O's to endure imprisonment and, if necessary, death. It seems that Lincoln had conscientious objectors shot. But even in America it did not seriously effect (*sic*) public opinion. [The letter is in typescript, and the last sentence has the manuscript addition, 'Worse luck!'].

From a reply to the above by Bertrand Russell, 17 April 1916:[63]

Most C.O's hold that under all circumstances it is wrong to take human life. Others, among whom I should be, are not prepared to lay down this proposition universally: they might concede that the Greeks were right to resist the Persians .... But they would say that killing is very seldom justifiable .... They consider wars between civilized States a folly and a crime on both sides ....

We, who believe that it is wrong to fight, are bound not only to abstain from fighting ourselves, but to abstain from abetting others in fighting. ... all schemes ... seem to many of us to embody a compromise which we could not accept without fundamental treachery to all that we believe.

In response to Murray's question on 'equality of sacrifice', Russell explained:

I must reply to this purely as an individual .... As to 'equality of sacrifice', I am astonished that you can mention such a thing in this connection. The sacrifice of the C.O's is immensely greater than that of men at the front.... The risk they run of being shot by the military authorities in France is as great as the risk the ordinary soldier runs of being shot by the Germans. They are being informed in barracks, with what truth I cannot judge, that they are to be sent to France; and the law certainly gives the authorities power to shoot them for disobedience at the Front ...

Every imaginative person knows that obloquy and the active contempt of those among whom one is compelled to live is far harder to bear than the prospect of death. ...

... you cannot expect men who disapprove of war to be in favour of conscription. But it is not our primary object to defeat the Act by agitation: our primary object is to take no part ourselves in what we regard as a crime.

From a copy letter from Gilbert Murray to Herbert Samuel, home secretary, 19 April 1916:[64]

> I see that my pupil, R.W. Postgate, has come to your notice. He chose to go to prison, rather than pay his fine and go straight to the barracks, in the hope that in the interval he might get permission to accept the work offered him by the Friends' Ambulance Unit. When the present crisis is over, I should much like to have a short talk with you … about some of these Oxford cases. Some of the Conscientious Objectors are obstinate as mules, but the Military Authorities are like rampant griffins, and I think there is a good deal of unnecessary friction and suffering.

Extracts from letters by or about conscientious objectors, 21 March to 19 April 1916

'He would be damned in history … if he was the man at such a crisis to break the coalition'

LEWIS HARCOURT DESCRIBES THE CABINET BATTLES OVER THE ISSUE OF CONSCRIPTION

Fault lines in the coalition became all too apparent over the issue of conscription as demand for manpower increased with continuing losses and the plan for a major offensive in the spring or summer of 1916 to take pressure off the French at Verdun. This was the most disputed issue from the formation of the Coalition in May 1915 to the passing of the Military Service Act, which came into force 2 March 1916. Having introduced conscription for single men aged 18 to 41, with appeal to military service tribunals being allowed for those who objected (though usually any exemption granted would be temporary or conditional), Asquith was soon forced to extend the Act to include married men. The issue nearly broke the Coalition, as Harcourt's dramatic account of the political brinkmanship shows. Conscription was not just an issue of liberal consciences against hard-nosed military men. Liberals such as Lloyd George supported conscription because as minister of munitions he was aware of the need to organize labour as well as provide men for the army. Labour Party members were suspicious of the Act for precisely the same reason. Many Unionists and a number of Liberals were also aware of the symbolic importance that the Act had in showing both enemies and allies that Britain was prepared to wage a form of 'total war'.

Harcourt describes Asquith and his supporters' struggle in mid-April 1916 to resist the conscription of married men. Under pressure from military demands for more men, and the threat of individual resignations and Unionist withdrawal from the Coalition if such conscription were not to be introduced, the second Military Service Act was passed in May 1916, and the political crisis was averted for the time being. However, the battles over the compulsion issue severely damaged Asquith's prestige and foreshadowed his eventual overthrow by Lloyd George. Harcourt's account suggests ambivalence in his own attitude, dislike of the Bill being offset by his overriding aim to preserve the Coalition for the sake of the appearance at least of unity.

17.4.16
Grave memo. by War Council of Sat. circulated this (Mon.) morn saying that any delay in conscription of unattested married men wd. have serious effect on results of the war.

Lunched with Asquith at 10 D[owning]. St. at 1.45. On the way there met McKenna in the Hall who sd. that though Ll. Geo. might resign Kitchener did not mean to go with him. Kitch told McK. this on Sat. afternoon.

Asquith late at luncheon, looking anxious. Margot nervous and full of notes from various colleagues to whom she had been writing—one from Walter Long saying he cd. not do what she asked viz. remain in Cabinet if Asq. resisted the military. After luncheon Asq. told me that B. Law had been to him this morning to say that it would be more difficult for him (B.L.) to get his party to vote against married men's conscription than for Asq. to persuade his party to vote for it. He (B.L.) therefore suggested the latter as the course of least resistance!!! What a man! And cur!

Harcourt recounts the adjournment of the Cabinet meeting scheduled for 4 p.m. while Bonar Law consulted his Unionist colleagues.

I took Kitchener to my room at H of C. and told him he wd. be a fool if he played into Ll. Geo's hands: that they wd. be a pretty pair if they resigned together and that political crises made strange bedfellows: that if he assisted to break up the Govt. for the sake of a problematical 200,000 men he wd. be cursed by the allies: that a break up here and now might end the war to our damage: Roumania might join Austria: America wd. be discouraged: Labour here wd. revolt with a good chance of a general strike and the finance, munitions and shipping of the allies wd. fail and Germany wd. triumph: it was doubtful if Asq. cd. reform his Govt. (though I think he shd. do so on a Lib. <u>Labour</u> basis) but it was <u>certain</u> the Unionist (*sic*) cd. not form a Govt. to last with Lib., Lab., and Irish against them and no majority in the Hof C. and it was hardly conceivable that <u>anyone</u> should dissolve at this moment.

I told Kitch that he should say in the last resort that though he wanted every man he cd. get, he realised the limitations and that sooner than destroy this Govt. he wd. surrender the chance of getting the problematic 200,000 by compulsion. I suggested that he should volunteer this at the 5 o'clock Cabinet: he sd. he cd. not do this, but he was in a more yielding mood when he left me after I had told him that he wd. be damned in history and by the allies if he was the man at such a crisis to break the coalition.

He knows nothing of constitutional or Parl[iamentar]y. Govt. being an Eastern satrap by nature and training.

After Kitchener departed at 4.35 p.m., Harcourt went to join Liberal Cabinet ministers who had gathered in Asquith's room. Lloyd George was pleading that the Committee of Cabinet, which included himself and the prime minister, with Bonar Law and Henderson added, should meet with the Army Council to find a 'via media'. McKenna and Lloyd George were in disagreement, with most of the Cabinet supporting the latter as they walked over to Downing Street, where the 'P.M. looked very grim'.

Harcourt recounts the complex political manoeuvrings as the government struggled for a formula that would save the Coalition. Before the Cabinet of 19 April the Labour party was refusing to accept Lloyd George's proposal or even that of their own leader, the Unionist Cabinet ministers were on the verge of resignation and Asquith 'will not fight but let the Tories try to form a Govt. and carry on'.

19.4.16   Cab. 11.30

... Curzon had another operation on his elbow last night but came to Cabinet reeking of chloroform. ...

Asq. complains bitterly of constant new figures produced by Army Council.

In the debate Harcourt claims that he himself pressed home the danger that the French would make peace if they thought Britain was not prepared to commit to compulsion (incidentally noting that they had the Cameroons to exchange for Alsace owing to the British blunder of handing the colony to France, a swipe at his successors in the Colonial Office). Grey said it was the most serious crisis since the 2nd of August 1914; Kitchener was threatening to resign though acknowledging that the break up of the Cabinet would be an 'appalling disaster'; Bonar Law said that even if he accepted a six week delay to try to persuade the Labour party (Henderson's proposal) the Tory Party would bring the Unionists out of the Cabinet. Harcourt then records the exchanges between a desperate Asquith, and the Tories Arthur Balfour, first lord of the Admiralty, Robert Cecil, Under Secretary at the Foreign Office, and Bonar Law:

Now 2.45

Asq. 'What am I to say in the H of C at 3.45'

Balfour 'that the Brit constitution is bankrupt, that we have broken down and are unfit to conduct the war and tell the allies to make the best peace they can and soon as they can'.

Asq. 'Am I to say that?'

Balfour 'It is the bare truth'.

R. Cecil 'The Unionist and Liberal Party ought to [be] told the situation and asked their views'

Asq. 'This wd. be the abdication of all authority'

R. Cecil 'I think that if the Tory Party knew the true situation they wd. never desire to drag the Unionist Ministers out of the Cabinet before Labour had been properly won over to possible future compulsion'

Bonar Law 'Might not the best way be to have the crisis, resignation etc to frighten the H of C. and so create a strong Govt.'

Balfour 'And frighten the Allies' ...

Henderson's proposal reconsidered. Cabinet not prepared at present to accept it.

Asq. thinks agreement probably unobtainable, though he wd. like Henderson's proposal to be accepted.

Henderson puts his proposal in writing. Kitchener says he can now accept it, on the basis of 75,000 men being got by voluntary effort in 6 weeks.

Asq. to tell the H of C. we are on the verge of [presumably agreement—Harcourt has not written anything further].

The Cabinet of 20 April moved forward on the agreement and various details were hammered out. Harcourt reports an evidently weary Asquith making a caustic remark about the War Office, which he said, keeps '4 sets of figures':

those which they use to deceive the enemy
those which they use to deceive the public
those which they use to deceive the Cabinet
the true figures which even the W.O. do not know.

Cabinet journal of Lewis Harcourt, 4–20 April 1916

'Such has been Good Friday of 1916!'

EASTER IN THE TRENCHES NEAR YPRES

On Good Friday Macmillan wrote to his mother from 'the shelter of my little "dug-out"', where, for the platoon, 'the whole day is spent in sleep and idling'. He goes on to describe in some detail the life of a platoon on the front line in the Ypres Salient. Although he depicts fairly intensive activity, his later comments indicate that this was exceptional.

There is a great deal of work to be done to try and make the trench rather safer, and also to try and join up with the other platoon of my company on my left. Night provides the necessary cover for this. But the work is naturally very slow, as 1 man in 2 has to be sentry. In the day-time the sentries use periscopes; at night they look over the top of the parapet.

We have been in here since Wednesday night. Tonight we shall be relieved by another of our own companies, and we shall go for another 2 days into Battalion Reserve. This will be much safer, of course, and more comfortable.

We have been very lucky since we came in. Yesterday was quiet all day. Last night we were much troubled by the German machine-guns; as I had to go out on a patrol to the right, in order to place a post or two in the gap, I took a strong dislike to their activities. But the trench itself is pretty safe now, altho' in some places the parapet needs a lot of thickening.

Later in the night, owing to a vigorous reply by our rifles, Lewis and machine guns, the enemy quietened down. Today has also been very quiet, considering the position. We have been troubled by a few rifle grenades, etc; and about 12 o'clock we got a few very heavy shells. These, luckily fell a little too far over our heads. Our artillery has been returning 3 shells for 1 all the afternoon; and here again these energetic tactics have been successful in cooling the ardour of the enemy.

The two lines are about 70 to 100 yards apart where I am. But the Germans have got a sap out to within about 20 or 30 yards of us. Here they have a sniper who bothers us a little. But a few gas bombs etc. have made him less forward.

I am, I confess, not sorry to think that my time is nearly over now. It is a little trying to be so cut off from every one, as we are here. But of course, it has the corresponding advantage of preventing C.O.'s, Generals etc. from coming along to bother and fuss.

Such has been Good Friday of 1916! I have got my little New Testament with me, and I have read the story of the Passion in St. Luke. Several of the men I found had also Testaments with them; one seeing me reading it in my dug-out asked me to lend it to him; which I have done. The men are mostly veterans, some have been here for 16 or 17 months. 2 in my platoon came out with the 2nd Battalion in August 1916 [*sic*—he presumably meant 1914] and have been here (unwounded) ever since. They are all sick of fighting, but sure of victory.

It is nearly 6 o'clock. The rain has stopped. Looking back towards our lines, one can see the sun setting over the still noble ruins of the city. One man (who had been at the battle of —— in 1915) said to me today; 'I nearly cried, Sir, when I saw the town again. They was the finest buildings as ever I saw'.

I hope you are having a fine Easter at home. We go out of the trenches altogether on Easter night; then we stay 4 days in the cellars; then 8 days rest. So for some time after tonight I shall be out of the front line.

Please give my love to all. The war is rather like being at a private school. I am already calculating the days till my first leave!

Goodbye now, my dearest Mother.

Your own

Harold.

P.S. Please send

2 indelible pencils

1 stick of shaving soap

Vanity Fair (pocket edition)

P.S. Easter Sunday. 12 midnight.

We are just safely back to our cellars in the town. Love to all.

MHM.

A little less than two weeks later, Macmillan characterized his experience at the front in a different way:

I am afraid that my letters contain but little news, and must be dull reading. But really nothing in particular seems to happen. Even in the trenches the feeling which is predominant is one of boredom.[65]

Letter from Harold Macmillan to his mother, Good Friday, 21 April 1916

'It is difficult to realise that we have really come through a winter campaign'

BUTTERWORTH DESCRIBES LIFE AT THE FRONT

George Butterworth continued to chronicle his war experiences in his diary and letters to letters to his father and Dorothea Ionides, who became his stepmother in January 1916. His experiences were not untypical of those of many soldiers in the period between the offensives at Loos in September 1915 and the Somme in July 1916. He regarded himself as fortunate not to be involved in any major actions, but this would not have been unusual in this period. As well as the round of trench duties and spells in reserve, Butterworth was sent for training in bombing and signalling. He gives an ironic account of leading a rescue party, and makes a few political comments on the conduct of the war around Easter 1916, when the government was under attack from many quarters. Like many serving soldiers, he appears to support conscription, but questions the motives of one of Asquith's severest critics, the newspaper and publishing magnate Alfred Harmsworth, 1st Viscount Northcliffe.

Saturday, Oct 2 [1915]
Although big things have been happening, I have very little news to give of the last ten days. We had a very quiet week in our bivouac, the time being occupied partly by work on reserve trenches, partly by the ordinary training (so called), of which everyone is heartily sick. In fact the men now regard the trenches as rest, and billet life as tiresome drudgery.

Then on Saturday, September 25th, as everyone knows, came the big push, preceded by a two days' bombardment, more or less continuous and at times extremely violent. We had known about this for some days before, but all details were kept dark, and even now we know very little more than has appeared in the papers.

As far as our share went, it consisted in being marched hurriedly about between the bivouac and a certain town where we are now billeted (7 miles)—apparently we were being used as corps (not divisional) reserve—ready to assist wherever required. ...

October 28.
... I will try and give some idea of what daily life in the trenches (i.e., ours) is like, so far as is permissible.

In the first place, there are practically no real trenches at all in this part of the country; we are here practically at sea level, and the spade finds water almost at once, hence protection has to be given with barricades of earth and sandbags. The front barricade is continuous all along the line, and behind it—for protection against shell fire—is a conglomeration of passages and cross walls; the geography of these is worthy of the maze at Hampton Court, and in striking contrast to the neat regularity of trenches built for training purposes. (Incidentally I had never seen a breastwork before coming over here).

As these walls have now been standing for nearly a year, they are in need of constant repair; there are enough rats in them to eat up the whole British Army. {One advantage of breastworks over trenches is that one can walk about behind them to a depth of about 25 yards without fear of being hit by bullets}.

As to our routine—by night we have a good number of sentries watching the front; these are relieved periodically, and the spare men are kept in readiness for emergencies.

By day there are, of course, fewer sentries, and they work entirely by periscope. …

The difference between day and night conditions is very great. By night, although spasmodic firing is always going on, we have not had a single man hit, and one could quite happily eat one's supper on the parapet, provided one retired below for one's smoke!

On the other hand, by day it is usually (though not always) extremely dangerous to expose even the top part of one's head for more than two or three seconds. A German sniper, even at 400 yards, can make pretty good practice at a six inch target, and we have already lost an officer and one or two men in that way. Moreover they frequently crawl out at night and take up a position from which by day they can pot away at our parapet without fear of detection. Of course it is the telescopic rifle that does it, and it is curious that the authorities do not think it worthwhile to put us on an equality in this respect. But in reality this sniping business is more of a nuisance than a danger, as it is quite unnecessary for anyone to expose himself by day, and by night the sniper can do nothing much. …

Now for a few incidents, chiefly connected with sorties into 'No Man's Land.'

(1) On one occasion we decided to attempt 'reprisals' against the German snipers; two men were detailed to go out before daybreak, take up a position, annoy the enemy as much as possible during the day, and return as soon as it got dark. We waited anxiously for their return, and eventually Headquarters 'phoned up that we were to send out a strong search party (of which more anon). This was not successful, and we had given the men up, but in the middle of the next morning, to our great joy, they turned up, having been in the open for 36 hours. …

(2) The rescue party.—This was a very tame affair. I was put in charge, and perhaps did not take it very seriously, but it seemed to me that we had a very small chance at night time of finding men, presumably wounded, without having some definite idea of where to look for them. However, it was a novel experience, and probably did us good.

We filed out (about 16 strong) by the usual exit, myself in rear, according to instructions. When just clear of our wire everyone suddenly lay down, and at the same time I heard a noise in a tree just to our left. Feeling sure that it was a man I got hold of a bomber, and together we stalked up to the tree. I then challenged softly, and no answer being given, the bomber hurled his bomb, which went off in great style. It struck me afterwards that it was foolish to give ourselves away so early in the proceedings, but I am only narrating this as an example how <u>not</u> to conduct a patrol. After satisfying ourselves that there had never been anyone there, we rejoined the others, and I passed up the order to advance. After ten yards crawling everyone lay down again, and this went on for about half-an-hour. By this time I was getting tired—also wet, and as we only had a limited time at our disposal, I decided to go up to the front—instructions notwithstanding—and push on a bit faster; our procedure, moreover, was beginning to strike me as rather ludicrous, as we were strong enough to frighten away any patrol likely to be out. So we went forward about 150 yards without meeting anything, and as time was getting short, I decided to circle round and return by a different route to our starting point. By this time everyone had acquired a certain degree of confidence—seeing that not a shot had been fired in our direction—and the last part of our journey was carried out at a brisk walk, and without any attempt at concealment. And so ended my first and (at present) only attempt at night patrolling—

Casualities, nil.

Results, ditto, except some experience and amusement. ...

Nov. 2.

I hope you have got my last budget.

We have now had a full fortnight's 'rest,' and for myself it has been almost literally rest. I have done practically nothing but eat, sleep and play chess! (No chess in the trenches, because one is glad to sleep all one's spare time.) There is nothing else to do here —no places to go to, the most frightfully dull country imaginable, and any amount of rain. ...

Nov. 22.

I am afraid I have left you some time without a letter, but there has been nothing to write about. I suppose you got my letter from the Bombing School. ...

Nov. 28.

We have just completed another turn in trenches—hard frost all the time, but on the whole we rather enjoyed it. I'm afraid the men found it difficult to sleep because of the cold, but we are managing to keep clear of frostbite and other trench ills. We had a very quiet time, and I think it was the first tour of duty in which the company had no casualties at all.

I hope the N.E.R. Battalion[66] will have luck—it is rather thankless work out here, and our Pioneer Battalion has certainly had more than its share of artillery and machine gun fire.

Many thanks for the books, which I hope to read in time.

Dec. 9th, 1915.
… I have been away four days…. The reason for my absence is that I got a chill, and went to a convalescent home instead of the trenches. Am all right again now. I'm afraid I have not sent you any news for a long time, but our existence is pretty monotonous —in fact, it is just bare existence, and nothing besides. I never know what the day of the week is, even Sunday. …

I read 'Aunt Sarah' in bed, and enjoyed it, though I don't think the author has been to the front and the chronology is poor; there was no trench warfare in August, 1914, and a new recruit would hardly be home wounded at the time of Ypres (No. 1)![67] …

Dec. 13 (in trenches).
Please tell the General [his name for his father] not to bother about the armour-plating, as it is not the sort of thing which can be done privately. …

Feb. 5, 1916.
I have been sent on a course of signalling (i.e., telephone, buzzer, etc.). It promises to be interesting, and at any rate novel. …

Easter Day.
All going on well, save the wet weather, which however now shows signs of improving. Except for occasional working- parties we are having a very easy week, in good billets. After this we shall probably go further back and have a week's manoeuvres, which will be a change. I shall be glad of a few books. If D. sent 'Count Bunker,' please thank her from me very much, and ask for more. Meanwhile there is a good deal of comic relief to be derived from home and American news—in Parliament the antics of that amazing idiot, P. Billing, M.P.[68]

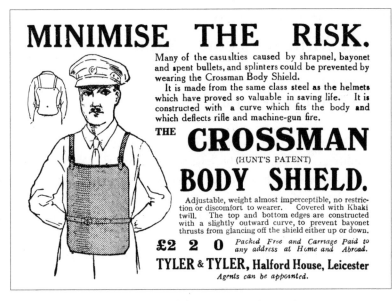

Advert for body armour from *Land & Water* magazine, 10 August 1916

The recruiting 'crisis' is too stupid for words. One can't understand how it ever arose, and Asquith is much to blame for allowing it. On the other hand the conscription campaign has been equally muddled, owing to the difference between those who want it for the sake of getting the numbers, and those who want it because they like it—like Harmsworth. Naturally the latter sort are objects of suspicion.

April 28.

… It is difficult to realise that we have really come through a winter campaign; I suppose one can consider it satisfactory as a test of physical fitness, though we have certainly been lucky, the worst weather nearly always having found us in billets. We have been equally fortunate as regards the attentions of the enemy, and there must be few battalions with seven months' trench experience whose total killed amount to less than fifty.

Butterworth was killed at Pozières on 5 August 1916, shot through the head by a sniper during the battle of the Somme.

Diary and letters of George Butterworth, 2 October 1915 to 28 April 1916

'One sympathises with the Prime Minister's complaints'

A FUTURE PM REFLECTS ON
THE POLICIES OF A CURRENT ONE

Harold Macmillan kept up to date with news from home, both domestic and political. In some of the letters sent from the Ypres Salient in the late spring of 1916 he reveals some of his political attitudes, and shows a degree of sympathy for Asquith, a prime minister increasingly beleaguered by the press and 'public opinion' on conscription, the Dardanelles and his war leadership in general. His dictum 'wait and see' was characterized in the Tory press as weak and dithering. Then on Easter Monday, 24 April 1916, Irish republicans staged an armed insurrection in Dublin which lasted for six days. The excitement in England that Macmillan refers to was over the issue of conscription. Macmillan was unclear about the Irish rebellion, but also uncompromising.

29 April 1916

> It seems that things in England are getting very exciting. But I think that it is very difficult for us to judge of our Government's successes or failures. Contemporary opinion rarely is confirmed by future generations. Mr. Asquith's 'Wait and see' is after all the watchword of Nelson, of Wellington and of Pitt. They waited for nearly 20 years, amid disloyalty and impatience at home, until the final moment came.
>
> The Irish troubles are rather hard to understand. And so far, the papers have had so little news (we always get yesterday's papers here, even in the trenches) that it is not easy to rate them at their proper importance. But I should imagine that it is only a small, if turbulent, minority of the Irish people that is disloyal to England. In some ways, it is rather a good thing that the traitorous movement should come to a head, in order that it may be more definitely and completely stamped out.

In a letter written on 30 April and 1 May, he reflects further on Ireland:

> The scenes in Dublin seem to be very much like those in Paris during the commune.

On 4 May he wrote:

> From the paper today it looks as tho' the Govt. has at last decided to take the plunge into Compulsion. I am very glad, as it has now become obvious that it is necessary. At the same time I think one sympathises with the Prime Minister's complaints. The press (or rather, a section of the press) seems to be even more bitter in its criticisms than in the old days of party warfare.

Interestingly, in this same letter, Macmillan reports that he has met 'young Tennant in this town (A) today and he is coming to lunch with us. He is in the 4th. Bn.'

The 'young Tennant' was Lieutenant Edward Wyndham 'Bim' Tennant (1897–1916) of the Grenadier Guards, a poet and a nephew of Margot Asquith. He was killed at the Battle of the Somme, a week before another Grenadier Guardsman, Raymond Asquith, met his death there. As an officer in such a prestigious regiment, Macmillan was never far removed from a social and political elite. Ideas and opinions would have passed from Whitehall to the front and back again in this milieu.

Letters from Macmillan to his mother, 29 April to 4 May 1916

'Many thousands of men somewhere, and yet not one is to be seen'

MACMILLAN DESCRIBES LIFE IN THE TRENCHES IN THE YPRES SALIENT

In this long letter Macmillan captures some of the strangeness of life in the trenches, a mixture of daytime tranquillity and frantic activity at night. Even as he describes the darting swallows he suddenly reports shelling, the ironic comments made at that moment being supplemented by a more hair-raising account of the incident on the next day.

As I have for the moment nothing to do, I am sitting down to start a letter which I shall not be able to post till Tuesday.

We are in a reserve line some 7 or 8 hundred yards behind the firing line. ...

We have been sleeping practically all day, as is customary in this strange life. It is a beautiful evening. As one looks out from the ruined cottage (now converted into a strong refuge from shells) one can see nothing in all the country round that shows any sign of life or being. Except for a shell now and then and perhaps an occasional crack of a rifle, it is the silence of the grave. All round are scattered ruins of villages and churches. Even the rows of trees bear marks of cruel usage, with split trunks and shattered branches. But no human being is visible. Perhaps now and then an orderly with a message is creeping along some path or hidden road. But it is extraordinary to think that in all the space that one can see there must be, of English and German, many thousands of men somewhere, and yet not one is to be seen. ...

What a lovely evening it is! The sun is too wonderful, setting majestically over the poor ruins of what must once have been a very fair city. There are ever so many swallows about, some of them almost tame. How beautifully they dive and swerve. Outside this little home of ours is the village pond, and round it the birds keep flying, low and swift.

'circleting the surface to meet
her mirrored winglets,'[69]

my swallow, reminiscent of the poet, perhaps, darts and turns, in happy ignorance of the grim landscape.

My trench had a charming cat inhabiting it last night. It seems that this cat lives permanently in the trench, and one takes him over with all other trench property (wire, shovel, picks, etc) at each relief.

The enemy has, with typical lack of decent courtesy, just begun to shell this house. In the last 5 minutes about 6 shells have pitched within 20 or 30 yards of us. With what reason he does this I don't know—there, I think he's stopped now—unless he has misjudged the range to a battery of ours which is some way behind us and which has done a lot of good work today.

Sunday—noon

Last night was rather an exciting night. I was having dinner with Parnell in the dug-out about 8 o'clock, when the enemy suddenly began a very violent bombardment. All round our dug-out was heavily shelled; a barrage was put on the road. All the working parties for the night were cancelled, as it was impossible to reach the 'dump' on the road to get the stakes, wire etc necessary. It was midnight before I could venture out to go over to the other post. Even then it was a hazardous journey. I had about 50 yards to go down the road to a cross-road, and then I turned off along another road and went along this about 100 yards before getting into my trench. I took an orderly with me, of course, as it is a rule that no one is ever to walk anywhere alone. This is a sound rule, as a man might be wounded and lie unnoticed for days and perhaps bleed to death, whereas if he had a companion he could get assistance at once. As we went down the road several shells were dropping round. We ran round the cross-road, which was naturally the hottest spot; just after we had passed the cross-road an enormous H.E. shell pitched right on the road. But we reached our destination in safety. When I got to this post, I found that they were shelling it rather severely. It was therefore impossible to do any work outside the trench, but there was quite enough to do in cleaning up inside, which I found them doing.

At about 3.30 a.m. this morning I came back here to Cy. headquarters and went to sleep quite happily and very tired. ...

Bertie Ponsonby (a brother of Myles Ponsonby, who was killed at Loos in the 4th Bn.) was wounded last night. He was transport officer, and was bringing the rations up the road, when the enemy began his artillery barrage—I hear that his leg is broken, and that he may lose it. I hope that rumour has exaggerated, as it often does.

I am rather sad because a Corporal Pryke, the 'bombing' corporal of this company was wounded (not severely) in last night's bombardment. He was a very intelligent man and is a great loss to me.

Also we had a sergeant (Sergt Cutler) killed. I only knew him slightly, but he was a good man. He had been out here without a break since Aug. 1914. It is very hard luck to escape for so long and then fall to a chance shell.

Letter from Harold Macmillan to his mother, Saturday 6 to Tuesday 9 May 1916

'Prepared to fight for another 50 years if necessary'

In this letter, after musing further on the strangeness of trench warfare, Macmillan talks about his feelings and beliefs about the war. Contrasting the 'glamour' of the days of the redcoats with modern warfare, and recognising the 'strain' and the 'horrors' of war, he nevertheless retains a belief that the struggle is worthwhile, and that 'great issues' are at stake. The modern reader may not find his sentiments comfortable reading, but they express an opinion found often in contemporary sources. It is a salutary reminder that for many people, probably the majority, the Great War still had a purpose and justification in the summer of 1916. Macmillan and many others had no doubt that they were fighting a just war, and were concerned that their sacrifices should not be negated by defeatism at home. Macmillan's reference to the memorandum on the 'lessons from Verdun' is interesting. Here we see a doctrine that most armies wished to promote in the face of the overwhelming firepower of modern industrial warfare, a belief that morale and character were still deciding factors. The idea flies in the face of what military thinkers knew about the nature of warfare, and indeed the French memorandum emphasizes sacrifice; but it is easy to see why a young officer like Macmillan would take to heart the idea that there was still a place for individual will and the hope that one could control one's own destiny.

> Your descriptions of the woods and gardens at Birch Grove, make me wish very much to be at home. England is really at its best at this time of the year. But Flanders (except on wet days) is not such a bad country; there is something rather fascinating in the long avenues on the roads, and the straight, hard lines of the landscape, like a chess board.
>
> Perhaps the most extraordinary thing about a modern battlefield is the desolation and emptiness of it all. I think I have tried to describe this to you before. One cannot emphasize this point too

much. Nothing is to be seen of war or soldiers—only the split and shattered trees and the burst of an occasional shell reveal anything of the truth. One can look for miles and see no human being. But in those miles of country lurk (like moles or rats, it seems) thousands, even hundreds of thousands of men, planning against each other perpetually some new device of death. Never showing themselves, they launch at each other bullet, bomb, aerial torpedo, and shell. And somewhere too (on the German side we know of their existence opposite us) are the little cylinders of gas, waiting only for the moment to spit forth their nauseous and destroying fumes. And yet the landscape shows nothing of all this—nothing but a few shattered trees and 3 or 4 thin lines of earth and sandbags; these and the ruins of towns and villages are the only signs of war anywhere visible. The glamour of red coats —the martial tunes of fife and drum—aide-de-camps scurrying hither and thither on splendid chargers—lances glittering and swords flashing—how different the old wars must have been. The thrill of battle comes now only once or twice in a twelvemonth. We need not so much the gallantry of our fathers; we need (and in our Army at any rate I think you will find it) that indomitable and patient determination which has saved England over and over again. If anyone at home thinks or talks of peace, you can truthfully say that the Army is weary enough of war but prepared to fight for another 50 years if necessary, until the final object is attained.

I don't know why I write such solemn stuff. But the daily newspapers are so full of nonsense about our 'exhaustion' and people at home seem to be so bent on petty personal quarrels, that the great issues (one feels) are becoming obscured and forgotten. Many of us could never stand the strain and endure the horrors which we see every day, if we did not feel that this was more than a War—a Crusade. I never see a man killed but think of him as a martyr. All the men (tho' they could not express it in words) have the same conviction—that our cause is right and certain in the end to triumph. And because of this unexpressed and almost unconscious faith, our allied armies have a superiority in moral [i.e. morale] which will be (some day) the deciding factor. We have had a very interesting memorandum circulated from French G.H.Q. on the lessons of Verdun. Most of it is technical, and of course secret. But the conclusions which he draws are hardly confidential. He says that in spite of the extraordinary development of mechanical contrivances for war, it is the human factor which is finally decisive. 'The

superiority of mind over matter, of the spiritual over the physical'
(queer language to us for an official document from a general!) [']is
indisputable and decisive.' And then he goes on to say that a body of
men properly trained and officered, with a high state of moral, can
do anything; can withstand any attack or bombardment, however
terrible; can in short, accomplish almost miracles. Finally, let this
maxim never be forgotten—

> 'Qu'aucun pouce de terrain ne doit être volontairement
> abandonné, quelles que soient les circonstances, et qu'une
> troupe, même entourée, doit resister jusqu'au dernier homme,
> sans reculer, <u>le sacrifice de chacun étant la condition même de la
> victoire</u>.'[70]

I have copied these words into my Field Pocket Book. They are very
fine.

I am afraid I have written a very long and didactic letter. But I
feel sure that you will be interested to know this direct evidence of
the spirit which animates the French Army.

Goodbye now. I must catch the post.

Love to all.

    Your own
      Harold

Letter from Harold Macmillan to his mother, Saturday 13 May 1916

'I am going to tell you something of what I saw in Mesopotamia'

T.E. LAWRENCE DESCRIBES
HIS EXPEDITION TO KUT AL-AMARA

In this twenty-page letter, Lawrence describes his journey to Kut,
where he had been sent to negotiate the extrication of the British
force trapped there by the Turkish army. The situation proved so bad
that in fact the negotiations were effectively about terms of surrender.
Lawrence wrote a scathing report about British generalship and

planning in the campaign on his way back to Cairo, and later there was a parliamentary inquiry into the whole affair. British and Indian forces had entered Mesopotamia initially to defend the oil refinery at Abadan at the mouth of the Shatt al-Arab, but had then pressed further up river, ultimately aiming for Baghdad. The Turks halted General Townshend's force at Ctesiphon, and he fell back on Kut, where he was besieged from December 1915. Townshend surrendered on 29 April 1916 after relief attempts had ended in failure with heavy casualties. Lawrence was clearly pleased to have escaped his desk at the Arab Bureau and to have seen the war at first hand, even if the circumstances were hardly satisfactory.

We are at sea, somewhere off Aden, I suppose, so before it gets too late I am going to tell you something of what I saw in Mesopotamia. You must excuse the writing, because the ship is vibrating queerly.

I went off ... about March 22: the transport I went on was the Royal George, a comfortable Canadian liner—and we got out to Kuwait without any happening of note.

At Kuwait ... we transhipped on to a fast mail-steamer, the Elephanta, of about 6000 tons. This took us across the bar at the mouth of the Shatt el-Arab, and up to Basra in the day. ... The river came down in a grey-green flood, and stopped abruptly in the sea, which was a heavy blue. ...

We went up to Basra—60 or 70 miles from the sea—at top speed, about 18 knots, and the river was never less than 300 yards wide. Generally it was a good five hundred. There was only one single-track phase, where the Turks had sunk three German ships in a line across the stream to block our passage. ...

On the way up we passed—at Abadan—the depot of the Anglo Persian Oil Company. You will remember the petrol wells in Persia in which the Admiralty bought a controlling interest, and whose protection was the first object of the Mesopotamia Expedition ... well they bring the oil down about 150 miles across country in a pipe, and refine it here. ...

I only stayed three days in Basra, as the G.O.C. and all his staff were up at the front. The people at the base gave me some biscuits, ten loaves, ten tins of jam, ten tins of beef, and put me on board a little paddle steamer that had been a ferry on the Irawaddy. Downstairs she was all engines, and the top was a flat deck partly sheltered by an awning. The front ⅔ of the deck was occupied by about 150 territorials: behind the funnel was a smaller space in which sat about ten of us, who all had ten tins etc. Each side of the steamer was tied a 100-foot steel barge loaded deep with firewood and forage and stores. ...

It took us six days to reach the front. The first night we anchored near Kurna [Al-Qurnah] which is a mud village just at the fork where the Euphrates comes in. ... To this point the Tigris is almost 500 yards wide, and runs slowly. Above Kurna the tide is not felt at all and the river for two days runs strongly, winding and twisting in all directions. ... The second night we spent at Ezra's tomb, which is a clump of trees and a few mud houses, and beside them, just on the bank, a domed mosque and courtyard of yellow brick, with some simple but beautiful glazed brick of a dark green colour built into the walls in bands and splashes. ...

The third night we tied up at Amara [Amarah]. ...

After Amara there were little places like Ali Shergi and Ali Gharbi and Sheikh Saad, between which we spent the fourth and fifth nights. ...

As for the country itself I should think it would be one of the hardest in the world to describe. As far north as Kurna you see only rows of date gardens which are ... just light green sunny tree tops and under them straight regular rows of brown stems hardly distinguishable in the shade. After Kurna though you run out into open meadow country, which you might be able to write about if you were on the spot—and if the precise spot was not the windy deck of a steamer full of people wondering when the next rain storm was coming down. To the west as far as your eye could see (with mists in foul weather and mirage in fine this is not far) the country looks like a shaggy Port Meadow. ...

In the East sometimes thirty or forty miles away, and sometimes only ten or twelve, you can see the long steep parallel ridges of the Persian hills. They were thickly covered with snow, and it was from them that the biting winds we had blew down. ...

The Arabs here are wonderfully hard, much rougher and poorer than our Jerablus [Jarabulus, Syria] men, but merry and full of talk. They are in the water all their lives and seem hardly to notice it. ...

At the front I found Headquarters living in a steamer with good awnings and a saloon! I stayed with them for about three weeks while Kut fell. We lost too many men at first in the relief and then tried too hard in the middle, and before the end everybody was tired out.

The weather cleared up and breeded [*sic*] myriads of flies. At sundown the awning over the deck used to change swiftly from grey to brown as the swarms alit on it to roost. The cavalry sometimes had to ride at foot pace, being blinded.

Colonel Beach, one of the Mesopotamian Staff, Aubrey Herbert (who was with us in Cairo) and myself were sent up to see the Turkish Commander in Chief, and arrange the release, if possible, of Townshend's wounded. From our front trenches we waved a white flag vigorously: then we scrambled out, and walked about half-way across the 500 yards of deep meadow grass between our lines and the Turkish trenches. Turkish officers came out to meet us, and we explained what we wanted. They were tired of shooting, so kept us sitting there with our flag as a temporary truce, while they told Halil Pasha we were coming—and eventually in the early afternoon we were taken blindfolded through their lines and about ten miles Westward (till within four miles of Kut) to his Headquarters. He is a nephew of Enver's, and suffered violent defeat in the Caucasus so they sent him to Mesopotamia as G.O.C. hoping he would make a reputation. He is about 32 or 33, very keen and energetic but not clever or intelligent I thought. He spoke French to us, and was very polite, but of course the cards were all in his hands, and we could not get much out of him. However he let about 1,000 wounded go without any condition but the release of as many Turks—which was all we could hope for.

We spent the night in his camp, and they gave us a most excellent dinner in Turkish style—which was a novelty to Colonel Beach, but pleased Aubrey and myself.

Next morning we looked at Kut in the distance, and then came back blindfolded as before. We took with us a couple of young Turkish officers, one the brother-in-law of Jemal Pasha, the other a nephew of Enver, and they afterwards went up to Kut from our camp in the hospital ships which removed the wounded. The ill feeling between Arabs and Turks has grown to such a degree that Halil cannot trust any of his Arabs in the firing line. ... After that there was nothing for us to do, so the Headquarters ship turned round, and came down again to Basra. We got there about the 8th and I spent four or five days settling up things and then came away. ...

There, I have written you a month of letters. I do not know how the Censor will find it in his heart to pass so Gargantuan a bale of manuscript ... but I'm afraid he will have to pass it, for there is nothing in it to help our enemies—nor is that a fair description of you. Hereafter I will again be nailed within that office at Cairo—the most interesting place there is till the Near East settles down. I am very pleased though to have had this sight of Mesopotamia in war time. It will be a wonderful country some day, when they regulate the floods, and dig out the irrigation ditches. Yet it will never be a really pleasant country, or a country where Europeans can live a normal life.

Extracts from a letter from T.E. Lawrence to his mother, 18 May 1916

'A weird and imaginative profusion of metaphor and slang'

HAROLD MACMILLAN ENCOUNTERS 'COLONIALS'

The war brought together men from all over the British Empire; it was a new and sometimes bemusing experience for many.

The 'Anzacs' are infinitely nicer and slightly more sober than the Canadians (at any rate, so far as represented here). But the chiefly amusing thing about Colonials is the way they talk. They seem to love to roll out long harangues about nothing, to ask obvious questions to which they know the answer, and (which is very delightful) to introduce into the most prosaic and technical matters a weird and imaginative profusion of metaphor and slang. They have great qualities—courage, good humour, and a cheery camaraderie. Unfortunately (not that many English officers now are any better) they have no self-respect whatever, and no conception of the dignity of the King's Commission. Last night a party of them went to a neighbouring town to dine and to 'beat —— into a dazzle, frazzle, just chew it up'. They fell into the hands of a watchful Provost-Marshal and have not returned.

Letter from Harold Macmillan to his mother, Saturday 20 May 1916

'The desire for an end of this business is deep and nearly universal'

LIEUTENANT DENMAN EXPLAINS THE ARMY'S VIEWS TO ARTHUR PONSONBY

The Honorable Richard Douglas Denman (1876–1957) was a graduate of Balliol College, Oxford. He was Liberal MP for Carlisle 1910 to 1918, and later joined the Labour Party. He served as a lieutenant and adjutant in the Royal Field Artillery in the First World War. The letter is an interesting example of the way information could travel from the front to politicians with particular agendas. In this case, Ponsonby might not have approved entirely of the message he was receiving, as Denman's radicalism was compromised by his identification with army opinion. Arthur, 1st Baron Ponsonby of Shulbrede (1871–1946), like Denman a Balliol alumnus, was opposed to Britain's involvement in the war and was one of the founders of the Union of Democratic Control (UDC), formed in August 1914 by radical Liberal politicians to oppose the government's war policy. From 1915 the UDC promoted the idea of a negotiated settlement, leading in 1917 to the publication of a manifesto calling for, among other things, peace with no annexations or indemnities, the restoration of sovereignty to occupied countries, plebiscites and disarmament. The UDC became increasingly associated with the Independent Labour Party, representing its position on foreign policy. Denman was one of a handful of MPs who joined the UDC.

In May 1916 when Denman wrote this letter he was keen to separate a desire to end the war from the demand for a peace at any price, a compromise between his political values and the needs of the army. His assessment of army opinion led him to put emphasis on the need to defeat Germany and restore occupied territories. Little more than a month before the launch of the Somme offensive, Denman is sceptical about the need for such an attack and suggests that the time is not yet right to carry it out. He also seems to concur with the Conservative critics of Asquith's government in his hopes for decisive measures to bring the war to an end, including compulsory service, which he notes would not be popular with Independent Labour Party supporters.

My dear Ponsonby

After nearly a couple of months of this life, I feel sufficiently saturated with the atmosphere of officers' messes, and of soldiers' letters which I have to censor, to make some generalisations on the sentiments of the Army in the West.

1. The desire for and end of this business is deep and nearly universal. The prevailing subject of conversation is when will the war cease? If you desire popularity, you cheerfully prophecy it will be over sometime this year. Most people, however, demand that peace shall be on terms which definitely indicated the failure of Germany. Of course men here think almost solely of the Western Front. Problems of the Eastern war and of the Colonies occupy little attention. Provided Belgium were set free again and rehabilitated at the joint cost of all other European Belligerents, and some portion of Alsace-Lorraine were restored to France, I believe the Army would welcome most heartily any terms of peace.

2. No sort of pessimism as to the military position exists. I judge the best military opinion as to the problems of the Western Front to be this. Our only danger lies in a premature offensive. A steady continuation of the policy of 'nagging' would in due course (shall we say another twelve months?) so weaken the Germans proportionately to ourselves as to make a Grand Offensive a sound proposition. A big success on the East might give us an opportunity this year. But unless Germany has to weaken herself drastically on this Front, it is quite vain to hope for a military end to the war this year.

3. No one seems to have any confidence in any of the leading politicians or journalists, or any certainty that they will not sacrifice the Army in the pursuit of aims not in the least military. From the point of view of the Army, I am sure Asquith's best course would be to examine seriously what are the differences between the German and British terms of peace, and frankly make them public. The Army of course will go on fighting indefinitely. But it would make a big difference if it were clear that there is some definite goal. The Army is sick of phrases and phrase makers.

4. Talking still of the Western Front alone, it seems highly probable that Germany in fear of a prolonged war (from which she cannot possibly gain) would be willing now to accept terms she would not again offer if, in the event, her powers of defence prove

greater than may fairly be expected. There is no doubt that the fighting quality of all the Armies in the West is deteriorating. The strain tells. And it is just possible that later on, even with superior numbers, we may lack the quality needed for a successful offensive. I've heard this argued. I don't myself believe it and don't believe the Germans do (or they would not be making their attempts to force an early issue). But it is a possibility to be faced in weighing the present situation.

I send these notes because I want to add to your fund of evidence that there is a strong desire out here for reasonable peace terms. I've met no one who was not in favour of compulsory service, so you see that my sources of evidence are not at all of the I.L.P. type. ...

I hope you all flourish

yours ever

    R.D. Denman

Of course this is not for publication.

Letter from Lt. R.D. Denman to Arthur Ponsonby, 24 May 1916

'We don't look so well as what we did when we were in Oxford'

LANCE CORPORAL A. COLLINGS DESCRIBES HIS LIFE WITH THE BRITISH SALONIKA FIELD FORCE

Anglo-French forces were landed at the Greek port of Salonika (Thessaloniki) in October 1915 to help the Serbs against German, Austro-Hungarian and Bulgarian armies. They were too late to save Serbia, and after a short winter campaign on the Serbian border the allies retired back to Salonika. The British now wished to withdraw their forces, but were persuaded by their allies to keep them there (see p. 158). Salonika was prepared for defence, and the allied troops moved into the surrounding country, to be reinforced with Serbian, Italian and Russian forces during 1916 in preparation for an offensive. There were several local actions on the Salonika Front from 1916 to 1918, but no great advances were made until the offensive by the allies in September 1918 brought about the capitulation of Bulgaria. Malaria was a major cause of British casualties on this front.

The harvest season is in full swing and it's rather amusing to see the folks at work. Everything is done by hand and the majority of the workers are women. They start rather early in the morning about three and rest in the middle of the day. Often wonder what they would think if they saw some of the latest machinery that is in use at home. Looks more like a Sunday school treat when the people go to work in the mornings. The men ride in state on a small donkey and the women walk behind. I must say that the women are rather good looking round this part a lot different to those against the other camp. With all the beauty of the country I shall be very pleased when we set our feet in that small island called England. We can see something here that we have not see [*sic*] before in the country and that is a train. It is quite a small railway but it makes me think we are not quite cut off from the outside world.

... Been living off bully beef and biscuits of late so you can tell how welcome the cake was. It was the first good feed I had had for a month. We don't look so well as what we did when we were in Oxford. If I did but know it that was our best days in the army.

... We have to be very careful over our personal cleanliness in a country like this or we should soon have fever break out. ... Very pleased to be able to say we are almost clear of vermin and that's a lot to be thankful for. Flies are our biggest trouble at present. They torment us almost to death during the day. It is rather quiet at present but we very often hear the guns going off. Seen but little of Zepps or aeroplanes since that one was fetched down in Salonica.

Letter, Lance Corporal A. Collings, 'British Salonica Field
Force', to Sarah Angelina Acland, 11 June 1916

'The cuckoo can be heard between the firing of the shells'

MACMILLAN DESCRIBES THE STRANGE INTERPLAY OF WAR AND NATURE

In this letter, Macmillan once again picks up on the theme of war and nature, effectively combining the picturesque and the grotesque to convey powerful images of life in the trenches.

24th 10. a.m.

... There is a tremendous artillery duel in progress at the moment. The guns are roaring and you can follow the progress of the shell by the noise, from its original roar as it leaves the mouth of our gun, all along its hissing and screaming journey, till the final consummation of its successful explosion in the enemy's lines. And similarly you can hear the Boche shells coming towards you, and bursting either short or beyond, and know from the sound which it will be. The sun is coming out now through the clouds. As I sit in my dug out, writing, I look out on a little ruined farm. No one wd. recognise it now, but the garden still struggles to keep a civilised look amid ruin and desolation. A few flowers are springing up, between the shell-holes. The birds (who seem quite unmoved by any bombardment) are singing merrily, for all the world as if they were in some peaceful countryside, stranger to High Explosive. The cuckoo can be heard between the firing of the shells. Nature does her best for us even here.

Save only in her vermin-life. Rats are surely among the less successful or meritorious of Nature's efforts. They infest the trenches—great big fat rats, as large as puppies. I fear them more than the Huns. They are odious. In the evenings we generally have a combined shoot. The men beat with sticks and we shoot the rats with revolvers. But we don't seem to be able to extirpate them. Whenever we come in to a new sector, they are particularly bad. I think this is due to carelessness in throwing food and refuse about, instead of burning. Now I must sleep again—Love to all. I will try and get this letter off today.

Your

Harold.

Letter from Harold Macmillan to his mother, written 'in the field', 23–24 June 1916

'The safest place is the front line'

MACMILLAN REASSURES HIS PARENTS

In this letter, Macmillan makes a point which may seem like a paradox to the modern mind, where trenches evoke images of the worst aspects of the Great War. During the autumn of 1914 the front line settled into trench warfare as the Germans responded to their failure to achieve a decisive victory in the West by creating a strong defensive system on high ground to enable them to concentrate their offensive efforts on their Eastern front. Trenches evolved into highly elaborate systems of defence, and although they were by no means safe from enemy fire, the huge casualties of the First World War generally occurred when men left the trench, either to attack enemy lines, or just to carry out the kinds of duties described in this letter. The letter begins with a touching indication of paternal concern, but ends with a story hardly designed to reassure parents.

Advert for ear defenders from *Land & Water* magazine, 31 July 1915

Your letters reach me very regularly. It is nice to have a letter from you every day. Father sent me back the ear-protectors. I'm afraid that you exaggerate in your minds the horrors of war! The noise is not really bad eno' to make them necessary. All the same, I will keep them by me.

General Heyworth wasn't killed in billets. He was killed in the front line, by a sniper, as he was going round the line. The reason that so many casualties occur during reliefs (surprisingly, really, they are) is that bodies of men walking down roads, communication trenches, etc. are always naturally liable to be caught by shrapnel. The artillery on both sides shrapnel the roads, in the hope of catching troops and transport. In our present position this can easily be done, as there are only a few main roads, which can be used. Then of course the machine gun fire which goes on blindly but practically unceasingly, throughout the night is bound to catch somebody, even if it be only with falling bullets. The safest place is the front line—then you have a trench. It is not really unnatural that casualties should be most common in reliefs and working parties, wh. altho' behind the front line, are in the open and unprotected. . . .

This morning about 10.30 a.m. we were all still sleeping. There was a good deal of shelling going on vaguely, which one could half hear in one's sleep. Suddenly there was a most terrific bang in my dug-out, and a great cloud of smoke. I share a dug-out (for sleeping) with one Oliver, an ensign. I was too sleepy to get up and see what had happened. So we both stayed in bed (it was obvious that the dug-out had not been much damaged) while excited orderlies and servants ran about, asking if we were buried etc. The far end of the dug-out (by the door) was certainly more or less blown in, but luckily the shell was a small one and only just caught the top sand-bags over the door. We were sleeping with our feet towards the door. The dug-out is a tubular one, about 10 ft. long and 6 ft. high. I have tried to find the nose-cap of the shell as a souvenir, but could not.

Letter from Harold Macmillan to his mother, 26 June 1916

'Some of the boys would realy rather stop in the trenches'

CORPORAL F.H. SMITH ENJOYS QUIET ON THE WESTERN FRONT

184th Trench Mortar Battery was formed 27 June 1916, and this letter appears to have been written shortly afterwards. The 184th (2nd South Midland) Brigade was part of the 61st (2nd South Midland) Division and served on the Western Front during the First World War. The Division was an unusual one on the Western Front, being a second-line Territorial force. Both the 2/1st and 2/4th battalions of the Oxfordshire and Buckinghamshire Light Infantry formed part of the brigade, and F.H. Smith appears to have been from one of these battalions.[71] The 'lazy life' referred to by Smith is a reminder that not all sectors of the Western Front were active all the time, and that some areas were comparatively quiet, to the extent that the men in his unit seem to have preferred being in the trenches to any other duties. Smith admits that he did not expect trenches to be like this. The Division was some 50 miles north of the area of the main action of the Battle of the Somme, but on 19 July 1916 it was thrown into the battle of Fromelles, in support of operations on the Somme, and met with bloody failure.

> I have been in France just over 3 weeks now, and we have had a good spell in the trenches … we went back for 8 days rest, but the next day we were called back, as the divisions which were holding the line went back for a few weeks rest.
>
> I have joined the L.T.M.B. and I think it is very much better job than what I had before. … Well I am as well as I have ever been, glad to say. … We have to cook our own food in the trenches, and it occupies our time a great deal, the time goes much quicker in the trenches than out, and some of the boys would realy [*sic*] rather stop in the trenches, (I mean the trenches were [*sic*] we are, as it is a very quiet part of the line) than be out, because we have to do drill etc when we are out. The life in the trenches is a very lazy life. I had a very different idea of the trenches before I had been in.

Letter, Corporal F.H. Smith, Light Trench Mortar Battery, 184 Infantry Brigade, B.E.F., France, to Sarah Angelina Acland, n.d. (late June 1916)

'The person who said the first five years of the war would be the worst doesn't err on the side of optimism'

GUY ACLAND RN WRITES AN OPTIMISTIC LETTER TO HIS AUNT

Hubert Guy Dyke Acland was the nephew of Sarah Angelina Acland. At this time he was a navy lieutenant, reaching the rank of lieutenant commander by the end of the war. The letter announces the birth of his first child, and reflects on the difficulties of communication at sea, and on hopes that the war situation is improving. It is dated 1 July, the first day of the Battle of the Somme, and expresses a widespread optimism that the great offensive would bring the war to an end. Horn's Reef, a contemporary name for the Battle of Jutland, was initially reported as a defeat, but news of German losses, and the realisation that despite sinking more ships the Germans had not changed the strategic situation or broken the British blockade, meant that it came to be seen as a strategic victory.

> Dearest Aunt Angie
>
> I hear from Mother that you are waiting for a letter from me .... It must be wandering the oceans and looking for an Oxford in the Anti-podes. ...
>
> I am sorry you didn't get it though, as I told you of the hopes of your being a Great Aunt therein. ... The third week of August the infant is due to make its bow into this turbulent world, but I hope its first views will be quiet and peaceful. Lalage [his wife] has found a cottage near Dorchester .... My chief moan as to the affair is the terrible irregularity of the mails. Sometimes she has had to wait a fortnight without a letter or word, and I have had a whole month without news. ... In a way that's a blessing as I couldn't do anything if the news were bad, and I have no opportunity of celebrating good news. As an example, it might amuse you to hear that my total expenditure on shore since the 9th Feb.ry has been 2/6. Sounds very gay and exciting doesn't it? There is no need for the War Savings Committee to send any of their pamphlets or posters to the Sutlej.

It is very hard to form any opinion from the fragmentary wireless messages and news from passing ships we get from time to time, but things certainly seem to be taking a brighter turn. Horn's Reef, the Russians, the Italians and our own push are all in the right direction, and the person who said the first five years of the war would be the worst doesn't err on the side of optimism.

Letter, Guy Acland, H.M.S. Sutlej, Plymouth, to
Sarah Angelina Acland, 1 July 1916

'We were all standing ready saddled up in our field praying and hoping for the order to move'

THE CAVALRY BRIGADE ON THE FIRST DAY OF THE SOMME

On 6 July 1916 Burgon Bickersteth wrote an extraordinary 31-page letter to his mother describing his part in the battle of the Somme. He did not yet know as he wrote that his brother Morris had been killed, along with more than 19,000 others, on the first day of the attack, 1 July 1916. This first part of the letter describes the tension in the 6th Cavalry Brigade as they awaited orders. As the battle went on, it became increasingly obvious that the cavalry were not going to be needed.

On Friday June 30 nothing of importance happened. On Saturday July 1st reveillee was at 5.0 am—and by 7.30 we were all standing ready saddled up in our field praying and hoping for the order to move. I do not think any of us really thought we should move—I am sure the higher command didn't—though perhaps some of us hoped we should move up much in the same way as we did at Loos.

About 10 am. information began to come in—and from that hour onwards at half hour intervals all day a continuous stream of telegrams flowed in. 'We are attacking so and so'. 'The — corps has reached Round Wood' 'The — Division has taken the front line at Beaumont Hamel but has been driven out.' 'The — Division is marching through Serre.' 'Third army reports attack on Gomme-court is making satisfactory progress'—and then after each of these statements more details would be given referring to our big scale maps which we had spread on the ground and eagerly were studying. Later in the day a telegram came saying '—Division driven out of Serre—two battalions believed cut off in the village.' Though I knew Morris [sic] battalion had not the job of actually taking the village I didn't much like this—and even as I write these words I have not the very least idea of how Morris has fared —nor shall I know for some days.

We 'stood to' all day at 2 hours notice—so we offsaddled and though no one could leave the field for any length of time life was fairly normal. Fortunately it was fine and we slept under the trees only rousing ourselves when new information came. It became evident as the attack progressed that we shouldn't be wanted that day—so we went back to our empty house which we had left rather hopefully in the early morning—had a meal and slept. Sunday morning (July 2nd) we were standing to at 4 hours notice —and then came orders that we could consider ourselves free till the evening.

Letter from Burgon Bickersteth to his mother, 6 July 1916

'One of the most amazing panoramas it had ever been our fortune or perhaps our misfortune to see'

BICKERSTETH OBSERVES THE SECOND DAY OF THE BATTLE OF THE SOMME

Burgon's 31-page letter continues with a remarkable eyewitness account of a part of the Somme battle seen through field glasses on 2 July 1916 (see map, Plate 9). The description of the attack on La Boisselle is very far removed from the commonly repeated idea that British troops advanced at a walking pace into a hail of fire; here Bickersteth sees the waves of attackers 'running and then lying down and then running again'. In reality, commanders on the spot were expected to attack in a way that most suited the nature of the terrain and the defences.

Some of us immediately decided to get as far forward as we could and watch the battle.

It was a glorious Sunday afternoon—and about 3 pm you might have seen three other subalterns and myself sitting on the side of a hill gazing through our glasses at one of the most amazing panoramas it had ever been our fortune or perhaps our misfortune to see. Directly below us was the town of Albert—a few kilometres to the east and just out of sight lay Fricourt at which point till two days ago the English and French lines had met. In front of you as clear to read as the maps which were lying on the grass at our sides stretched the eastern slopes of the valley of the Ancre and here right under our very eyes was raging a battle, momentarily as fierce as anything that has been experienced by the defenders of Verdun. The scene as it presented itself to us is almost beyond description. The long lines of heaped up chalk betrayed the position of the trenches with which the green background of the hillside was seamed and scored as if by some gigantic white pencil. But the battle had passed on—and behind our former front and support lines were now massed troops in reserve. Above, the higher slopes gave place to a gently rising plateau and here we could recognise those villages the names of which are now household words—Thiépval, La Boiselle [La Boisselle], Ovillers, Pozières, Contalmaison, Montauban, Mametz. Our view was extensive and yet distances seemed much smaller than I expected. We could almost have put our hand on La Boiselle and Ovillers and Pozières seemed ridiculously close. One realized what terrible obstacles the ingenuity of man has been able to invent, to make it so difficult to advance even a thousand yards.

All we could see of La Boiselle was a heap of bricks—the Southern part of the village was hiden [sic] by some rising ground. Ovillers was little better. One end of what was once a large barn still stood, a gaunt framework, the sole structure in the village which stood as far as we could see even a few feet above the ground. In Pozières the church tower was still standing battered almost beyond all recognition and looking like a white skeleton the bones of which might at any moment crumble and sink to the ground. Immediately below us in the valley were our own guns so thick that in one small wood alone we counted eight.

At the moment we arrived we seemed to be giving Thiépval most attention. The village itself is hidden by the Thiépval wood which here clothes the side of the valley. But had the wood not been there, there could in any case have been no village to see. A sheet of flame and smoke enveloped what was once Thiépval and the line of German trenches which lay just north of it. Thiépval was very important in the early open fighting between German and French in September 1914 and lying like Gommecourt in a very dominating position it has long been a thorn in the side of the British. Never have I seen anything to touch the bombardment. Shells of every size and strength were hurled into that place for some twenty minutes. The whole area round and between Ovillers and la Boiselle was an inferno. All the gunning seemed to be by us—the Germans replying with a very small output of shells. On Pozières, Contalmaison and the trench lines between these places rained an almost continuous stream of shells, so that a haze which was hardly dispersed by the light summer breeze hung over the whole front. Green, brown, light blue, brick red clouds of smoke showed where a gas shell or some other diabolical invention had just burst and scattered death. Away to the South Montauban and the woods round it were being subjected to an equally stiff bombardment. Very occasionally there was a lull in the roar of our own guns and then still further to the South we heard the thundering chorus of the French artillery. The road leading from Albert to Bapaume was full of troops waiting under the shelter of the hill to go up to the attack. Hundreds of infantry and guns by the dozen were all visible to us but hidden to the Germans who were on the plateau above. Although, therefore, one could detect little sign of life in the actual new front lines except bombs and gas-clouds, yet owing to the fact that from our point of vantage we could see so many reserves moving up and getting into position, the picture seemed to resemble an old fashioned battle field far more than anything I have seen even including Loos.

You will hardly believe it when I tell you that there were large patches of properly sewn red clover in full flower and hay cocks neatly arranged in rows between the former British front and support line. That is to say that in the quieter days before the actual 'push' had started enterprising farmers had worked their land right up to the within 400 yards of the front line trenches. In many of the woods the trees still wore the full green of midsummer, though round Thiépval, Ovillers and Pozières all was blasted and gaunt. On the slope which ran from where we sat to the houses of Albert were ripening crops. Scarlet poppies, blue cornflowers and wheat were swaying in the gentle breeze of a perfect summer afternoon. The sky was blue and covered with light fleecy clouds. The atmosphere after the wet weather extraordinarily clear. In the same field as ourselves were two men in civilian clothes and a woman with a white parasol protecting her from the sun—all three spending the leisure of a Sunday afternoon in watching this terrific struggle.

La Boiselle alone seemed immune from our shell fire at the moment and the reason for this we were soon to know. We were sitting along the parapet of a well-made trench dug along this dominating ridge on a reserve line. Suddenly a colonel of the Scots Guards popped his head up from under an archway where we saw a telephone installed and asked if we would care to know all that was happening. He proved to be an advance intelligence officer of the Corps—and he proceeded to give us much interesting information. 'At the present moment', he said, 'we are shelling Thiépval like hell with the idea of deceiving the Bosch and making him think we are going to attack the village. The ruse seems to be succeeding as I see the Hun is beginning to put a barrage across our front in that sector'—and he pointed to where a fresh hurricane of shot and shell was falling along the front line before Thiépval. Really what with our own fire and this added German barrage I have never in my life seen anything so terrible and awe-inspiring as the square mile or so in and about Thiépval at 4.30 pm that Sunday afternoon. The Colonel continued—'What we are really going to do is to attack La Boiselle from the South and you will be able to see all the early part of the attack from here. Do you see the German sausage over Contalmaison Wood?' We nodded. 'Well follow down directly underneath that and you will come to a large white chalky patch of soil.' We all saw it—'Well, the waves of infantry will advance across that in 10 minutes' time.'

We riveted our glasses to the spot and sure enough at 5.pm exactly what must have been a couple of Companies in extended order came across the patch at the double. A third of the way across they halted—and we could see them lying flat on the ground. So far they were hidden by a rise in the ground from the Boche who had no idea they were there. A few seconds rest and then up they got and raced on again—and behind them appeared another extended line. The first Companies were still hidden—but evidently the Enemy had some observation post as shrapnel began to burst above them, and although the range was not correct at first, the shooting rapidly became more accurate. Evidently the Company Commander was waiting for something —the first line was lying just under the brow of the hill for fully ten minutes. Then a man on the extreme left flank—evidently an orderly with a message—detached himself from the rest and ran off at a terrific pace. We kept him in sight for a couple of hundred yards and then he disappeared. Finally the front line moved on and disappeared over the brow—and after them came wave after wave, running and then lying down and then running again. Sometimes several black heaps would be left lying on the ground when the line moved on—but generally speaking there seemed few casualties—until they got over the ridge and found themselves almost among the first houses of La Boiselle—what happened there I don't know—we could not see. But we learnt afterwards in the day's summary of fighting that La Boiselle had been taken and I wondered whether this good result had anything to do with our little messenger whom we followed so clearly with our glasses speeding away to the left flank over the shell swept area. After this attack from the south had gone forward—several Companies of infantry who had long been sitting under the shelter of our original first line suddenly formed up ready for the attack. They too went over the brow from the west—and attacked the village frontally, moving forward in artillery formation. The village was now getting a pretty good strafing from the Huns—and we in turn were putting a barrage on behind to prevent the bringing up of reinforcements. The bombardment seemed to have been transferred from Thiépval to La Boiselle. The air was full of shrapnel and the varied-coloured smokes of different stink-shells—huge columns of earth flew heavenwards as some allmighty 'crump' burst churning up the soil already pounded incessantly for the last five days. Machine gun and rifle fire filled the air whenever there was a lull in the artillery fire. Bombs and trench mortars there undoubtedly were too, though they were hardly noticeable in the perfect inferno which surrounded that little hamlet of 230 people on this lovely Sunday afternoon.

This was the finest panorama of a battle I have ever seen or am likely to see—and it was hard to tear ourselves away. But we had to get back and so rolling up our maps and putting away our glasses we walked back off the rise to where our horses were waiting and rode home down the valley which joins Amiens and Albert.

Continuation of the letter from Burgon Bickersteth to his mother, 6 July 1916

'There is not a word about our troops'

ANDREW CLARK RECORDS A LACK OF NEWS FROM THE SOMME

In marked contrast to the detailed description of the battle that Bicker-steth provided for his mother, those who were dependent on official news had very little to go on. Andrew Clark was evidently infuriated by the War Office's attitude. The bulletin does not in fact contain *any* news about the British sector.

> Su. 9 July 1916
> … I give, opposite the official bulletin as posted in Great Leighs Post Office on Sunday 9 July 1916. It exhibits the heartless insolence of the war office in its most heartless form. With the guns in Flanders thundering in the ears of villagers here, whose relatives are at the front, there is not a word about our troops.
>
> Official Bulletin as posted at Great Leighs Post Office on Su. 9 July
>
> Summary of Saturday's
> Official War News.
> ———
>
> French Official. We captured 350 prisoners in successful dash near Belley-en-Santerre. We progressed east Estrees with grenades in enemy saps and took 50 prisoners.
>
> Russian Official. Lower Styr progress continued 75 officers 2000 men prisoners. Near Optovo many Austrians sabred after cavalry charge 6000 prisoners much material taken. Masses further prisoners still arriving east Monaster-Jiske. Village Gregorev captured with 1000 prisoners.

> *Diary of the Revd Andrew Clark, rector of Great Leighs, Essex, 9 July 1916*

'A wild and impracticable scheme, pure lunacy'

BRIGADIER MAKINS, THE CAVALRY AND THE SOMME OFFENSIVE

Had the Somme offensive achieved the breakthrough that Sir Douglas Haig hoped for, the role of the cavalry would have been highly important in pressing home the advantage in what might once again become a war of movement. Brigadier Makins's diary gives us a glimpse of the thinking of a senior cavalry officer at the opening of the offensive, the hopes, fears and ultimate disappointment. Makins indicates a good deal of scepticism and some confusion as to what his role would really entail, and his comments about Rawlinson's HQ in the chateau at Querrieu suggest that opinion about strategy was not unanimous.

On 26 June 1916 Makins had a 'quiet morning'. There was a conference at Divisional HQ at 6 p.m. at Frohen-le-Grand 'where the scheme of operations is disclosed somewhat. It looks like bloody work.' He went on to St-Ouen to rendezvous by car, noting that it was a wet night and a 'bad march' for the men. On the next day they marched to Noyelles via the outskirts of Amiens. Leaving St-Ouen at 8.45 p.m he notes that they marched 'along the Roman Road along which hardly anyone can have travelled since Caesar'.

On 28 June it 'pours with rain at 1 p.m.—Goughy says the attack is off for 48 hours.' After a tour of the camp, which he describes as 'a nice spot except under the present wet conditions', he dined with '"Rawly"—he has a splendid chateau at Querrieu'.[72] On the 29th it was still unsettled, and Makins went to

> reconnoitre the line from about 1½ [miles] S.W. of Albert. See the gilt figure of the virgin and child hanging from the church. ... Up again at 4 p.m. and see a bombardment of the line and also an emission of smoke S. of Albert where the Huns put a barrage behind expecting an attack.

On 30 June Makins received more detailed instructions at a divisional conference at 11.30 a.m., followed by a brigade conference 'in the marquee in camp':

> The Div is to cross at Aveluy and Albert. I am to cross at Aveluy and lead the way to Mouquet Farm and on to Loupart Wood and on to Grevilleirs [sic] if all goes well. I cannot imagine the situation, and I think many people's imaginations run mad. But if all goes well and if we go through 'like butter' as the phrase is, that is my role.

On the first day of the Somme offensive, Makins wrote in his diary:

> A glorious morning. The Brigade starts at 3.45 am for Bresle by a side track. Slug and I go by car. The attack starts about 7.30 preceded by a heavy bombardment. We are told to be ready to start at noon, but later by 2 pm and finally ordered at 5 p.m. back to Noyelles. I hack[73] home but our brigade has to follow the 2nd who are ¾ hrs late in starting. Things have gone well in the South and our troops have Mametz and Montauban and the Huns retreating but they stick on to more of the first line at Ovillers and to the N. The Brigade does not get in till 9.15 p.m. owing to the 2nd Brigade.

On Sunday 2 July Makins noted that it was his wife Flo's birthday:

> A good rest last night. People not very satisfied with yesterday. But things have gone pretty well to the S. … There is to be an attack at 4 p.m. today on La Boisselle. Apparently our troops went through the place yesterday to Contalmaison but did not dig [out] the German so the latter are a bit in the air.

This was the attack described by Burgon Bickersteth (see pp. 197–201).

On the next few days the cavalry found themselves called forward and stood down on several occasions. On 4 July Makins went to Fricourt by car: 'an awful scene of desolation and the Huns give it a few shells'.

On the 5th the brigade moved back once more:

> Starting Point at X Rds at Querrieu at 8am. Get off at 8.30 after 2nd Brig are clear. 'Rawly' comes to see us off and is very cheery. I pass him on the march and he says we are only moving back because of

the congestion at railheads and he may call on us suddenly, and if he does that he promises us some pig sticking—just like his talk.

On the 6th he walked down to the River Somme near his billets in Amiens, and saw 'Red X barges full of wounded' before receiving the order to be ready at 1¾ hours notice by 6 a.m. tomorrow: 'There is to be a big attack tomorrow all along the S of our line.'

On the 7th he heard that the British had taken Contalmaison, but had been driven out, and then on the 8th that their move had been postponed. After another reprieve on the 10th, on the 11th his unit was ordered to march to the 'old bivouac' at Querrieu:

> I wonder what will happen?! I don't think it looks rosy. The cavalry cannot get much chance or else they will be sacrificed.

Slug and Makins attended the divisional conference at Allonville on the 12th:

> A wild and impracticable scheme, pure lunacy. They intend to launch the cavalry between the 2 present German lines. Kirby agrees that the originator of the scheme is mad and B Brown calls Querrieux Chateau a lunatic asylum.

On the 13th they were ordered to march to Buire sur l'Ancre:

> A general order from Rawly saying the battle is ½ won and urging the men to do their best.

Diary of Brigadier Ernest Makins, 26 June to 13 July 1916

'In the capacity of "Prisoners' Friend"'

MACMILLAN ACTS AS DEFENCE IN A COURT MARTIAL

Junior officers could expect a whole range of duties to be thrust upon them by the army. As well as acting as bombing, billeting, signalling and intelligence officers, and undertaking a whole range of other military responsibilities, they could be called upon to sit on courts martial. Like most men in this situation, Macmillan had no legal training, though he appears to have benefited from the advice of his brother Arthur, who clearly had.

I am afraid I have not had time to write during the last two days, altho' we were not actually in the line. We came in last night, and had a very good and quiet relief. But yesterday and the day before my time was taken up with several duties, including that of getting up the cases and attending the courts-martial of certain men in the Battalion, in the capacity of 'Prisoners' Friend'. I wish the duty had fallen to Arthur instead of to me. But I tried to remember any scraps of law which I have heard from him, and I laboriously studied the rules of evidence, procedure etc. The men whom I had to defend were, unfortunately, of the worst possible character. One did not create a favourable impression by insisting on addressing the president of the court as 'Me Lud'—thereby showing that in civilian life he had had experience of the proceedings of a criminal trial. The only points wh. cd. possibly be raised were of a legal and technical nature. These points, therefore, I produced; I cross-examined the witnesses for the prosecution and called many witnesses for the defence. The details of the case I am not able to describe in a letter; but you can tell Arthur that I will tell him all about it some day, if it interests him. At all events, my labour was rewarded. And I had the enormous satisfaction of seeing a complete miscarriage of elementary, if not of technical, justice, and the two men who should have been shot, are still serving with the Bn. The C.O. twits me very much about this, and says that I am never to appear again in this learned capacity, as it is bad for discipline! Such are the advantages of a legal brother!

All these labours have occupied my time during our period of rest. But I was much amused and interested by this change of work and novelty of duties. The most charming thing about the law is its vocabulary. I loved to 'submit' things to the Court and to 'put it' to the witness. Even to 'suggest' (in a calmly indifferent way) that something the direct opposite of what the witness has sworn, is the real truth—all this is very delightful. Also (but this a great secret) in my legal argument I quoted as a leading authority the well-known case of Rex v. Dyson 1899., which certain rude persons have since asserted to be entirely imaginary—a calumny which of course Arthur could easily disprove. Inter arma silent leges!—well, not with us.[74]

Letter from Harold Macmillan to his mother, written 'in the field' 16 July 1916

'They began throwing bombs at us at random'

MACMILLAN IS WOUNDED ON PATROL

In this letter Macmillan describes how he was wounded during a patrol in no-man's-land. He explains that out of a sense of duty to his regiment, and to his men, he has forgone the opportunity to come home on leave. Although he is in part influenced by a chance of promotion, he seems to be genuinely concerned about the effects on his men, whose opportunities for leave were very few compared with officers.

I don't know whether my postcard has reached you. I hope it didn't frighten you. I wrote it as soon as I got down to the Bn. dressing station and had seen the Doctor.

Both wounds are luckily very slight. As we are going out tonight for 4 days in reserve and then for 8 days rest, I have decided not to go back to any Ambulance behind the lines, but to stay with the Bn. The doctor thinks that I shall be quite all right again in a fortnight or so.

The way in which it happened was this. A patrol was wanted to go out across No Mans Land as near to the enemy's lines as possible, in order to obtain certain, I believe, important information. The idea of this patrol was only to listen, not to fight or capture a prisoner. It was to consist of only 3 or 4 men and an officer.

I said I would go, and I took 2 men, both of whom I knew and trusted.

We got out a good way and I think we obtained all the information that was wanted. Unfortunately, just as we were going to come home, about 2.30 a.m. we were spotted by a German bombing post in a sap. They challenged us, but we cd. not see them to shoot, and of course they were entrenched while we were in the open. So I motioned to my men to lie quite still in the long grass. Then they began throwing bombs at us at random. The first, unluckily, hit me in the face and back and stunned me for the moment. One of the other men was hit with a bit of bomb in the right arm. We still lay where we were. The men never moved or ran till I gave the word. I waited a few moments, and then gave the word to run for it. We ran back about 50 yds, while the force in the sap (wh. was a strong one) fired and threw bombs at us, but without hitting us. A lot of flares were fired, and when each flare went up, we flopped down in the grass and waited till it had died down.

We got back all right after this—about 200 yards—to our own trench.

Of the 3 of us, one man was wounded in the arm with a bit of bomb, but not badly. He also had a tiny wound in the leg. The other man was untouched. The bomb wh. hit me, (the first throw) landed just behind my left foot. A piece of it hit me in the back, but this is only a very superficial wound. Other pieces rained down on my helmet, and the force of the explosion laid me out for a few seconds. But I was able to master myself, and it was not till I got back in the trench that I found that I was also hit just above the left temple, close to the eye. The pair of spectacles wh. I was wearing must have been blown off by the force of the explosion, for I never saw them again. Very luckily they were not smashed and driven into my eye. As it is, this wound is also a superficial one. The eye and temple are swollen, of course, but otherwise all is well. I felt rather dazed last night, but I have been resting all today, and have had a long and refreshing sleep.

When I had been dressed, at about 4 a.m. the Doctor told me that I could either go back with some other cases (including my man) to the Ambulance and Clearing Station, or stay with the Bn. If I went on, I might very possibly go home to England, as the hospitals are all being cleared very rapidly, in view of the 'push'. But he felt sure that I should be quite well by the time our 'rest' from the trenches is over. So I said I would stay.

Of course, I know, dearest Mother, how anxious you are about me and how glad you would be to have me home. But if I had gone home (it is not at all certain that I should have gone) it could only have been because of the accident of the hospitals being very full just now. My first duty is to the Regiment in wh. I have the honour to serve. And not only are we very short of officers of any experience just now (there is no one to come out from Chelsea but boys and other officers who have not been out before) but I was told confidentially by the Adjutant the other day that the C.O. wd. prob. give me command of the next company vacant, when I had had a little more experience of trench work. So I feel doubly bound to stick it out, and I am sure that you and Father wd. think that I was right. Also, on general grounds, the fact of an officer not going away when the men know that he might have done so with little difficulty has, I'm sure, a very good effect on the 'morale' of the Battalion. The men have to stay if they are slightly wounded, and the officers shd. too. And I feel sure, dearest Mother, that you will say that I have done right. I am sure Father or my grandfathers would have done the same so please don't worry. I feel sure that Providence wh. has been so kind, will keep me all right till the end. My escape this time was really wonderful.

Letter from Harold Macmillan to his mother, 19 or 20 July 1916

'Longueval was being subjected to the most awful shelling'

BICKERSTETH DESCRIBES THE BOMBARDMENT OF LONGUEVAL

As Bickersteth explains, the bombardment was part of a German counter-attack nearly three weeks into the battle of the Somme. His description provides a particularly vivid picture of the effects of the war on the landscape, and of the frantic activity during an action. The events took place on 17 to 18 July.

Our progress to Montauban was slow. We did not enter the village as it was being shelled but kept away to the left (West). ... we found an excellent artillery O.P. (observation post) and as luck would have it the major in charge proved to have been at Winchester with Irwin.

When we arrived at this point Longueval was being subjected to the most awful shelling. ... All these villages are clothed in trees. All over this part of France a village resembles a wood more than a visible collection of houses. Montauban ... was once hidden by trees ... now the trees are so battered and slashed that broken heaps of masonry can be seen peeping out of the twisted boughs. Of Longueval village of course nothing remains—but at 4.30. this particular afternoon the site of Longueval was shrouded in a black haze. We were about a mile and a half from the village. The noise was indescribable—the whole scene most awe-inspiring. ... Longueval ... looked like some great volcano in eruption sending up smoke and flame to the heavens—along the ridge in front of us black German 'crumps' were falling on our new secondary line with the greatest regularity. First the flash and then fountains of earth soared upward like some enormous waterspout. ... on our left flank seeming to run up from Fricourt was Mametz Wood on much lower ground than ourselves—so that over the tree tops we could see the battered church tower of Contalmaison and behind that Pozières. Guns everywhere—men moving up—wounded coming back, carried in stretchers or walking with bandaged heads—'This way—walking wounded' said one large notice board. 'Trench crossing' with a large arrow pointing, said another. Guns moving to new positions, ammunition columns or led horses belonging to limbers passing and re-passing. In the middle of this Irwin and the gunner major discussed Winchester and recalled old friends. I got the subaltern to explain to me what was doing. He had laid his guns on a windmill away to the left—had gone two degrees to the right, come down 600 yards and hoped he was hitting the new Switch Trench. The Huns have constructed a new trench between their 2nd and 3rd lines—it is called the S.T. because it is switched off from their second line somewhere round Pozières and runs due East—taking in the top corner of High Wood. The tremendous bombardment we were actually witnessing was that preceding the great German counter attack on Longueval and Delville Wood which began at 5.30. on Tuesday afternoon July 18, when they got back from us part of Delville Wood and the northern corner of Longueval village. This you will have seen in the papers.

Letter from Burgon Bickersteth to his mother,
20 July, a continuation of the letter of 6 July

'We were about 3500 feet up and fast approaching the line'

BURGON BICKERSTETH
FLIES OVER THE SOMME BATTLEFIELD

Bickersteth's long letter was not sent until late in the month. Instead, he continued it on 25 July, to describe another new experience, his first flight in an aeroplane.

Yesterday I had the most marvellous experience of my life. I flew over our own front line and over the German front line penetrating two miles into German territory and circling about the further side of Flers and Martinpuich.

How <u>am</u> I to describe this to you?

There is an aerodrome near here on the hill and we heard that Miller was a Flight Commander there. Miller you may remember at York by name. He is a small rather insignificant looking S. African— he joined the 5th Reserve Cavalry in the autumn of 1914 but soon fell ill with internal trouble. ... He left to join the R.F.C. He is now a Captain and in charge of 4 machines. ... We found Miller in the mess, and he offered to show us round the machines. We never asked to go up, as we knew these R.F.C. fellows get so bored with people asking for a flight. But Miller himself suggested taking us up for a little run—and at ten minutes past four you might have seen me duly habited in fur cap, goggles and long leather coat and gauntlets climbing up into a Morane monoplane behind Miller. ... I had never before been in an aeroplane. ... 'Where are we going?' I said. 'Oh well!' said Miller, 'I think we might go to Pozières. We took it last night you know'. ... 'And what about the Boches?' 'We shan't meet any Boches' he said with so much quiet certainly that I felt he knew.

'We shan't need a Lewis Gun. I shall merely take a revolver'. ...
We began to run along the grass—then the men turned us. We ran
back past the aerodrome at a terrific pace—and then suddenly I was
conscious we had left the earth. It is a wonderful sensation—up–
up–up—the land flew away below—a vast green map below me. ...
At last I was actually looking at the map in reality .... We were
flying along the valley towards Albert ... and now nearing Fricourt.
Once I felt bad. We climbed. The machine turned ... almost half
over—our nose stuck up in the air and a great white pall of cloud
seemed to engulf us. But we were soon through this. ... We were
about 3500 feet up and fast approaching the line. The predominant
green vanished—and predominant yellow took its place. The land
was seamed with endless tracks crossing and re-crossing. Fricourt
seemed a rather yellower patch in a yellow land. What green there
was seemed dull and blasted. From that height woods appeared like
small patches of gorse, and even here the yellow peeped through.
This of course was where endless shelling had at last eradicated all
signs of trees and had left only yellow shell holes in their place.

... The noise of the engines and the fearful rush of wind—so
great at times that I was forced to put my head between my legs
and so get the advantage of Miller's back—prevented any spoken
word. Sometimes there is a telephone (to telephone 8 inches!) but
there wasn't one on this machine—but a small writing block was left
on the side—and on this Miller wrote. First he wrote Fricourt and
pointed to this yellow patch. Then he wrote Delville Wood, then
Longueval ... each time he pointed first to the paper—and then we
looked over the edge (3500 feet!) and he pointed to the place. ... on
the paper appeared High Wood .... Below I could see batteries in
action—flashes and puffs of smoke mostly white sometimes green
smoke. But no sign of movement at all. Trenches to the untrained
eye are hard to detect .... On we went. Below us were several of our
standard biplanes circling about, and on the paper there appeared
Flers, and then Martinpuich .... We went right beyond Flers—and
then I got one of those views which will be for ever imprinted on my
mind's eye—a view of a vast country beyond—Hun territory—roads
and avenues leading right into it —villages and woods untouched—
our Promised Land—and even as I looked I could see tiny black
streaks along some roads—Hun transport! Puffing trains—and a
dim hazy horizon. We turned and I suppose it was wise—we were
2 miles in Hun territory. ... On the paper appeared 'Cavalry'. This
showed me the exact spot where the cavalry had charged.

And now we were vol planing[75] down pretty fast. We had to land between Catterpillar Wood and Montauban owing to the magnets going wrong—and I came back in a motor ambulance.

The somewhat abrupt ending to the flight was in fact much worse than he was prepared to say. In a letter in to his mother of 28 October we find that his brother Julian has given away the truth, and he admits that the aircraft hit the ground at eighty m.p.h., turned over and was 'smashed to atoms'. He and the pilot had to be cut free from the wreckage, emerging before a crowd of astonished onlookers 'ghastly white but neither of us any the worse'.[76]

Letter from Burgon Bickersteth to his mother,
25 July, a continuation of the letter of 6 July

'Machines fly over Oxford every day'

ANDREW CLARK RETURNS TO OXFORD

While travelling to Oxford, Andrew Clark made a note of war posters, and paid particular attention to a note of warning to railway passengers:

In view of possible attacks by hostile aircraft, it is necessary that the blinds in the carriages of all trains should be pulled down after sunset.

Clark was not only keeping a diary of the effects of the war on everyday life; he was also collecting all kinds of documents and printed ephemera which he felt in some way reflected the impact of the war, including posters, advertisements and bulletins. These were carefully preserved with the diary or in separate albums and passed on to the Bodleian Library. In Oxford Clark encountered men of the Officers Cadet Battalion. The drive to expand the number of officers lay behind the creation of this organization, and it was also a route to a commission for men from the ranks. By 1917, 50 per cent of officers commissioned had served in the ranks that year.

<u>Th. 20 July 1916</u>

... noticed at Paddington Station that there were very few advertisement-slips in comparison with former years. I preserve the only one that seemed attractive enough to take.

[On the following page is pasted a very vibrant pamphlet for 'G.W.R Inland Health and Pleasure Resorts. The Delightful Bristol Channel Watering Places.']

At the O.U. Society's rooms I found many notices in connection with hardships incurred through the war by the society; subscriptions to tide over financial troubles; deaths in battle of former officers. These I did not feel equal to copying at present. But I took for preservation one of the river steamer advertisements, hoping to be able to go down for a day to Sandford and correct papers there. ...

<u>Friday 21 July 1916</u>

... From O.U.S. entrance hall I brought an advertisement of the Cinematograph Theatre in George Street. To a man of any standing there is no more astonishing feature in Oxford than the way in which the whole central block of the town from Beaumont Street and Broad Street in the N. to the South side of High Street and Queen Street has become occupied by restaurants, tea-shops, places of amusement.

At this point Clark pasted into his diary several pamphlets related to events in Oxford, including an advertisement for Serbian music at Pembroke College Hall and New College Chapel, a brochure for the George Street Cinematograph Theatre, and an advertisement for soldiers to go to C.H. Brown saddler in Market Street.

<u>Sat. 22 July 1916</u>

... Oxford is very full of strapping young fellows, some of whom have on their shoulder strap, covering the regimental mark, a green cloth patch, with on it in big brass letters

O.C.B.

I asked what this meant, and was told it meant

Officers Cadet Battalion.

These, I was informed, were young fellows who had enlisted, done good service, and were now in training for Commissions. I was told that there might be as many as 800 to 900 of them in Oxford. Those of them who wore flat caps had a white band round it above the snout, under the bulging out top. Many of them had glengarries, and a good many were kilted. I asked one of these what his battalion was—it proved to be 4 Camerons (Highlanders, of course). He came from Inverness.

I saw also in the street a number of people with a little glengarry-shaped bonnet, of greenish khaki, worn cocked on one side of the head, half folded. It has no ribbons. These I were [sic] told were Royal Flying Corps. There is a flying-school in Portmeadow, and machines fly over Oxford every day. ...

Thursday 3 Aug 1916
About 11.40 a.m. I went to buy three fat volumes of Smith's Dictionary of the Bible. Which I had seen offered at a 1/- a volume at the shop of F.W. Chaundy, opposite the old Clarendon building. As I emerged from the stair-case, the porter's boy rushed across the Quad shouting to his father that an aeroplane was 'looping the loop' over the College. I heard the engines very distinctly, but I could see nothing of it. But when I got down to the open space between Radcliffe Camera and Hertford College (at S.E. corner of Bodleian) I found a crowd gazing up. The air-craft was just overhead, flying low, not much higher than St. Mary's steeple. ... I could see not only its outline, but the markings on its wings. ... The sun was in my eyes. It was probably a bi-plane, but flying on so even a keel that from below it looked exactly like a tailed, two winged, bird, floating along.

Diary of the Revd Andrew Clark, rector of Great Leighs,
Essex, 20 July to 3 August 1916

'P.M. says his opposition to female suffrage is vitally affected by women's work in the war'

SOMERVILLE COLLEGE, WOMEN'S WAR WORK, AND THE PRIME MINISTER AND FEMALE SUFFRAGE

A glance at the annual reports produced by Somerville, the Oxford women's college, reveals a snapshot of the kind of work educated women found themselves involved with during the First World War. The *Annual Report and Oxford letter* published by the Somerville Students' Asssociation in 1917 includes a list of members and records their war work. This was a new departure for the Association, and reflects both their increasing involvement in the war effort, and the growing scale of that work nationwide. Mrs E.H. Thruston of Machynlleth in Wales, for example, is recorded as undertaking 'Work for Belgian Refugees. Visiting hospitals and BRC [Belgian Refugee Committee] work.' Also the report recognizes her 'domestic work releasing other labour'. Charlotte Tibbits of Bromley had undertaken 'holiday work in canteens' and as a hospital orderly. Una Tilley of Blackheath was a history mistress in the County School for Girls, but had also worked from January 1916 in the War Trade Intelligence Department. Janet Tree of Worcester did VAD [Voluntary Aid Detachment] and canteen work. Agnes Tuke of Cheltenham had since 1915 been 'taking officers and their families as paying guests' and had worked in the house and garden of a VAD home. Helen Vaudrey of Birmingham had worked in the VAD since September 1914, and was now 'Joint officer-in-charge, H.Q.'

The VAD had been founded in 1909 to help in hospitals. By 1914 two-thirds of the 74,000 'VADs' were female, and the war led to an influx of new volunteers. Although it was not intended that they should serve overseas, the shortage of nurses soon changed the situation, and women aged over twenty-three with more than three months' experience in hospital work were taken for overseas service. The Somerville student Vera Brittain, whose *Testament of Youth* is one of the most famous war memoirs, delayed her studies to serve with the VAD, first

Sylvia and Venetia Stanley, 1905

in London, then later in Malta and France. VADs were largely from middle- and upper-class backgrounds (reflected in the large numbers recorded in the Somerville annual report). Sometimes this could lead to difficulties in military hospitals where professional nurses might criticize their lack of aptitude or experience, but as the war went on their competence increased and they became an accepted part of the service. There were VAD hospitals in most of the large towns in Britain, and VADs were to be found serving behind the Western Front, and near other fronts in the Dardanelles and in Mesopotamia.

Somerville students could be found in a great variety of war-related occupations. Hilda Walton of Kensington was from 1916 lady super-intendent of the munitions factory, Waltham Abbey. Helen Waters of

217

Kingston Hill had since July 1916 been a 'Member of Almeric Paget Massage Corps', an organization founded at the outbreak of the war by Mr and Mrs Almeric Paget. These privately funded masseuses were placed in the major military hospitals in the United Kingdom, and were involved in therapies such as hydrotherapy and electrotherapy as well as massage.

The prime minister, H.H. Asquith, was opposed to female suffrage before the war, but underwent a change of heart as the war progressed. His own friends and family, including his confidantes Venetia Stanley and Sylvia Henley, and his daughter Violet, were all involved in voluntary war work. Lewis Harcourt recorded in his journal the change in thinking of both himself and Asquith, and explicitly relates it to women's war work, though clearly not all Cabinet colleagues thought the issue worthy of discussion. Harcourt had voted against both the Parliamentary Franchise (Women) Bill in March 1912 and the Representation of the People (Women) Bill in May 1913, and in 1912 his house at Nuneham had been attacked by militant suffragists.

> 9.8.16   Cab. 11.30
> ... 11 Zeppelins raided our East Coast last night—some casualties— no material damage. ...
>
> P.M. says his opposition to female suffrage is vitally affected by women's work in the war.
>
> I said the only logical and possible solution is <u>Universal</u> suffrage (including women). This upset most of the Cabinet, but the P.M. agreed with me.
>
> Long and confused discussion.
>
> Grey says this is a criminal waste of time when we ought to be devoting our energies to winning the war.
>
> Agreed to introduce a minimum Bill with possibility of amendments being made by House of C.
>
> *Somerville Students' Asssociation Annual Report and Oxford letter (1917);*
> *Harcourt's Cabinet Journal, 9 August 1916*

'At last we have had a go at the enemy'

CORPORAL F.B. WOOLLEY GOES INTO ACTION IN SALONIKA

The letter conveys a mixture of relief and elation as Corporal Woolley's battalion sees action for the first time. His sentiments match those of Macmillan and other junior officers, a desire to see the war end, but not until the Germans have been defeated.

> Thank you very much for such a nice parcel. I very sorry to say the cake had gone bad it was a shame and a great disappointment ....
>
> I received your letter and read it as the shells were bursting all round, at last we have had a go at the enemy and we reached our object allright. I am sorry to say some poor chaps went under but all were eager to do their bit it was grand to see our boys go at them I can tell you the old honour of the Regiment was upheld. ... I hope this war will soon be over but not until our enemy is completely crushed if its years I'm willing. I know we mean to stick at them until they are completely beat. I hope all your kins men are keeping all right. You must feel proud to have so many serving their country.
>
> *Letter, Corporal F.B. Woolley, 7th battalion Oxfordshire and Buckinghamshire*
> *Light Infantry, Salonika, to Sarah Angelina Acland, 27 August 1916*

'This is not the weather for killing people'

HAROLD MACMILLAN ON THE SOMME

The war diary, written in pencil on seventeen loose sheets from a notepad, is enclosed with Macmillan's letters to his mother. It covers the period from 21 July to 14 September 1916, including the transfer from the Ypres salient to the Somme and the battalion's operations there. It is mostly written in the form of an official war diary, but contains numerous characteristic personal remarks and impressions. Macmillan periodically includes references to his current reading matter.

<u>August 1st</u>

... The whole Bde. is on the march—1st line transport with each Bn. We are the rear Bn. of the Bde. today. We marched to SARTON, S.E. of DOULLENS. ...

It is extraordinary how much better one feels after a little exercise. Trench warfare is deadly to the digestion. One gets very tired without taking much exercise. Also the SOMME country is so much more attractive and healthy-feeling than FLANDERS. We are all thoroughly glad to have left the YPRES salient. In this village also we encamped in an orchard. Below the orchard runs a very pleasant stream. All the afternoon we bathed and basked in the sun. ...

<u>2nd</u>

... It is quite heavenly to sit beneath the shady trees and idle the day away, with talk and books and, it must be confessed, dozing. The gramophone is in great form. But we all shudder to think of a battle on such a day as this. This is not the weather for killing people. It is far too charming.

(The Winter's Tale)...

<u>10th</u> Left SARTON. Bn. marched at 5.40. We arrived at BETRAN-COURT at about 7 p.m. We are in a camp. We passed H.M. The King on the road. He was with Sir Douglas Haig. A most uncomfortable camp and very crowded. (The Greatest Wish in the World—Temple Thurston)

<u>11th</u> We relieved 2nd Bn. SHERWOOD FORESTERS in trenches opp. BEAUMONT-HAMEL, North of THIEPVAL. The Bn. marched by Coys at 1 hr interval, the 1st Coy. at 7.50. We were last and marched at 10.50 a.m. We got into the line about 2 p.m. A very hot day and a very tiring march. The trenches here are a great change. They are very deep, 8 or 9 feet. The soil is hard chalky. The Communication trenches are very long. WITHINGTON AVENUE, up which we came is over 1 mile long. The posn. overlooks the enemy wh. is a change for us. You can see a long way—right round to THIEPVAL on the right, and MAILLY MAILLY [he means Mailly Maillet] and BEAUCOURT.

<u>13th</u> (Sunday)—A heavy bombardment of the enemy's lines opp. took place last night (12th) 10.50–11.50 p.m. Also there seemed to be a good deal of activity in the direction of POZIERES, with bomb fighting. A quiet morning; the hot weather has given way to dull, coldish days. ... One officer must always be on duty by day now, as

well as by night. Went round front line in afternoon and evening. Very interesting. Watched our artillery cutting the wire in front of THIEPVAL, but was sniped at and went away.

16th Marched from the camp at 11.15 a.m. to billets in village of COURCELLES. We arrived at 12. noon. Quite decent billets. (Boswell) ...

18th ... No 1 Coy's concert in evening. Very amusing. 2 machine gunners (who are professionals) gave a good sketch. Willie and the Doctor came to dinner. We are billetted in the Abbé Duhamel. He (with all the inhabitants) has of course left the village. We have a nice set of 5 or 4 rooms. His candlesticks come in very useful. Is it sacri-religious? They are doubtless from the altars of the church. ...

20th ... We are in WARNIMONT wood. The men are in huts—we are in tents, 4 subalterns to a tent—Irish Gds band came and played to us. ...

24th: Marched off 7.40 a.m. and reached FLESSELLES (about 10 miles) near MONTVILLERS at about 11.30 a.m. A good march, and good roads. Billets poor. The village is filled with Senegalese troops. We move on tomorrow by march and train. ...

30th: Wet. No parades—Boswell is finished at last, and with Much Ado most of the Shakespearian comedies. Now I must pass to the tragedies. Major Kirby Ellice to lunch. Roumania has come in at last.

Extracts from Harold Macmillan's war diary, 1–30 August 1916

'It was like one large flaming cigar'

ETHEL WHITEHOUSE DESCRIBES THE SHOOTING
DOWN OF A ZEPPELIN NEAR PLAISTOW, LONDON

This eyewitness account of a Zeppelin raid conveys something of the outlandish appearance of these great airships. The original letter contains very little punctuation, adding to the sense of breathless excitement.

We had another raid early this morning about ¼ past 2. I saw the Zepp and the bombs dropping from it, and saw the fire from our guns going for it. It seemed as though it would hit it but it just missed. Then it seemed to be hidden above the clouds as the guns stopped and it seemed as though they had used all their bombs as they stopped dropping them about. A few minutes after we heard such a lot of cheering and shouting hooters going and the noise was terrible. We all rushed to look out and saw the Zepp being brought down all in flames. We saw it so plainly and was quite near us. It is thought our aeroplanes brought it down. We could see them following the Zepp down. We could see three and the search lights. It was a wonderful sight but I am afraid the men in the Zepp must have been burnt to death as it went to earth so slowly. It was like one large flaming cigar. We are near the Victoria Docks and East India Docks and Matron has a branch home at Victoria Docks. We are not so far from Woolwich either.

Letter, Ethel Whitehouse, District Nurses Home, Howards Road,
Plaistow, to Sarah Angelina Acland, 3 September 1916

'Noble and glorious … revolting and horrid'

HAROLD MACMILLAN CANNOT RECONCILE TWO FACES OF WAR

In this remarkably frank letter, surrounded by death, Macmillan still clings to his belief in the nobility of war, though clearly now sickened by the increasing carnage. Where this ambivalence might have led Macmillan by 1918 we cannot know—this was to be his last letter from the front before his war was ended by a severe wound. He begins the letter by trying to reassure his mother that all is well, but then does not spare her from a graphic reflection on his situation.

11.10 a.m.

My dearest Mother—

We are in the trenches, in an interesting position. Everything has been fortunate for us so far. There is no reason to be alarmed

222

about us. The news seems to be good lately and the enemy must be suffering on every side.

There is nothing to tell you in particular. The flies are again a terrible plague, and the stench from the dead bodies which lie in heaps around is awful. We do all the burying that we possibly can, and this will of course help. But there is not always time to do everything. The act of death in battle is noble and glorious. But the physical appearance and actual symptoms of death are, in these terrible circumstances, revolting only and horrid.

The weather is not so good now, and we are afraid of rain, but it has held off up till now fairly well. The night was rather a trying one. I shall sleep again now. I do not know when I shall be able to send this letter, but I hope tomorrow.

Letter from Harold Macmillan to his mother, 13 September 1916

German prisoners carry a wounded officer of the Grenadier Guards near Ginchy, 14th September 1916. Harold Macmillan was wounded early the next morning during this attack

'I am wounded—not badly'

MRS MACMILLAN RECEIVES NEWS
OF HER SON'S WOUNDING

At 6.20 a.m. on 15 September 1916 Macmillan led his platoon in an advance on Ginchy, part of the battle of Flers–Courcelette. He was wounded in the left thigh and pelvis by machine gun fire from the left flank and fell unconscious for a time into a shell hole. Only once night had fallen was he found by a rescue party. Unable to walk, he was taken back to British lines by stretcher-bearers, whose activities brought further shelling. He was met by Neville Talbot, chaplain of XIV Corps, who coincidently had been Macmillan's chaplain at Balliol College. Talbot forwarded Macmillan's note to his mother, written in a shaky hand on a small scrap of paper. In fact his wound was severe, and his active service was over.

> Dear Mrs Macmillan—
> I enclose this from Harold. You need not be anxious about him. He has two wounds one in the left buttock and the other in the right leg below the knee. There is nothing broken, and no danger.
> He has had a trying time but is full of courage—I am so glad that I was able to see him go through this Dressing Station.
> Yours sincerely,
> NS Talbot
> Chaplain
> Head Qrs. XIV Corps.
> Sept 16.16.

MACMILLAN'S NOTE

> Dearest Mother—
> I am wounded—not badly. I am in the clearing station, where Neville Talbot has given me this paper.
> I shall be home soon.
> Your own
> Harold.

> *Letter from Neville Talbot to Mrs Macmillan, enclosing a*
> *note from Harold Macmillan, 16 September 1916*

'I felt extremely doubtful and very cynical about the whole affair'

BURGON BICKERSTETH IS DOUBTFUL ABOUT
THE CAVALRY'S ROLE AT FLERS-COURCELETTE,
SEPTEMBER 1916

In this letter Burgon Bickersteth continues his account of his part in the Somme campaign, this time in the Battle of Flers–Courcelette, 15 to 22 September 1916. This third and last general British offensive of the battle of the Somme had the aim of cutting a hole in the German line with massed infantry and artillery attacks, to be exploited by the cavalry. Although some advances were made, the overall objective was not achieved. Bickersteth begins to show signs that he has serious doubts about the progress of the battle, and like Brigadier Makins records cynicism among cavalry officers about the role they are expected to play (see pp. 203–5).

My dear Father and Mother

I see that my last long letter ended with the day we left CAURON-ST-MARTIN once again for the SOMME this time as cavalry. Forty-eight hours was not long to post through the transference from infantry to cavalry establishment but by the morning of Sept 10th all was ready. ... From NEUILLY L'HÔPITAL we moved on to LA CHAUSSÉE which lies in the AMIENS–ABBEVILLE valley .... Here on the evening of Sept 13th with the portraits of eighteenth century grandees looking down upon us from the walls we were told the plan of battle for the cavalry. The cavalry were on its trial—and it was said we were to be now at all costs—neither man or horse to be spared—and if necessary whole brigades would be sacrificed. The GAP through which we were to pass was between GUEUDICOURT [he means Gueudecourt] and MORVAL—a distance at the most of some 4000 yards. It did not seem very great—but the role of the cavalry was to enlarge the lips of this hole and it was confidently predicted by no less a person than Sir Douglas Haig that once we were through and the Germans saw we were behind them, they would surrender to us in large numbers. Well as we sat round that table and heard the objective of the 2nd Indian Cavalry Division and the 1st British Cavalry Division which were to go first and the subsequent task of the 1st Indian and 2nd British Cavalry Divisions with ourselves (the 3rd Cav: Div:) in reserve I confess that I (and I know a good many others too) felt extremely doubtful and very cynical about the whole affair.

Next day Sept 14 we started early and marched via Amiens to some fields just outside BONNAY … the encampment presented an extraordinary picturesque appearance—all the hills were dotted with camp fires and lights—away at the end of the valley beyond Albert we saw the continuous flashes of the guns lighting up the eastern horizon and the evening we arrived the bombardment prior to the great attack on Sept 15 was very great. A most beautiful harvest moon lit the countryside with a soft ghostly light.

As happened before on July 1st and on July 14th news began to come in a few hours after the attack—and it soon became clear that towards MARTINPUICH, FLERS, and GUEUDICOURT our progress was good, whereas in front of LES BOEUFS, and MORVAL we were being held up—and it was just this holding up on the South which entirely spoilt our chances—we knew it at once—and as the day wore on—and the next day came and the initial general attack resolved itself into more local affairs everyone realised we should never be wanted. The only chance of the cavalry was to get through on the first wash, so to speak. Personally I believe Loos just a year ago today was the nearest we have ever been to being used. Certainly by the evening of Sept 16th it was clear that for us July 1st and July 14th had merely been re-enacted.

Letter from Burgon Bickersteth to his parents, written 26 September 1916, describing the events of 10–16 September

'We talked of the sheer wickedness of this great European struggle'

BURGON BICKERSTETH HAS SEVERE DOUBTS ABOUT THE WAR

Bickersteth's long letter continues to tell the story of his part in the Battle of Flers–Courcelette. This battle marked the first use of the tank in warfare. Despite the optimistic reports Bickersteth notes here, the tanks were not a great success owing to their slowness and mechanical difficulties, but they had some psychological impact, as Bickersteth remarks.

Bickersteth's experiences on the Somme, and the high price the soldiers were paying for little territorial gain, had a profound effect on him, and for the first time he expresses severe doubts about the purpose and direction of the war. His brother Morris had been killed on the second day of the campaign. Another brother Julian was a padre; ministering to the wounded, he was never far from scenes of death. Discussions with Julian, and his meeting with a war-weary Neville Talbot on 18 September (just two days after Talbot had written to Harold Macmillan's mother to inform her that her son was wounded, one of the 29,000 casualties of the Battle of Flers–Courcelette—see p. 224) had perhaps crystallized ideas that Burgon had been turning over in his mind. He has begun to see hope in a socialist vision of the future.

> On Sept 17th we moved camp to the outskirts of QUERRIEU and PONT NOYELLES....
> That afternoon I went to 4th Army HQs at QUERRIEU to find out where the 56th Division was—The HQs are installed in a beautiful chateau, guarded by very smart Guardsman. I penetrated to the General Staff room and was received by a sleek well-groomed staff officer, who gave me the information I wanted. I decided it was too far to attempt to reach Julian [his brother] that afternoon, so went back to camp and got leave from King to have the whole of the next day off.

I met Somers that evening—he had been to Army HQs and was full of information about the Tanks. On the whole they had been successful—Their chief fault had been that they had in most cases fired too high. As you probably know they are not unlike a huge toad in shape, when viewed from the side. Their outline is one enormous wheel—on the same principle as the catterpillar [*sic*] wheel, only very much larger. ... The body of the Tank is the shape of a stubby cigar—and is merely a chamber the walls of which are entirely composed of armour plating. ... As you have read they will go through houses, over trenches, negotiate shell craters and indeed overcome any obstacle. ... Certain it is that the sight of these uncouth engines of war lumbering along over no mans land, over first and second line trenches, undamaged by machine gun fire, and untroubled by holes, trenches, walls, houses fairly put the wind up the Boche. We know now that they were seen the night before coming up and German officers were warned to be prepared for an attack, but were ordered not to mention the matter to their men, for fear they might be afraid. One was hit east of FLERS and lies even now derelict between the two lines—the men in it were killed—and the Huns did attempt to get it away, but as it weighs 40 to 50 ton the attempt was not a success.

... early next morning Sept 18 I started off to try and find Julian. ... I started at 9.0 am with the faithful Hunt in attendance. We rode via BONNAY to HEILLY, DURNENCOURT, MÉAULTE, FRICOURT to CARNOY. The traffic as usual was terrific. Divisions being relieved, new divisions going in. Near MÉAULTE I met Rodocanachi who used to be at the House with me—He was riding at the head of his company, having just come out of the line. He is in the Oxford and Bucks Light Infantry (14th Div) and they had had a terrible time. He seemed utterly knocked up and could hardly talk coherently. The high ground between CARNOY and BRAY-SUR-SOMME is one vast camp—horse lines, lorry parks, huts, tents, light railways, hospitals ...

At Divisional HQs I was most hospitably received, my man and horses fed, and myself invited into lunch—As it was 1.0 pm I accepted—all the more readily as an obliging APM offered me fresh horses to take me on to CHIMPANZEE trench, where I should have to walk to ANGLE WOOD to find Julian. Of Julian everyone talked most warmly. 'He is doing splendidly. He is everywhere popular, always up in front under fire, and works himself to death for everybody.' The rain continued in driving sheets. You can imagine the lakes of liquid mud splashed sky high by every passing vehicle and horse. Immediately after lunch I walked to BRONFAY FARM, where there is a large dressing station and where I hoped to get definite information about Julian's whereabouts. The first person I saw on arriving there was Neville Talbot. He was superintending the building of a shed in the padre's lines. We were both surprised to meet and at once began an interesting conversation. There seemed to be a number of badly wounded pouring up to the hospital in motor ambulances and as Neville surveyed them he said 'This is the only part of the war I see, day in and day out. It is almost more than one can bear.' He could tell me nothing definite about Julian but offered to walk back with me to the Div[isiona]l HQs and as we went we talked of the sheer wickedness of this great European struggle. I admit my views about the war have somewhat changed and the question constantly presents itself. Is the thing we are fighting worse than the methods we are forced to use in trying to fight it? In other words war has now come to be such a horrible, fearful thing, that one wonders whether for sheer wickedness it is not worse than the domination of the world by German ideas. After all what are German ideas? Chiefly, at the moment, to get world power. An aspiration which I am bound to confess I am pretty certain we too should have, were we in German shoes. Her methods to attain this end have been ruthless—involving the violation of small countries, but this is merely part of a carefully thought-out and very thorough plan. In our own past though we have no such black blots on our history, we have not been always over-careful of how we come by additional territory. (Though here please do not mistake me and say I am one of those who say graft is the foundation of the British Empire.) Were Germany to get what she wants or rather were she to get what she now would be ready to accept—a place in the sun instead of the sun—I do not think we should have to fear the over-running of the world by German autocratic ideas—Hohenzollern tyranny, Prussian oppression could never exist in the 20th century. Quite apart from the rest of Germany never allowing it, Socialism and other international forces are far too strong to brook any such nonsense. I have before me a copy of The Round Table. In an article on war-aims it says '...for there can be no peace until the power of Germany to dictate to Europe is overthrown and until the national liberties she has destroyed are restored.' Somehow or other I feel it would be much more difficult to write this, if the author saw for himself the horror of it all out here. We cannot and we shall not crush Germany. ... I do not believe that this 20th century which is going to see the triumph of labour, of Socialistic tendencies, of democratic ideals will ever again be troubled by sheer, undiluted militarism which since 1870 has been Germany's rôle. Labour simply would not stand it. This being the case what exactly are we fighting for? People at home fondly believe that having gained crushing military and naval victories we shall be able to limit the size of the German fleet, limit, too (like Napoleon tried to do and failed) the size of her army, dethrone Junkerism, dictate to the Hohenzollerns and so forth. I repeat we shall never do that. And I believe the only way—(and perhaps the most Christian way?) of bringing the German nation to a proper understanding of its crimes is to make peace.

Bickersteth then rounded on the newspapers and their partial telling of the story:

And without the shadow as well as the light how can people at home really form any idea as to what is really happening? The report that Thiepval has at last fallen fills everybody with delight, and people at home picture our cheering men and the great ludicrous tanks lumbering ahead and the surrendering Boches and so on. They don't realise or rather the nation as a whole does not realise the horrors which have accompanied that gain of a few thousand yards.

Continuation of Bickersteth's letter to his parents,
26 September 1916, describing the events of 17–18 September

'In him and his future I had invested all my stock of hope'

ASQUITH MOURNS THE DEATH OF HIS SON RAYMOND ON THE SOMME

Raymond Asquith (1878–1916) was the prime minister's son by his first wife Helen, who died in 1891. Raymond won a scholarship to Balliol in 1896, was elected a Fellow of All Souls in 1902, and called to the bar in 1904. The war brought an end to a possible political career. He was commissioned as a second lieutenant in the London Regiment, and then transferred to the 3rd Battalion, Grenadier Guards, on 14 August 1915. He had been assigned as a staff officer, but requested to be returned to active duty before the Somme. He was killed in an attack near Ginchy at the Battle of Flers–Courcelette, a phase of the Somme Offensive, on 15 September 1916. On the same day Harold Macmillan of the 2nd battalion Grenadier Guards was seriously wounded in the same attack.

The Wharf ... Wed 20 Sept 16

Most dear—it was a comfort to get your letter. I knew you would feel as I do the waste of such powers and possibilities, with so much radiance and charm. I have never seen the like. I can honestly say that in my own life he was the thing of which I was truly proud, and in him and his future I had invested all my stock of hope. That is all gone, and for the moment I feel bankrupt.

We are still without any but the meagrest particulars: but he seems to have been shot 200 yards in advance of the trenches through the lungs, and to have died on his way back to the dressing station. He was buried the next day, the clergyman being a Mr McCormick, I believe of some West End London Church.

I drove from here yesterday to Mells, nearly 80 miles, to see Katharine [Raymond's wife] who wanted me .... I have never seen anyone so stunned and shattered: all she wants is to die. I spent an hour with her and I hope did her some little good. Only yesterday morning she had received a letter from him, written last Thursday: she showed it to me—a delightful little love letter.

The Wharf ... Sat 30 Sept 16

... We heard today how poor bimbo [Edward Wyndham 'Bim' Tennant, Margot Asquith's nephew—see p. 177] came to his end: he was shot in the head by a sniper and died instantly: I wonder if he was wearing his helmet. They have buried him close by the side of Raymond. Did you see his poem in the 'Times' yesterday? I had a letter from a Dr in R.A.M.C. who met Raymond as he was being carried in from the first dressing station to the rear. He asked to be turned over on to his left side. The Dr would have given him an opiate, but saw that it was unnecessary, as he was quite free from pain and just dying. We probably know now all that we ever shall. ...

I get through my work after a fashion, but with a good deal of absent-mindedness at times, and I have read literally nothing.

Among the Gilbert Murray papers is a draft letter of condolence in Murray's hand:[77]

Dear Mr Asquith,

Though I know you must have innumerable letters I cannot refrain from sending you a word of deep sympathy about Raymond. He was among the friends of a very glorious band. Those Oxford scholars who gave up ~~everything happy lives and~~ brilliant futures and successful lives to serve their country. I always ~~remember~~ think of him as he was when I examined him for the Ireland.[78] I was struck then as much by his personality as his scholarship. ~~But he seemed to me afterward to grow in mellowness as well as in dignity and power.~~ And he grew afterward to be man of such rare dignity and power.

I always remember a conversation we had at a time when it seemed that your life was in danger from the militant suffragists and the indignant affection that showed in his words and voice.

Letters from H.H. Asquith to Sylvia Henley, 20 and 30 September 1916

Raymond Asquith in the uniform of the Grenadier Guards.
He joined the 3rd battalion in August 1915

'You are in the habit of taking notes of what goes on at the Cabinet'

THE PRIME MINISTER REBUKES LEWIS HARCOURT FOR RECORDING CABINET DISCUSSIONS

The prime minister had been notified by other Cabinet members that Harcourt was keeping notes at Cabinet meetings, and sent this reprimand. As the letter shows, this was not the first time that such complaints had been made, but it had not deterred Harcourt. He had noted in July 1914 that Winston Churchill had remonstrated with him on the matter (see p. 28). No official diary of Cabinet meetings existed until Lloyd George instituted the practice in December 1916 after the fall of the Asquith government and the end of Harcourt's period in the Cabinet. The Cabinet made collective decisions so that individual contributions to discussions and decisions were not on the official record. Harcourt's journal would have seriously jeopardized the government had it become known, though, as we have seen, Asquith too was divulging highly confidential information to Sylvia Henley at this time.

> Confidential
>
> It has been represented to me by some of my colleagues that you are in the habit of taking notes of what goes on at the Cabinet.
>
> As I have more than once pointed out in the past, this is a violation of our unwritten law, under which only the Prime Minister is entitled to take and keep any record of Cabinet proceedings.
>
> Yours always
> H.H.A.

> *Letter from H.H. Asquith to Lewis Harcourt, 5 October 1916,*
> *found inserted into Harcourt's Cabinet journal*

'The really serious thing at the moment is not any of the land operations'

ASQUITH EXPLAINS A SHIFT IN THE FOCUS OF THE WAR

In these letters Asquith's weariness with the burdens of office is apparent. After the expenditure of so much blood and treasure on the Somme, and the death of his own son, the war continues to throw up new problems. The reference to the submarine threat in fact highlights a major problem for Germany; the Allies' continued naval dominance and maintenance of a blockade forced Germany to extend the submarine war, and this brought the United States to join the allies in April 1917. A little more than a month after this dinner at Lloyd George's residence at 11 Downing Street, the chancellor of the exchequer would take over from Asquith as prime minister.

1 Nov 16. Midnight
… Our people cut a rather sorry figure in the House to-day, and (as usual) I was called in to make the best of a surrender. 'Crosses'— aren't they? … I have just come back from my dinner next door. Only 4 of us. Our host (Ll.G) A.J.B[alfour], E. Grey and self. Welsh mutton and partridges. We had quite a good, discursive, survey of the whole situation—with the usual conclusion: more co-ordination 1st among the Allied statesmen and 2nd among the Allied Staffs. …

Thurs. 2 Nov 16
… I am not at all satisfied with your way of life: you go underground from time to time like a South African river, while I am left to plod along the Veldt. It is true (to be quite just) that I occasionally come across a pool from which I can get a more or less refreshing draft. I don't know that last night's dinner with Ll. G. quite answers that description. The only other guests were E. Grey and A.J.B. We had quite a good talk about the future of the war. The really serious thing at the moment is not any of the land operations, whether on the Somme or in Rumania, but the way in wh. the German submarines are lapping up the tonnage, both allied

and neutral, wh. keeps us all alive. We had a War C[ommitt]ee
this morning at wh. Jellicoe was present, and spent much time and
thought upon this lurid topic.

Letters from H.H. Asquith to Sylvia Henley, 1–2 November 1916

'He is "mad" to get out again'

A WOUNDED OFFICER OF THE SOUTH LANCASHIRES, NOVEMBER 1916

Andrew Clark records the experiences of Lieutenant Kenneth Sadgrove,
a young Cambridge alumnus wounded on the Somme. Despite the
wound and the 'bad time in the front trenches', Sadgrove appears to
have wanted to get back to his men.

Fr. 24 Nov. 1916
Kenneth Sadgrove, elder son of the rev. T. Sadgrove, rector of
Fairsted, is (wounded) in a hospital in London. He is Lieutenant
in the S. Lancashires .... His men in the trenches were too close
together. He held up his left hand, with his stick, to wave them to
spread themselves out, and was hit in the arm. His servant had
to use, to stop the bleeding, the pair of socks and the vest he was
wearing and they made the wound foul. It was 24 hours before he
could be brought to the field hospital, and the arm had become all
black, and it was at first feared it would have to be amputated. Had
he been 6 days longer in the field he would have got his captaincy
.... The servant was only a rough miner before the war, but was
extraordinarily kind. He was brought to England in a Belgian ship
which took three days to make the passage, being delayed by gales
and the intricacy of the passage through the mines. The hospital he
is in is in Mrs Hall Walker's house in Regent Park. Mr. Hall Walker
is a very wealthy man, and a great racing man. They have fitted up
their house as a hospital, most beautifully. The doctors promise that
K.S. shall get home for Christmas, but must then see a doctor every
day. Unless he can get skin grafted on the wound he is in danger of
losing the use of the arm, the muscles are so shrunk. He is able to

236

sit up. He is 'mad' to get out again, but will not get his old company, the men of which he was very fond of.

He had one specially bad time in the front trenches. Germans were in front and behind, and only a small trickle of support could get through to where he was. He and his men were without food for 24 hours, and afterwards were fed very irregularly.

When Mrs Sadgrove visited her son in hospital the next bed to him was occupied by a man suffering from shell-shock. His eyes were very strange, and he kept moaning all the time. She thought her presence was disturbing this patient, and she cut short her visit to her son.

Diary of the Revd Andrew Clark, Rector of Great Leighs, Essex, 24 November 1916

'To expect a war with Germany to be carried through by adroit palavering is to expect too much'

THE VICARS OF ADLESTROP AND BOXLEY ARE PESSIMISTIC ABOUT THE PROSPECTS FOR 1917

These letters indicate an increasing pessimism among some churchmen who had set great store in hopes that the war would bring about a national spiritual revival. Asquith's apparent lack of dynamism in prosecuting the war was the subject of loud and persistent criticism in the right-wing press, a view supported by the writers of these letters. Asquith resigned five days after they were written. The 'Archbishop of Canterbury's National Mission of Repentence and Hope' was an attempt to encourage a renewal of faith across the nation, but its impact was minimal.

Allowing a clear month for transit [to Japan], this letter must convey to you my best wishes for the new year. I look forward to it myself with much misgiving and anxiety. I expect that for the purpose of God's dealings with us we have not yet suffered enough, and must be prepared to suffer more. Only as we comfort ourselves under the discipline of felt suffering can we recommend ourselves to God for a restoration of the blessings of peace. I no longer apologize for posing as something of a pessimist: the optimists have disappointed me too often. To expect a war with Germany to be carried through by adroit palavering is to expect too much. It would be funny if there were nothing to show for all the money we have been pouring out like water, but something which no money can buy is needed before any good end can come in view. Our public men have for the most part talked themselves silly in times of peace, and it must be really a very troublesome sort of war that does not admit of being negotiated on the same terms.

On the same day, the Revd Edmund Best Dalison wrote to Lionel Cholmondeley from Boxley in Kent:

We are still living through this nightmare, and do not seem to get much more forward in spite of our lavish expenditure of noble lives and treasure. If only we had some energetic leader who was whole-heartedly for winning the war, instead of these incompetent rulers who are more than half German in all their sympathies. One feels in despair sometimes, nor can one see how the country can shake off the trammels of this old man of the sea that has sat astride her back these many years. As far as we are concerned the actual preaching of the National Mission has come and gone. I suppose it remains to be seen whether it has done anything. I don't myself feel that it has stirred the people at all definitely.

Letters, from F.G. Cholmondeley, vicar of Adlestrop, to his brother Lionel Cholmondeley, and from the Revd Edmund Best Dalison to the same, 1 December 1916

'Asquith's delay very foolish and unintelligible'

LEWIS HARCOURT'S ACCOUNT OF THE END OF ASQUITH'S PREMIERSHIP

Lewis Harcourt recorded in his journal the political wheeling and dealing that led to Asquith's resignation on 5 December 1916. If his own account can be taken at face value, he seems to have played a significant part in advising both Asquith and his Liberal colleagues on the best course of action. The hope that Lloyd George would be undermined by Asquith's resignation proved a false one, and Harcourt reveals his own doubts about the outcome, and also anger at Asquith's failure to head off the danger. The fall of Asquith was also the end of Harcourt's political career.

4.12.16

During Questions in H of C. today A. Chamberlain told me of the meeting of Unionist members of the Cabinet yesterday (Sunday) at which they unanimously decided that under the circs. Asquith ought to resign and that if he did not, they would all (9) collectively do so. ... He told me their object was that by Asquith's resignation Lloyd George should be 'put in his place' by finding that he could not form a Govt. and that their decision was in no way unfriendly to Asq. ...

At 4.30 I got a message from 10 Downing St to go there and found Grey, McKenna and Runciman in the Private Secy's room where I joined them. ...

Grey said he wanted tea and presently a tray was brought in for us (not for Asq. who never drinks tea).

Asq. sd he wanted our advice and he proposed to act on the advice of his <u>Liberal</u> colleagues and no others. He told us that B. Law came to him yesterday afternoon with the resignations ... and when asked why said 'general dissatisfaction with the conduct of the war'. Asq. thought he was deserted by all his Unionist colleagues and did not realise till this morning ... that this was meant to strengthen his hand against Ll. George.

George has demanded that A. Balfour should be removed from the Admiralty and that Carson shd. be brought into the Govt.

Asq. absolutely refused to remove Balfour whom he says he has good reason to believe is well regarded by the sailors.

He (Asq.) asked Ll. Geo whom he wd. put at the Admlty and Ll. G. replied 'Bonar Law'.

Asq. 'Do you think he wd. do it well?'

Ll. G. 'No, but the country think he is a man'.

Ll. G. demands a War Committee consisting only of himself, Bonar Law, Carson and (as an afterthought, to nobble Labour) Henderson. (All this appears in today's Times!).

Asq. told Ll. G. that he wd. not discuss Balfour and that he wd. not agree to a War Committee so constituted: Asq. sd. that he felt that a smaller War Committee was desirable: that it ought to sit every day and twice or thrice a day and that he cd. not devote the time necessary for this, but he was prepared to agree to a War Committee such as proposed of which <u>he</u> remained a member, that he attended when he could: that when he did he took the chair: that the agenda was submitted to him before its meeting, and its decisions afterwards and that he should have an absolute veto over all its decisions: without this he would not remain P.M.

Ll. Geo. had agreed to all this and Asq. thought he might proceed on these lines. To avoid Unionist resignations he asks for all of ours so that he shall proceed to 'reconstruct' with a clean slate. We agreed to this, but we 4 (joined at 5.30 by H. Samuel and at 6.30 by Henderson) said we thought Asq.'s position wd. be fatally weakened by what wd. be represented in the press as a triumph for Ll. Geo. and that the proper step for Asq. to take was to tell the King that under present conditions he (Asq.) cd. not go on and that the K. shd. send for Ll. Geo. or B. Law to form a new Govt.—B. Law wd. certainly refuse at once: Ll. G's action I think more doubtful—yesterday to Asq. he said the idea was unthinkable and wrote him this morning that he (Asq.) was essential and that he (Ll.G.) had never held any other view!!!

We 4 and Asq. thought that if Ll. Geo. tried to form a Govt. he wd. fail—then Asq's position wd. be greatly strengthened and he cd. make concessions as to the War Committee <u>then</u> without loss of prestige which he cd. not do now.

Ll. G. cd. hardly refuse to serve under Asq. when he (Ll. G.) had failed to form a Govt. and it wd. appear that he remained on Asq's terms.

I sd. 'But what if Ll. G. <u>does</u> form a Govt. I assume that <u>we</u> refuse to join it'. This was agreed and it was thought that most of the Tories wd. do so too.

Harcourt records further discussions about the attitude to a hypothetical Lloyd George government, and on asking if they should oppose it in the Commons, received the reply from Grey that if they give him the chance to form a government, they must also give him the chance to conduct it. Harcourt then asked:

'What if we think his Govt. incompetent for and fatal to the war?' and I got no reply.

The group then pressed on Asquith that his best way to bring Lloyd George down was to resign as they had suggested. At the end of the day Harcourt felt that they had convinced Asquith but he was not sure, and on 5 December he wrote in his journal that they had heard that Asquith had not resigned but had instead sent a letter to Lloyd George rejecting all his demands. This he thought would compel Lloyd George's resignation, but then later his own:

Asq's delay very foolish and unintelligible. Runciman says Asq. was not quite frank with us last night as he did not tell us that Ll. G. demands the dismissal (besides Arthur Balfour) of Grey, McKenna and Lansdowne.

Asquith summoned his Liberal colleagues (apart from Lloyd George) and Henderson to a meeting in the Cabinet Room at Downing Street. They learnt that the Unionists in the Cabinet had once again asked Asquith to resign to counter Lloyd George's manoeuvre, and Asquith explained his reasons for not going:

… such as the effect on the allies of disappearance of himself and Grey who represent a concrete fact to them: the danger of the great spread of the pacivist [*sic*] movement here if Liberal control was removed (there is already a very serious movement throughout the country in this direction)….
    I admitted all this but I sd. 'by not resigning last night and writing your letter to Ll. G. you have allowed <u>him</u> to get in first

with his resignation and now you will follow as if <u>yours</u> was the result of his: but yours must come and must come tonight and be in tomorrow's papers. You cannot contemplate going on ... with only a Liberal rump...'. All my colleagues agreed with me, and pressed the same view on Asq. Most of them believed that Ll. G. wd. try to form a Govt. and would succeed in getting something together though it might be a scratch affair. ...

At this point a letter was delivered to Asq. from B. Law stating the final decision of the Unionists that they must resign unless Asq. did so. G. Curzon was the messenger .... Asq. asked if we would like to see him [Curzon]: we sd. yes and he came in.

Asq. told him that his Lib. colleagues had unanimously come to the same conclusion as the Unionists and that he would at once (this was about 6.30 p.m.) convey his resignation to the King.

Cabinet journal of Lewis Harcourt, 4–5 December 1916

'The end of the war is not in sight'

OPINIONS OFFERED TO ANDREW CLARK
AFTER THE END OF THE BATTLE OF THE SOMME

The opinions recorded by Clark just after the Somme offensive had ground to a halt indicate the pessimism that was becoming widespread in the winter of 1916. Two particular aspects have caught his attention: the apparent resilience of the Germans and their ability to continue the war on land and sea; and the disillusion of a British officer who was clearly alienated by civilian attitudes. This became a strong theme of later war memoirs and reflects the huge gulf of experience and understanding that could open up between those who had experienced the war at first hand and those who had not.

Sat. 25 Nov. 1916

7. P.M. Major James Caldwell called. He was very depressed about both the war, and about commerce—rather an unusual thing for him.

(i) he says the most extraordinary thing about the war is the prodigious use of high explosives by Germany. Germany is not only the most self-contained country in the world, having in its own great territory all things, vegetable and mineral, in adequate supply for its needs, but the German people, as a whole, are prepared to sacrifice everything for Germany. Germany's resources and resourcefulness are far from exhausted, and the end of the war is not in sight. ...

(vi) This Curate's [The Curate of Chelmsford] elder brother _____ Colley was, at the outbreak of the war, home for vacation. He was a professor of English in the University of Posen [Germany; now Poznan, Poland]. He obtained a commission at once, and went out to the front almost immediately. When he was last home, he said that from all his experience he knew Germany was perfectly organized for war in a way people in this country could not grasp. He said also that, commercially and socially, there never was in Germany that hatred of this country which people are now trying to make out. He travelled up with his brother (the curate) from home to London, on his way out, and, on the steps of the hotel, he stood and looked at the thoughtless crowd and said—'I have, of course, not been in Germany since the war broke out, but I know that nowhere there would a state of things like this be allowed or even possible. Here I am, back from mud and danger, and going back into them; and all these people are carrying on as though there were no war.' This was just before the advance on The Somme. He was killed in the first 'push' on the Somme. ...

Monday, 11 December.
... Dr R.P. Smallwood called this morning .... .

... he was very pessimistic about the war. 'The war is really over and we have lost. The Germans have command of the North Sea. I met last week an officer just landed from a submarine, and he said he was never so thankful to be back to port in his life. Last year we chased the Germans, now we have to turn round and they chase us'.

Diary of the Revd Andrew Clark, rector of Great Leighs,
Essex, 25 November to 11 December 1916

'This is a bit of a cataclysm isn't it?'

ASQUITH WRITES ABOUT HIS RESIGNATION

In these letters Asquith appears to be resigned to his fate, and relieved to relinquish the burdens of state. He cannot, however, hide his bitterness towards Lloyd George. The Coalition and Asquith's premiership had been under mounting criticism following setbacks on all fronts: the Somme offensive had ground to a halt; a Balkan ally, Romania, had been overrun; and Russian and Italian offensives had failed. Lloyd George had become increasingly critical of the government, and from 20 November had opened negotiations with Bonar Law and the Irish Unionist Sir Edward Carson about re-forming the Cabinet. The involvement of Asquith's bitter critic, the Conservative MP and newspaper owner Sir Max Aitken (later Lord Beaverbrook), an ally of Bonar Law and admirer of Lloyd George, made it clear what the intended outcome of these talks was. A challenge to Bonar Law by his own backbenchers precipitated the end of the Coalition. After much political manoeuvring, Asquith accepted a proposal to set up a supreme war cabinet of three men under his continued leadership, on 3 December. But then, with the crisis apparently resolved, Asquith changed his mind after consultation with Liberal colleagues and rejected the proposal. There followed a crisis which split the Liberal Party, as not only Unionists but also many Liberals threw their support behind Lloyd George, believing that he would prove more able to win the war. The resignation of Lloyd George and Bonar Law triggered the collapse of Asquith's coalition, and Lloyd George took office as prime minister on 7 December 1916. On 19 December he made a rousing speech in the Commons in which he committed himself 'to the rescue of mankind from the most overwhelming catastrophe'.[79] Asquith, however, sitting in the House as an ordinary MP for the first time in eleven years, found the speech 'dull and ineffective'. Europe was on the brink of a precipice at the end of 1916: the way forward was a negotiated settlement or a more vigorous prosecution of the war. All the main powers chose the latter, as the support for Lloyd George demonstrates in Britain's case. The illusion that the

244

war would be short had gone, and Lloyd George could only offer prolonged sacrifice:

> What is the urgent task in front of the Government? To complete and make even more effective the mobilisation of all our national resources, a mobilisation which has been going on since the commencement of the War, so as to enable the nation to bear the strain, however prolonged, and to march through to victory, however lengthy, and however exhausting may be the journey. It is a gigantic task, and let me give this word of warning: If there be any who have given their confidence to the new Administration in expectation of a speedy victory, they will be doomed to disappointment.[80]

10, Downing Street,
Whitehall. S.W.

Wed 6 Dec 16

Most Dear—this is a bit of a cataclysm isn't it? As all my colleagues of both shades agreed, there was no other course that could be taken.

There is by the way in the Times this morning a <u>most</u> mendacious narrative of my dealings with Ll. G, which I fear must have been inspired by himself. The King was a good deal distressed, but behaved very well.

It is impossible yet to say what is likely to happen, and I know no more than the rest of the world. The probabilities point to a junction of the Unionists <u>plus</u> Carson with Ll. G.

I confess to feeling a certain sense of relief. Nothing can be conceived more hellish than the experience I have gone through during the last month. Almost for the first time I have felt that I was growing old.

You have been an angel of goodness and understanding, and I bless you

Your Ever Devoted

Forbes House,
Halkin Street, S.W.

... Tu night Dec 19.16

... I went to the House and for the first time for 11 years took my seat on the left of the Speaker's Chair: quite a new point of view. I was very well received. Ll. G. Spoke for the best part of 2 hours: far too long and for the most part dull and ineffective: long slats of type

245

written stuff on different topics, interlarded when one came to the end and it was time for the next to begin by a series of perorations of the platform type. The House got rather tired, and I did not keep them for more than 1/2 an hour. I think it was all right: at any rate my friends were pleased. If I were a journalist I should entitle my article to-morrow on the new government's policy, if it can be called a policy: 'Slapdash and Eye-wash'.

[address printed, the rest handwritten]

10, Downing Street,
Whitehall. S.W.

Wed 20 Dec 16

My very Dearest and Best—

I have spent most of this morning and aft. at my writing table here (this is the last letter I shall ever write from it) rummaging my drawers, transferring all sorts of papers historic and otherwise to tin-boxes and despatch boxes, and generally winding up.

What a tragic occupation! I have tried to be brutal and callous, and have destroyed a lot. But every now and again I have felt constrained to linger, as one piece of paper and another recalled vividly the touch of vanish'd or distant scenes and persons, and made the past live again.

Nine years is a long spell in anyone's life, and these nine have been coloured almost from first to last by every kind of moving kaleidoscopic incident and emotion. There have been some moments—not a few—of Inferno; many of Purgatory; and now and again real glimpses of Paradise.

What I want to tell you my beloved is that you, more than anyone, have held the golden keys which in rare and blessed hours have unlocked for me that gate. You don't want thanks: you couldn't help it; but you have done for me what I can never forget, and I bless the day when we came close together, as please God we shall always remain. I need you now more than ever.

Your truly devoted and <u>eternally</u> Loving.

Letters from H.H. Asquith to Sylvia Henley, 6–20 December 1916

'I fear your Govt. had got a little out of touch with public opinion'

LEWIS HARCOURT DISCUSSES THE FALL OF ASQUITH WITH KING GEORGE V

With the fall of Asquith, Harcourt too left the government. He had been suffering from a heart condition for some time and decided that now was the time to give up the strains of political life. On 3 January 1917 he was raised to the peerage as Viscount Harcourt. On the occasion of his audience with King George V he had a frank discussion about the end of Asquith's government.

20.12.16

I had my farewell audience of the King from 11.45 to 12.10 this morning. He was extremely kind, sd. it was sad to say goodbye after my 11 years of service and expressed great appreciation of all I had done at the Office of Works. ...

I sympathized with the King in the loss of Asquith's sound judgment and wise guidance. The K. sd. 'I feel his loss very much and I stuck to him and fought for him to the end, but I fear your Govt. had got a little out of touch with public opinion, you allowed them to push you instead of leading them, and then you had all that d—d Press agitation against you.' I sd I wondered how long it wd. be before Northcliffe turned agst. Ll. Geo. and that when he did I expected Ll. Geo. wd. close up his papers and shut Northcliffe up. The King sd 'And a good job too or this country will be ruled only by the newspapers'.

I sd. I hoped the Govt. wd. succeed because if they failed it meant the failure of the War but I sd. I was nervous of the naval situation as I feared lest Ll. Geo., Carson and Beatty[81] might try something rash in the North Sea and lose half our fleet. The King sd 'There is no chance of that with Jellicoe at the Admlty: he wd. stop it.' I sd. 'But cd. he against the others[?]' The K. 'Beatty is <u>not</u> a rash man, you are quite wrong to think that and now that he is in supreme command in the N. Sea he will more than ever [be] cautious'.

The K sd he did not know much of Carson and had not seen him since his appointment. He sd. 'Milner[82] is a curious appt. but Ll. Geo said he wanted him in his War Cabinet, heard he was a clever man but no one had attacked Milner more than he (Ll. Geo)'. The K. asked me what I thought of Milner and I sd. 'an inferior mind and judgment. I knew him at the Inland Revenue and watched his failure in S. Africa: the Tories never thought of bringing him in at the time of the Coalition—his reputation is purely from Press puff'.

I begged the King not to lend himself to a possible early 'snap' Election which I sd. would be a national scandal. He replied 'I entirely agree with you and I am utterly opposed to it and told Ll. Geo. so when he suggested it to me. I told him that dissolution was my prerogative and that I was against it strongly. Ll. Geo. said "it might become necessary" and I said that I should be the judge of that when I saw how his Govt. was received in the Country and supported in Parliament. Ll. Geo. assured me that he too was opposed to an early Election but that if one became necessary he wd. pass a bill to have all Elections on the same day'.

I warned the King that Ll. Geo. might try for this in order to strengthen his position but that there cd. be no justification for it so long as the Opposition and all other parties were giving him effective support in the H of C. which we intended to do: that an election now on the state register, the soldiers absent and unable to vote, the munition workers away from home and unable to vote except by leaving their work, the great cost and disturbance to the country wd. be a scandal and wd. react on him (the King) as being the ultimate source of the dissolution. I emphasised his special prerogative in the matter and this he sd. he had impressed on Ll. Geo. I think it is clear Ll. Geo. made no condition of a dissolution, when he wanted it, when he took office.

The K. asked me whether it wd. not be a good thing to get rid of some members of the H of C. (by dissolution) but I replied that it was unthinkable to put the country to an expense of £2,000,000 and the upset of industry, war work etc. in order to get rid of 10 or 12 men who had no influence in the H of C. or the country and who wd. acquire influence in the country if they became martyrs.

I finally begged the King to stand firm in his own judgement on this matter and—as Party is suspended in war—to seek other advice and support if he found himself unduly pressed.

I told him I thought the new idea of having no Cabinet for the consideration and decision of questions not wholly and specifically

'War' wd. never work and that I thought it mischievous and bad in every way that the S[ecretarie]s of State and other big officers should not meet frequently to discuss policy outside the war and compare differences. The King seemed to think the War Cabinet of 5 sufficient and said our late Cabinet of 23 was an impossible body, but I explained to him that we never discussed or reversed the decisions of the War Committee and that we only concerned ourselves with general policy, that few of us spoke—except on subjects on which we were expert, and that I thought we were an invaluable adjunct to the War Committee.

I thanked the King for my Peerage and told him the health circs. which made it necessary. He asked what my title wd. be and I sd. 'That of the Ld. Chancellor—Visct. Harcourt.'[83]

Cabinet Diary of Lewis Harcourt, 20 December 1916

Notes

1. *Hansard* 5C, 88.1334-58.
2. *Douglas Haig War Diaries and Letters 1914-1918*, ed. Gary Sheffield and John Bourne, Phoenix, London, 2006, p. 83.
3. *Inside Asquith's Cabinet: From the Diaries of Charles Hobhouse*, ed. Edward David, John Murray, London, 1977, p. 229.
4. *The Bickersteth Diaries 1914-1918*, ed. John Bickersteth, Leo Cooper, London, 1995 pp. 183-4.
5. Extracts published in ibid. The original letters from Burgon that formed part of the 'Diaries' are among the Bickersteth papers in the Bodleian Library.
6. *The Home Letters of T.E. Lawrence and His Brothers*, ed. M.R. Lawrence, Blackwell, Oxford, 1954, p. 232.
7. John Morley (1838-1923), 1st Viscount Morley of Blackburn, Lord President of the Council; Walter Runciman (1870-1949), President of the Board of Agriculture and Fisheries; Thomas McKinnon Wood (1855-1927), Scottish Secretary; Joseph Pease (1860-1943), President of the Board of Education; Reginald McKenna (1863-1943), Home Secretary; William Lygon (1872-1938), 7th Earl Beauchamp, First Commissioner of Works; John Burns (1858-1943), President of the Board of Trade; Sir John Simon (1873-1954), Attorney General; Sir Charles Hobhouse (1862-1941), 4th Baronet, Postmaster General; Augustine Birrell (1850-1933), Irish Secretary; Herbert Samuel (1870-1963), President of the Local Government Board; Charles Masterman (1873-1927), Chancellor of the Duchy of Lancaster.
8. Theobald von Bethmann Hollweg (1856-1921), chancellor of Germany 1909-17.
9. Sir William Edward Goschen (1847-1924), British ambassador in Berlin.
10. Robert Crewe-Milnes (1858-1945), 1st Marquess of Crewe, Secretary of State for India.
11. Andrew Bonar Law (1858-1923), leader of the Conservative and Unionist Party.
12. Admiral Sir Cecil Fiennes Thursby (1861-1936).
13. Hugh Makins (1881-1915), an alumnus of Oriel College, Oxford; served as captain 16th battalion London Regiment (Queen's Westminster Rifles). He was killed in action at Vlamertinghe on 4 November 1915.
14. Another brother, Geoffrey Makins (1877-1915), captain in the 3rd Battalion King's Royal Rifle Corps. Like Ernest he was a professional soldier, and had served in the Boer War. He was killed in action on 23 August 1915.
15. Sir Charles Philips Trevelyan (1870-1958), Parliamentary Secretary to the Board of Education 1908-1914; founded the Union of Democratic Control (see p. 187).
16. John Edward Redmond (1856-1918), leader of the nationalist Irish Parliamentary Party 1900-1918.
17. Joseph Jacques Césaire Joffre (1852-1931), French general.
18. Sir Reginald Herbert Brade (1864-1933), Permanent Under-Secretary of State for War 1914-20.
19. Reginald Owen Morris (1886-1948), composer and music teacher.

20. John Scott Haldane (1860–1936), physiologist, Fellow of New College, Oxford.

21. My thanks to Professor Richard Sheppard, who provided the translation. The German text is published in *Dichtungen, Schriften, Briefe*, ed. Klaus Hurlebusch and Karl Ludwig Schneider, C.H. Beck, Munich, 1983.

22. General Sir Edward Stanislaus Bulfin (1862–1939).

23. Lieutenant General Samuel Holt Lomax (1855–1915) died of wounds received five months later, one of the highest ranking British officers to be killed in action during the war.

24. Lieutenant Colonel Arthur Jex Blake Percival (d. 1914).

25. Millicent, Duchess of Sutherland's hospital at Dunkirk.

26. Henry Tennant (1897–1917), 2nd Lieutenant Royal Flying Corps, was killed in a flying accident on 27 May 1917. He was just seventeen years old when Margot met him.

27. General Henry Seymour Rawlinson (1864–1925), commander of IV Corps 1914–15, and 4th Army 1916–18.

28. Lord (Arthur) Francis (Henry) Hill (1895–1953), a captain in the 2nd Dragoons (Royal Scots Greys).

29. William Le Queux, *The Invasion*, London, 1906, pp. 122–6.

30. Cd. 6231, Harcourt Cabinet Journal, 4.8.14.

31. Cd. 6242, uncatalogued Butterworth war diary.

32. MS. Eng. d. 3045, fols. 38–39.

33. Eleftherios Venizelos (1864–1936), prime minister of Greece.

34. My thanks to Sandrine Decoux, who translated the letter.

35. Lloyd George and others believed that control of drinking was necessary to increase industrial efficiency, and had considered state control of the licensed liquor trade and prohibition, but these schemes proved impracticable.

36. Edgar Algernon Robert Gascoyne-Cecil, 1st Viscount Cecil of Chelwood (1864–1958), Independent Conservative MP and Parliamentary Under-Secretary of State for Foreign Affairs from May 1915.

37. The text of this letter, written either to George's father or to his future stepmother, is taken from the book privately printed by his father, *George Butterworth, 1885–1916* (York, 1918). The original letter is not among the Butterworth papers in the Bodleian.

38. John William Gulland (1864–1920), Liberal politician. He was Parliamentary Secretary to the Treasury (Chief Whip) under Asquith, a position he had to share with the Conservative Lord Edmund Talbot with the formation of the Coalition in May 1915.

39. Francis Octavius Grenfell (1880–1915) received the Victoria Cross. He was a cousin of Julian Grenfell—see p. 120.

40. Maurice Bonham Carter (1880–1960), Asquith's Principal Private Secretary. He married Asquith's daughter, Violet, in November 1915.

41. William Robertson (1860–1933), Chief of Staff with the BEF. In December 1915 he was made Chief of Imperial General Staff (CIGS).

42. General Hubert Gough (1870–1963) had been prominent in the 'Curragh Incident' of 20 March 1914 when many British officers at the main army base in Ireland threatened to resign rather than take military action against the Ulster Volunteers who opposed the Home Rule Bill. The War Secretary J.E.B. Seely and the CIGS Sir John French were forced to resign in the aftermath.

43. Ferdinand Foch (1851–1929), French general.

44. Sir Edward Carson (1854–1935), leader of the Irish Unionist Alliance and Ulster Unionist Party 1910–21; Attorney General in Asquith's Cabinet May–October 1915.

45. Letter from Julian Grenfell to his mother, 24 October 1914, in *Julian Grenfell, Soldier & Poet: Letters and Diaries, 1910–1915*, ed. Kate Thompson, Hertfordshire Record Society, Rickmansworth, 2004, p. 231.

46. Admiral John Rushworth Jellicoe (1859–1935), commander of the Grand Fleet, was a protégé of the former First Sea Lord 'Jackie' Fisher. Admiral Sir Frederick Charles Doveton Sturdee (1859–1925) commanded the 4th Battle Squadron of the Grand Fleet. He had been Admiral Charles Beresford's chief of staff. The Beresford–Fisher feud after 1900 had split the Navy.

47. Major General Frederick Hammersley (1858–1924) and General Sir Bryan Thomas Mahon (1862–1930).

48. Lieutenant Thomas Edward Geoffrey, 13th Kensington Battalion London Regiment, alumnus of Christ Church, Oxford, killed in action at Laventie, 11 January 1915.

49. A V-shaped plantation of trees planted on the South Downs for Queen Victoria's Jubilee, 1887.

50. *The Bickersteth Diaries 1914–1918*, p. 56.

51. Walter Long (1854–1924), 1st Viscount Long, President of the Local Government Board.

52. Lieutenant General Fenton John Aylmer (1862–1935).

53. William Waldegrave Palmer, 2nd Earl of Selborne (1859–1942), President of the Board of Agriculture.

54. Aristide Briand (1862–1932), Prime Minister and Foreign Minister of France.

55. This appears to be the nickname for a friend or relation of Sarah Acland.

56. Adrian Gregory, *The Last Great War: British Society and the First World War*, Cambridge University Press, Cambridge, 2008, pp. 70–111.

57. MS. Gilbert Murray 375, fols 3–4.

58. MS. Gilbert Murray 375, fol. 10.

59. Major A.K. Slessor, 1/4th Oxfordshire and Buckinghamshire Light Infantry, employed in Recruiting Service, 1916–18.

60. MS. Gilbert Murray 375, fol. 8.

61. MS. Gilbert Murray 165, fol. 151.

62. No-Conscription Fellowship, a body that encouraged men to refuse war service.

63. MS. Gilbert Murray 165, fols 152–9.

64. MS. Gilbert Murray 375, fol. 11.

65. MS. Macmillan dep. d. 2/1, fol. 73b.

66. A Pioneer Battalion raised by the North Eastern Railway Company (17th Northumberland Fusiliers).

67. *Aunt Sarah and the War, A Tale of Transformations* was written anonymously by Wilfrid Meynell, a 62-year-old newspaper publisher and editor.

68. Noel Pemberton Billing (1881–1948) was an extreme right-wing Independent MP who believed that British society was being undermined by homosexuality, promoted by German agents. He publicly attacked, among others, Margot Asquith for her alleged involvement in the conspiracy.

69. The quotation is from *Love in the Valley* by George Meredith.

70. No inch of ground must be voluntarily abandoned, whatever the circumstances, and a unit, even surrounded, must resist to the last man, without flinching, the sacrifice of each man being the condition for victory.

71. TNA WO 372/24/150292, Medal card of F.H. Smith, Lance Corporal, Oxford-shire and Buckinghamshire Light Infantry.

72. This was the headquarters of Sir Henry Rawlinson, general of the 4th Army, which played the major role in the early part of the Somme offensive.

73. *OED*: hack—to ride on horseback at ordinary pace, to ride on the road; distinguished from cross-country or military riding.

74. A maxim of Cicero: 'In times of war, the law falls silent.'

75. *OED*: volplane—to make a steep controlled descent in an aeroplane with the engine stopped or shut off.

76. MS. Eng. d. 3047, fol. 163.

77. MS. Gilbert Murray 119, fol. 101.

78. Dean Ireland's scholarship, founded in 1825 for the promotion of classical learning and taste.

79. *Hansard* 5C, 88.1357-8.

80. *Hansard* 5C, 88.1338.

81. David Richard Beatty (1871–1936), 1st Earl Beatty, succeeded Jellicoe as Commander-in-Chief of the Grand Fleet, November 1916.

82. Alfred Milner (1854–1925), 1st Viscount Milner, was appointed to the new five-man War Cabinet, though his political views were diametrically opposed to those of Lloyd George. Despite Harcourt's assessment he became a key figure, being appointed War Secretary in 1918, and then Colonial Secretary in 1919.

83. This Viscount Harcourt was his forebear Simon Harcourt (1661–1727), Lord Chancellor 1710–14.

Further reading

Asquith, Margot, *The Autobiography of Margot Asquith*, ed. Mark Bonham Carter, Methuen, London, 1985.

Barlow, Michael, *Whom the Gods Love: The Life and Music of George Butterworth*, Toccata Press, London, 1997.

Bickersteth, John (ed.), *The Bickersteth Diaries 1914–1918*, Leo Cooper, London, 1995.

Brock, Eleanor, and M.G. Brock (eds), *H.H. Asquith: Letters to Venetia Stanley*, Oxford University Press, Oxford, 1982.

Brown, Malcolm (ed.), *The Letters of T.E. Lawrence*, Oxford University Press, Oxford, 1991.

Butterworth, Alexander Kaye (ed.), *George Butterworth, 1885–1916*, Delittle, Fenwick & Co., York and London, 1918 (printed for private circulation only).

Cassar, George H., *Asquith as War Leader*, Hambledon Press, London, 1994.

Clark, Andrew, *Echoes of the Great War: The Diary of the Reverend Andrew Clark, 1914–1919*, ed. James Munson, Oxford University Press, Oxford, 1985.

Clifford, Colin, *The Asquiths*, John Murray, London, 2002.

Oxford Dictionary of National Biography, online edition, ed. Lawrence Goldman, September 2013.

Gregory, Adrian, *The Last Great War: British Society and the First World War*, Cambridge University Press, Cambridge, 2008.

Horne, Alistair, *Macmillan 1894–1956*, Macmillan, London, 1988.

Hurlebusch, Klaus, and Karl Ludwig Schneider (eds), *Dichtungen, Schriften, Briefe*, C.H. Beck, Munich, 1983.

Moore-Bick, Christopher, *Playing the Game: The British Junior Infantry Officer on the Western Front 1914–18*, Helion, Solihull, 2011.

Prior, Robin, and Trevor Wilson, *The Somme*, Yale University Press, New Haven CT and London, 2005.

Sheppard, Richard, *Ernst Stadler (1883–1914): A German Expressionist Poet at Oxford*, Magdalen College Occasional Paper 2, Magdalen College, Oxford, 1994.

Stevenson, David, *1914–1918: The History of the First World War*, Allen Lane, London, 2004.

Strachan, Hew, *The First World War*, Volume 1: *To Arms*, Oxford University Press, Oxford, 2001.

Strachan, Hew, *The First World War, a New Illustrated History*, Simon & Schuster, London, 2003,

Thorpe, D.R., *Supermac: The Life of Harold Macmillan*, Chatto & Windus, London, 2010.

Manuscript sources

The following manuscript collections have been used. Unless otherwise indicated, the collections are held at the Bodleian Libraries.

Letters to Sarah Angelina Acland, MS. Acland d. 151
Letters of H.H. Asquith to Venetia Stanley, MS. Eng. c. 7093
Letters of H.H. Asquith to Sylvia Henley MS. Eng. lett. c. 542/1, c. 542/2, c. 542/4
Diary of Margot Asquith, MS. Eng. d. 3210, d. 3211
Letter from Clement Attlee to his brother Thomas, MS. Eng. c. 4792
Letters of Burgon Bickersteth, MS. Eng. d. 3045, d, 3046, d. 3047
Diary and letters of George Butterworth CMD 6242 and Pr. bk. 17402 d. 828
Letters to and from Lionel Cholmondeley, MS. Eng. lett. d. 99
Diary of the Revd Andrew Clark, MS. Eng. hist. e. 88, e. 89, e. 90, e. 101, e. 111,
    e. 129, e. 138, e. 140
Letter from Charles Fisher, MS. Eng. d. 3781, fol. 121
Letter from Commandant Paul Giron, MS. Harcourt adds. 299
Cabinet Journal of Lewis Harcourt, CMD 6231
Letters from T.E. Lawrence, Dep. c. 760, MS. Eng. c. 6740
Letters of Harold Macmillan, MS. Macmillan, dep. c. 4529, dep. c. 452, dep. d. 1/1,
    dep. d. 2/1
Diary of Ernest Makins, MS. Sherfield 101, 102, 104
Letters of Harry Miller-Stirling, MSS Afr. s. 2051
Letters to Gilbert Murray, MS. Gilbert Murray 25, 26, 119, 165, 375
Letters to Arthur Ponsonby MS. Eng. hist. c. 664
Somerville Students' Asssociation, *Annual Report and Oxford letter* (1917), Pr.bk. Per.
    G.A. Oxon 8° 859
Diary of Ernst Stadler, Deutsches Literaturarchiv Marbach, A: Stadler

Image sources

Index

28 May 16

Sunday

My dear Father,

As you probably guessed
we have been in the trenches
again — rather sooner than
I expected. You may also
have imagined that things
have been more lively than
usual — as a matter of fact
on our immediate front things
have been quiet — casualties
below normal, which is
astonishing considering what
was going on within a
mile or two of us, i.e.
the battle of ———, which